D0058337

CHILDREN
UNDER FIRE

CHILDREN
UNDER FIRE

AN AMERICAN CRISIS

JOHN WOODROW COX

An Imprint of HarperCollins*Publishers*

HarperCollins books may be purchased for educational, business, or sales promotional use. For information, please email the Special Markets Department at SPsales@harpercollins.com.

Ecco® and HarperCollins® are trademarks of HarperCollins Publishers.

FIRST EDITION

Designed by Paula Russell Szafranski

Library of Congress Cataloging-in-Publication Data has been applied for.

ISBN 978-0-06-288393-3

21 22 23 24 25   LSC   10 9 8 7 6 5 4 3 2 1

For the children who told me their stories,
and for the ones who could not.

And to Mom and Dad, to Gram
and to Ed, and, of course, to Jenn.

CONTENTS

"I HATE GUNS"

Ava, Tyshaun, and the Bullets that Changed Them

The boy had come to the end of another bad week, and now the girl he adored wanted to know how he was doing. He hated when people thought of him as a troublemaker, one of those kids who frustrated his teachers and disappointed his mother, but more and more often, he feared that's how they all felt. He had struggled to keep buried what was inside him, a swirling, combustible blend of emotion that the tiniest spark could ignite. It had started as disbelief, even denial, before turning into grief and then, at last, this simmering rage that had clung to him for months. It had erupted again a few days prior, so the true answer to the girl's question would have been that he wasn't doing well, but the boy didn't want her to know the truth.

"Good," Tyshaun McPhatter, age nine, told her instead as he stared through the screen of his mother's cell phone at Ava Olsen, age eight. It was, for late spring, an unusually brisk afternoon in his neighborhood, just fifteen minutes from the U.S. Capitol Building in Washington, DC. Dressed in black sweatpants and a gray hoodie pulled low over his head, Tyshaun stood barefoot as he slumped over the side of an armchair in his mother's modest living room, the cell phone in one hand and a chocolate chip granola bar in the other. Ava, who was 520 miles away in South Carolina that afternoon, told him her week had been hard.

"Why?" he asked.

"I've just been mad and sad and stuff," said Ava, her hair honey blonde, brown eyes serious, and accent tinged with the South. She wore a blue T-shirt and pink SpongeBob SquarePants bottoms as she sat atop her bed beside a half-dozen stuffed animals and a fat brown cat named Charlie.

"Why?" Tyshaun repeated, between bites of the granola bar.

Ava didn't know what to say. She also didn't want her friend to know the truth, both because it pained her to discuss it and because she dreaded what he might think of her if he knew. For seven seconds, she didn't answer. "I don't know, just—" she said, then stopped and changed the subject.

Ava had first heard about Tyshaun nearly a year earlier, when she walked into her living room and noticed her mother, Mary, crying on the couch. "Why are you upset?" asked Ava, who suspected that, yet again, *she* was why. No, Mary assured the girl. It wasn't her fault. Her mother explained that she had just read a story I'd written for the *Washington Post* about a child named Tyshaun who was a lot like Ava. The boy also felt angry and confused and unhappy sometimes because he, too, had lost someone he loved.

"His dad is where Jacob is," Mary said, and Ava understood. Mary hadn't let her read my story, but she showed her daughter pictures of Tyshaun—posing next to his dad and flashing the deuces sign in a family photo; playing with a toy, alone, on his father's couch; staring out a window, his dark eyes empty.

The boy looked like he needed a friend, Ava announced, so she got a pencil and a sheet of paper and sat down at her kitchen table. "Dear Tyshaun," she began to write, in neat block letters.

Before their lives came apart, the two kids had little in common, other than their ages. Ava, who is white, was a Daisy Scout and wanted nothing more than to become a cheerleader. Day after day, she practiced cartwheels in the dirt and grass behind her home, which overlooked a neighbor's bucolic horse farm. She had lived almost all her life in Townville, a quiet, four-thousand-person swath of countryside in the northwest corner of South Carolina known as the Upstate. Her dad had always worked in security or law enforcement, and he had always carried a gun, which she'd never thought much about, if at all. In a community with a single stoplight, at least six churches, and an abundance of backyard shooting ranges, most people believed in God and, just slightly less, in their right to bear arms. Townville sat on the eastern edge of a county in which seven in ten voters supported Donald Trump in 2016. Gable-roofed chicken houses stood among cow pastures and rolling fields of hay, wheat, corn, and soybeans, and everyone shopped at Dollar General, nicknamed the "Townville Target." It was a world that, in Ava's mind, had always been safe and always would be.

That changed one afternoon in late September 2016, when she walked outside her school for recess just as a teenager drove up to the playground in a Dodge Ram, jumped out of the pickup, and pointed a gun. One of the bullets he fired struck six-year-old Jacob Hall, a classmate whom Ava loved dearly. Three days later, Jacob died.

She was so overwhelmed by the loss, and the terror of what she'd witnessed, that a pediatrician later diagnosed her with post-traumatic stress disorder and recommended that the girl be home-schooled. Ava, who was prescribed both antipsychotics and antidepressants, began hitting herself and yanking out her eyelashes. In the months that followed, she detailed her torment in journals: "I can't stop feeling mad." "No one ever listens to me." "I hate guns."

By then, Tyshaun, who is black, had known since as far back as his memory stretched about the bad things people could do with guns. On his dad's dresser in Southeast Washington was a reminder: a three-inch button inscribed with REST IN PEACE that honored a family friend shot two blocks away. Tyshaun was growing up in a time of rapid gentrification across the seven-hundred-thousand-person city, but the change had yet to reach his side of the Anacostia River, where more than half the District's homicides occurred and nearly every other child grew up in poverty. It was amid this chaos that the boy lived part time with his father, Andrew McPhatter, in a row of seventy-year-old duplexes around the corner from a liquor store. The vast majority of his overwhelmingly black section of the city rejected Trump in 2016, as did the rest of Washington, which cast just 1 in 25 votes for him. Parents in Tyshaun's neighborhood viewed firearms less like sacred objects than like carriers of an infectious disease, but they were everywhere, despite the District's strict gun laws, thanks to the demand from drug dealers and gang members and a supply from surrounding states with much looser laws. The impact was perpetually devastating on the community, where many boys and girls learned to navigate peril before they learned to read. For kids in Tyshaun's neighborhood, the unrelenting threat of gun violence informed almost every aspect of their lives: the streets they walked down, the parks they visited, the pictures they drew, the nightmares they had, the number of parents they came home to.

Tyshaun's mom, Donna Johnson, had fretted since he was born about how that environment would affect her son, so she decided that the best way to keep him safe was to keep him busy. He made s'mores at Cub Scout gatherings and took lessons for hockey, swimming, and software coding. He liked football and decided, at a wiry four foot four, that he would play linebacker in the NFL for his hometown team when he grew up. Donna, a thirty-year-old State Department security officer, was desperate to protect his goofy innocence, the quality that led him once to secretly record himself rapping an original song she discovered later. "What are thoose on your toooes, they can't be Doritooos," he rhymed, then nodded to the camera, feeling good about his track. "That's the new one."

She struggled to preserve that piece of her boy, who had both a deep well of compassion for people he sensed were suffering and a tendency to explode in anger, often with his fists, when he was being teased or challenged. "I just want him to be different," Donna would say, because she had already seen too many tough young boys who, when they turned into tough young men, ended up in prisons or caskets. By age seven, Tyshaun had narrowly escaped harm from gunfire twice, and three of his father's friends had already been killed. Then came that week early in 2017 when, over seven days, six people were shot on a single street that ran through their neighborhood. The last of them, and the only one who didn't survive, was Tyshaun's father.

The loss unmoored Tyshaun, whose dad was also his best friend. They were twins, said people who knew Andrew as a boy, before the dreadlocks. Same chocolate eyes, strong chin, quiet smile. Andrew was the fun parent, the one who stayed up with Tyshaun well past his bedtime playing the violent video games Donna didn't like. But Andrew was also the parent who, while Donna worked, attended parent-teacher meetings and seldom missed a school performance or ball game.

As the weeks passed, and the signs of the boy's sorrow waned, his fear and fury bloomed. At home, he began to talk less of the things he missed about his dad and more about the man who'd killed him, and whether he would come after Tyshaun, too. At school, he shoved a boy who he suspected had laughed about the shooting, later threatening to punch another who he thought had done the same. One day, after a long stretch of quiet during a drive home, he told his mom he wanted to die, so he could be with his dad again.

Tyshaun McPhatter didn't get shot, and neither did Ava Olsen. Their small bodies bear none of the grisly physical wounds that our nation assumes to be the direst consequence of gun violence, but the damage that bullets did to both of them was immense. Their experiences, as young Americans, were not in any way unique, though. Every moment of every day, gunfire reshapes our kids' lives, because of whom it takes away or what it makes them witness or how it forever changes their view of the world. And time after time, the people who love them wonder the same thing that the people who love Tyshaun and Ava wondered about them: would these children ever recover?

FOR KIDS ALL across the country, gun violence is, and long has been, a public health crisis that's both dramatically underestimated and widely ignored. The trend lines are ominous. On average, one child is shot every hour in the United States, and since the 1990s, the country has made no progress in its limited efforts to curb the rates at which children die. Over the past ten years, about thirty thousand kids and teens have been killed by gunfire—recently overtaking cancer as their second-leading cause of death.

On this issue, America stands in isolation. One study found that among the world's high-income countries, including Canada, Germany, and the United Kingdom, 91 percent of kids younger than fifteen who were killed by gunfire lived here. Another study concluded that older teens were eighty-two times more likely to die from gun violence in the United States than in any other wealthy, democratic nation.

The difference between America and those places isn't crime or race, class or culture, all of which has been argued before. Exorbitantly more people are killed by guns here because we have exorbitantly more guns—nearly four hundred million, by one estimate—and laws that are less effective at regulating them. Researchers have consistently found that America's rates of other serious crimes, including assault and robbery, are comparable with those in other rich countries. Only on the issue of gun violence are we exceptional.

"It's not as if a nineteen-year-old in the United States is more evil than a nineteen-year-old in Australia. There's no evidence for that," explained David Hemenway, director of the Harvard Injury Control Research Center. "But a nineteen-year-old in America can very easily get a pistol. That's very hard to do in Australia. So, when there's a bar fight in Australia, somebody gets punched out or hit with a beer bottle. Here, they get shot."

How it's come to this, and how to fix it, is a point of unending political debate between gun safety activists, some of whom argue that the weapons should all be banned, and gun rights activists, some of whom argue that any new laws infringe on their Second Amendment rights. Central to America's continued inability to protect its kids, however, is that many people, if not most, on both sides of the issue fail to understand its scope or, by extension, its true ramifications.

The children who are killed or maimed dominate headlines, but they represent only a fraction of the problem in the United States, where not thousands, but *millions* of children are affected every year. These are mostly the Avas and Tyshauns—the kids who weren't shot and aren't considered victims by our legal system but who have, nonetheless, been irreparably harmed by the epidemic.

In this country, where the number of citizens killed by guns since 1968 exceeds the number killed in all of its wars *combined*, bullets now routinely take the lives of well more than thirty thousand people a year. Many of those who've been lost, and hundreds of thousands more who were injured but survived, had sons and daughters or were wounded in close proximity to other parents' children.

One study concluded that kids who witness an attack involving a gun or knife can be just as psychologically damaged as children who have themselves been shot or stabbed. When the victim is a close friend or family member, the distress may, in fact, be worse, according to one of the study's coauthors, clinical psychologist Sherry Hamby. Even kids who just come near acts of gun violence can be changed by them. In Chicago, researchers discovered that kids who simply lived in a neighborhood where a murder had occurred scored worse on vocabulary and reading tests in the week immediately after the killing.

"We don't do enough to acknowledge the collateral damage of

gun violence," Hamby told me. "We are asking too many to carry this burden."

The most vulnerable bearers of that burden are our children, and yet, in the world's wealthiest nation—one that claims to cherish its youngest above all else—this uniquely American crisis rages on. And that's how a black boy from a neglected neighborhood in the nation's capital came to know a white girl from a tiny town in the rural South.

IT WAS NEARING Tyshaun's bedtime when I arrived at his mom's house one evening in June 2017. We hadn't seen each other in a few weeks, but emails and notes of support from people who had read his story in the *Post* had continued to pour in, and I had a pair of special letters to deliver to him in person.

The first was from Justice Sonia Sotomayor, the first Latina to sit on the U.S. Supreme Court: "I have no words that I can tell you to explain the sadness of the loss of your father. We live in a world in which people like you and your father pay the price of violence that we do not control enough. You are living proof that we must do more." Sotomayor also sent a copy of the children's book that described her youth in the Bronx. On the first page, just above her signature, she'd added, "There is hope that you can someday not just live in a better world but that you will play a part in making the world a better place."

The second letter was the one from Ava.

I sat with Tyshaun in his family's living room, trying to explain to him what it meant to receive a handwritten note from a member of the Supreme Court. Justice Sotomayor was among the most important people in America, I said, and she wanted to encourage him. That was amazing, I said. He should feel very special, I said. Tyshaun, though, fixated on the second letter because it was from a *girl* who lived somewhere far away and knew what he had gone through and who had gone through something similar—and she wanted to be his friend. In that moment, nothing mattered more to him. Dressed only in blue boxer shorts and a white tank top, he was riveted, running his finger beneath each of her words as he read them aloud.

"Hi my name is Ava. My mom read about you online. I saw your picture and would like to be your pen pal. I get sad and mad sometimes too. I am 7 years old. I am in first grade. I used to go to Townville Elementary School. I don't anymore because something scary happened there. Do you like video games? I do. I like *Minecraft*. Do you? Do you like ice cream? I love chocolate!"

When he reached the end, Tyshaun sprinted upstairs and sat at his desk, beside the *Daredevil* superhero decal pasted to the wall. He grabbed a pencil and pulled out a sheet of notebook paper, proceeding to write as fast as he could.

"Dear Ava, I no that you are sad and want to no if you can come over some time," he scribbled, before jotting down his address and his mom's phone number. "And i like dogs i like to play 2K17 and my favorite sport is football and i love you"—followed by two hearts—"And i am in 2nd grade and am 8 years old."

Donna didn't let him send that one because his rushed handwriting was nearly illegible. She told him to slow down and think about what he really wanted to say. In the next draft, he started with his name and his age.

"I heard about your school. I hope are having a bless day. Stay strong I'm praying for you," he continued. "Sure I'll be your pin pal."

Back and forth the letters went in the months that followed. Ava thanked Tyshaun for his prayers and asked who his favorite football team was. "Mine is Clemson Tigers," she wrote. She asked what his favorite kind of dog was and what he liked to do for fun and what movie he liked best. She asked when his birthday was. She told him she hoped he was having a blessed day, too.

He told her he'd had a busy summer and listed all that he had done at a camp that a group of *Post* readers had raised money to send him to: baseball, soccer, ziplining, fishing, bouncing atop a trampoline on the water. He asked if she had an Xbox or PS4 and said he had just returned to school. Before sketching her a puppy, which he made sure she noticed by writing "puppy" and drawing an arrow pointing to it, he encouraged her: "I hope you go back to a school with kids. time heal all."

That December, Ava wished him a Merry Christmas and told him of her plans. "We make a gingerbread house and then we put my toy Godzilla in it." Included with the letter was a $25 gift card that Ava had bought with change she'd been saving for months.

He sent back a rainbow-colored stuffed dog that he had picked up on a trip with his mom. "I went to Las Veags and seen some of the biggest buildings in the world over winter break," he wrote. "i got you a little some thing in this bag and it came from the biggest gift store in the world."

In February, during a particularly bad week for Ava, she thought he might be having one, too, so she sent him something that could help. "They are squishies," she wrote, describing the miniature polyurethane animals. "You can squeeze them, or throw them, or pinch them when you are worried, sad or mad. I like them a lot and they sometimes make me feel better and they are a lot of fun. They didn't have any red, but I hope you like the colors I picked out for you. They are 2 bears, and an Octopus." She also added a puppy, and the word "puppy" with an arrow, then she signed the letter to him the same way she signed all of them: "Your friend, Ava."

Now, on that afternoon in 2018, the two of them were looking at each other over the phone, and Tyshaun was asking *why* her week had been so hard, and Ava was changing the subject.

"How did you like your science kit?" she asked, referring to the latest gift she'd sent, a box of ingredients and recipes that taught children how to make candy. He hadn't opened it yet, he said, but he planned to the next week. The kids, chatting through Facebook

Messenger, had already begun to cycle through the app's silly masks, and at this moment, they both appeared on the screen with pink cat noses and fluffy brown ears.

"I'm going to get you something, but I can't tell you what it is," he said, considering the right approach. "What would you want—if I bought you something?"

"Anything, really," Ava said, her lips now coated in a deep-red digital lipstick.

"What? Teddy bear? Game?"

"Anything."

"I'm gonna think about it," Tyshaun said. He told her he looked forward to her parents getting a new TV, since their old one was broken.

"Me, too."

"Then we can play Minecraft," he continued, before asking her about an incident that had gotten her into trouble a few weeks earlier. She had figured out a way to get online through an iPad so she could play the game and look up cat pictures on Instagram.

"How did you hack into your mom's account?" he asked.

"I just did. I just went online and figured out what their restrictions code was for a tablet and then just . . ." she said, trailing off because Mary was sitting in the room with her.

Silence.

"Can you teach me how to hack?" he sheepishly inquired. Ava glanced over at her mom, then back at Tyshaun.

"No!" Mary shouted in the background.

"No," Ava repeated dutifully, and both kids laughed in a way that neither of them had in a long time.

"I got in *big* trouble" Ava told him. Tyshaun stood from his chair and, with the phone in hand, walked over to a storage closet and grabbed a bag of pretzels.

"I can't wait until I see you in person," he said.

"Me, too."

He sat back down, his mind still on what she had told him earlier.

"Why were you sad?" Tyshaun asked, and her smile faded.

Earlier that day, she had heard neighbors firing guns in the nearby woods, a common occurrence in and around Townville, but one that had begun to torture Ava, who couldn't stand the noise. She paced the living room, muttering to herself and breathing deeply. She finally fled to her parents' bedroom and into their bathroom closet, which the family had converted into her safe space. She lay down on the floor and wrapped herself in a blanket.

"I don't want to die," she told her mom.

When the anxiety didn't pass, Mary gave her a clonidine to help soothe it, but the medication made her so groggy that her mother feared she wouldn't be up for her call with Tyshaun that evening. She had her daughter take a bath to help wake her up, knowing how upset Ava would be later if she missed the conversation. It was because of all that, and so much more, that Ava was sad, but even when Tyshaun asked why, for a third time, the girl couldn't bear to tell him.

"I don't know," Ava said.

Tyshaun didn't ask again, moving on to favorite sports teams and his weekend computer coding class before asking where her younger brother was.

"He has a sleepover at my grandma's house," Ava said of Cameron, who was seven. He had also been on the playground during the shooting, and though he'd struggled at moments, her sibling had kept attending school and fared far better in the aftermath.

"I see you go over to your grandmother's house a lot," Tyshaun said.

"Yes, he does, too. Every weekend, he likes to go there," Ava said, though she didn't know that the reason Cameron liked to be there, instead of in his own home, was because of how sad and stressed and angry his sister had become.

Donna, listening from a chair near Tyshaun, was thrilled that he and Ava had developed this friendship. It gave her hope that the kids could help each other, that maybe they could find some relief from the pain of what each had lost and from the deep sense of shame both felt over who they had become since. She looked at her son.

"Ty, maybe you can share with her some stuff Dr. Gan shared with you?" Donna said, mentioning the psychologist he had finally started meeting with at school. He ignored her.

"You heard me?"

No answer.

"Do you hear me, Ty?"

"What, Mom?" he snapped. "What?"

She smiled, staying calm.

"Maybe you can share with her some stuff Dr. Gan shared with you. You could share with Ava?"

"I don't remember that," Tyshaun said dismissively. "All he has me do is just play with toys."

"Y'all talk."

"Yeah, we do talk sometimes, then go right to playing," he said.

Donna wouldn't give up. She walked over to the couch Tyshaun was sprawled across and stood behind him so Ava could look at her.

"I just wanted to see how you're doing, Ava," she said.

"I had a bad week," the little girl admitted.

"Well, hopefully you have some good days coming up," she said. "Tyshaun had a bad day, too, this week."

"Only one time!" he objected with a mouth still full of pretzels. He didn't want Ava to hear that five days earlier he had exploded in his third-grade class after a trivial miscommunication with his teacher, flipping over a desk and storming out into the hallway. "Leave me alone," he had screamed when someone tried to calm him down. That sort of thing wasn't uncommon at his charter school, a campus founded to serve an impoverished and crime-plagued community in DC, but it had been an uncommon thing for Tyshaun to do, at least until his father died.

It was because all that, and so much more, that Tyshaun had had a bad day, but when Donna brought it up in the hope that hearing about his challenges might help Ava, the boy couldn't bear to tell her.

"*Mom*," Tyshaun interrupted, his patience gone. "Bye-bye, Mom."

"I can talk," Donna responded.

"Hello, Ava," Ty said, raising his voice, trying to drown out his mother's.

"Oh, don't worry," Ava's mother, Mary, offered on the other end. "She'll try to shove me out, too."

"Okay, I'm going to let him. I'm going to sit down," Donna said, relenting as she returned to her seat. "Don't try to push me away."

"But is this *your* conversation?" Tyshaun said.

"I wanted to say some encouraging words to her," she whispered, but Tyshaun ignored that, too.

As he asked Ava to show him her stuffed animals, he drooped backward off the end of the couch like a slug, until his shoulders reached the floor and he was holding the phone upside down. Donna shook her head.

"What are you going to do tomorrow, Ava?" he asked.

"Umm, work some on my scrapbook maybe and just play and eat," she said. "Would you send me a picture of you so I can put it in my scrapbook?"

"All right. Okay," he said, and then Tyshaun decided he wanted her to see something that meant as much to him as anything in the world. It was time, he thought. Ava was his friend.

"I'm going to show you my hoodie," he said, and he stood up and handed the phone to Donna, so she could point the camera at his back. On the sweatshirt was an enlarged photo of a man with a thick beard, dark eyes, and long dreadlocks, and beneath his image were three words: HAPPY BIRTHDAY DADDY.

CHAPTER 2

"WHAT HAPPENED TO JACOB?"

Twelve Seconds on a School Playground
and the Town that Would Never Be the Same

The smallest first-grader at Townville Elementary approached a half-moon table in the back of the classroom, where his teacher, Meghan Hollingsworth, awaited him. It was just before recess on the afternoon of September 28, 2016, and only a month into the new school year, Jacob Hall faced a big moment. Not often did the kids get to read to Miss Hollingsworth one-on-one, among their favorite things to do, but Jacob's turn had arrived, so he climbed onto a chair and opened *Curious Cat*, the book she'd selected. Through the chunky lenses in his oversize black-rimmed glasses, the six-year-old's blue eyes stared down at the first page.

"'Dad opened the car door. In climbed Curious Cat,'" Jacob began, except he misread "climbed," on that page and every one to follow, in a way that was so adorable that Meghan had to suppress a smile.

"'Purrrrrrrrr,'" Jacob continued, each word awash in his thick, plodding South Carolina drawl. "'Purrrrrrrrr.'"

Meghan, then thirty-five, had first been introduced to him along with the rest of Townville Elementary at the school's talent show two years earlier. Jacob dressed as a Teenage Mutant Ninja Turtle and, in a focused, earnest performance, showcased his "karate moves." Legs kicked, arms flailed. At the end, he bowed. Meghan, a teacher for thirteen years, loved it. Many students were far too shy to get up onstage in front of the whole school, especially in their first year of kindergarten, but here was a kid, so tiny he could have passed for a toddler, who didn't hesitate. She couldn't wait for him to join her class. *This*, she thought, *is going to be fun.*

He had an uninhibited joyfulness that, even among first-graders, was rare. When Jacob found something particularly amusing, he didn't laugh so much as cackle, throwing his head back and his hands out in a way that made his classmates giggle, too. He wanted to make friends with everyone he met, though no one more than Ava, whose timidity stood no chance against him. He would hold her hand on the playground when no one was looking, and even when someone was; he'd undo her ponytail because he liked how her hair smelled, which Ava thought was very funny. She called him "Jakey." He was the only boy she'd ever kissed.

Nineteen days before he read the story about the cat aloud in class, Ava had written him a note: "Come play with me please," she scribbled in pencil. "You can play with my cats. Do you want to get married when you come? My mom will make us lunch." At the bottom of the page, she'd drawn herself in a pink dress standing next to a bespectacled Jacob, who appeared about half her height. "I love you!" she added beside a red heart.

There was much about Jacob's young life that Ava, and even Meghan, knew nothing of, though, and that was largely because his bright spirit masked the realities of what he'd survived. The boy had been born six weeks early, when Renae Hall had an emergency C-section on Mother's Day in 2010. He spent his first month alive in a hospital. At birth, he weighed four pounds, two ounces, and measured sixteen inches in length—so small, his mother recalled, that many preemie clothes didn't fit him. He had one lazy eye, turned in toward his nose, and another that was nearsighted, leaving him virtually blind until he got glasses at eighteen months. In the years that followed, he suffered from debilitating asthma, brought on by allergies and exercise. An episode around age two was severe enough that doctors placed him in the intensive care unit, one of many emergency visits. The doting nurses so adored Jacob that they began to call him their "happy wheezer." As he got older, Renae struggled off and on with drug abuse, sometimes leaving her parents with the responsibility of caring for Jacob and his younger sister and brother.

A complainer, however, he was not. Jacob's family dropped him off late for school nearly every day, but he felt no shame. Lugging a backpack that looked as big he was, Jacob always announced his arrival while hurrying through Meghan's classroom door and to his diminutive desk: "Good morning, Miss Hollingsworth!" The boy's defining physical quality, his height—he had reached just three and a half feet by that year—also never seemed to bother Jacob, nor did it make him a target for teasing among classmates. He was, instead, the one they all looked out for—everybody's kid brother. The others also liked to work with him, in part because he was kind but also because he took his schoolwork seriously, always eager to please.

And that's what he aimed to do that fall day, when he read the final pages of the book about the cat to Miss Hollingsworth. He had described the animal's journey into the car, the shopping bag, the shoe box, the closet, the laundry bin, and now, at last, the washing machine, leading to the book's final, all-caps word, which Jacob delivered with gusto: "'MEOW!'"

As the kids finished up the day's work, the time for recess drew near, a moment in which they tended to grow antsy. Even six weeks into first grade, they were still adjusting to the disappointment of not getting to go outside twice a day, as they had in kindergarten. At the beginning of the school year, Meghan's students had asked her so often when recess began that she'd put up on the wall a drawing of a clock that showed where the little hand and big hand would point when the time came.

Now, as the hour arrived once again, someone called from the front office, and Meghan knew she'd made a big mistake, at least by the exacting standards of her first-graders: she had forgotten to retrieve a student's birthday cupcakes. Her aide, Pamela Sanchez, hustled upstairs to get them, and when she returned, the kids lined up at the back of the room to go outside. Townville Elementary, the bones of which had been built more than a half century earlier, had two floors. The upper contained the front entrance, the main offices, and third through sixth grade, while kindergarten through second grade held classes below. Because the school rested on a slope, the lower floor was even with the playground out back, a source of constant temptation for Meghan's students. By the time their celebratory desserts arrived, the kids could see that the other first-grade class had already swarmed the slides and monkey bars.

As Meghan took the tray and headed to the back of the room, Jacob, who prided himself on being a gentleman, realized his teacher needed help, so he volunteered. At his size, though, holding both his own cupcake and the hefty green metal door proved difficult. Meghan maneuvered next to him, propping it open with her back while balancing the tray of chocolate and vanilla treats, all covered in blue frosting. On their way past her, the students selected which one they wanted.

Ava, who was near the front of the line, had just picked a chocolate cupcake when, at 1:41 on that balmy, blue-sky afternoon, the girl noticed something she had never seen before. A black Dodge pickup curled around the back corner of the school and rumbled toward them. Without waiting for the truck to come to a stop, out of the cab stepped a thin, towering figure wearing dark clothes and a black baseball cap over his wispy blond hair. To the first-graders, he looked like a teenager, and before his truck rolled into the chain-link fence that surrounded the playground, several of them assumed he had come to help with something or to say hello. Then they saw the gun.

"I hate my life," the children heard him say as he raised a black pistol and fired the first shot.

Pop, pop, pop, pop.

Near the door, Collin Edwards listened to Meghan scream, "Go! Go! Go!" but when the six-year-old darted back toward their classroom, he felt his foot vibrate, then burn, as if he'd stepped on a white-hot coal. A bullet had blown through the inside of his right ankle and popped out beneath his big toe, punching a hole in the sole of his Velcro-strapped sneaker. He kept running.

Another round struck Meghan, ripping through her jean vest and gouging her left shoulder. Dazed, but unaware of the wound, she dropped the tray and ordered her students to return, ushering inside the ones who were nearby before stepping back into the room and away from the door, which swung shut under its own weight.

Standing on the wood chips near a yellow tube slide, Siena Kibilko, who was in the other first-grade class, felt stunned. Until that moment, her most serious concern had been which *How to Train Your Dragon* toy she would get for her upcoming seventh birthday. "Run!" Siena heard a teacher shouting, and she did. Karson Robinson, one of the biggest kids in class, hadn't waited for directions. At the initial sound of gunshots, he scrambled over a fence on the opposite side of the playground and briefly headed toward the baseball fields where, as a Townville Giant, he had gotten his first recreation league single. A few seconds later, with nowhere else to go, Karson turned back toward the school.

On the sidewalk, Ava had dropped her cupcake. The Daisy Scout remembered what her mom had told her: "If something doesn't feel right, run." She sprinted toward the far side of the building just before Siena did the same, rounding a corner to momentary safety. Nowhere in sight, though, was Jacob. Ava had been enamored of him since they met at church three years earlier. At recess, she often helped him climb up on the green swings, where they'd sit next to each other and talk about cats (which she liked more) and dogs (which he liked more). He called her "Big A," because, like everyone else, she stood several inches taller. Ava didn't mind, though. She had decided to spend the rest of her life with Jacob. Just before the shooting, the girl knew he had been near her at the door, but amid the pandemonium, she'd lost track. Ava hoped he was okay.

Meanwhile, Meghan, who feared that the shooter would chase them inside the building, rushed Collin and the rest of the kids with her through a hallway and into another room. Her aide, Pamela, was trying unsuccessfully to call someone in the front office when she noticed that one child remained in the first-grade class. It was Jacob, crumpled atop a rug decorated with brightly colored squares, where the kids got to sit when they needed a break from their desks. At first, Pamela thought that the boy had fallen and that perhaps, because he was so small, someone had stepped on him.

"Miss Sanchez, my leg hurts," he said. "Something's wrong with my leg."

"Hold on," she said, scooping the boy up and bringing him into the hallway. Already, the pink in his cheeks had begun to fade. "Baby, I'm coming right back. I'm not leaving you," she told him, before hurrying into Meghan's room to make sure the door had been locked and that no more kids were on the playground. When she returned to Jacob, just seconds later, he'd stopped talking or moving, and blood had seeped through his clothes.

On the other side of the building, at the opposite end of the long hallway where Pamela had brought Jacob, Karson caught up with Ava and Siena and a few others kids outside, some of whom were beating on the double doors, begging for help. "Let us in," Siena yelled, and soon the kids were hustled inside—seconds before the gunman rounded the corner.

By then, the school nurse, Angie Langdale, had reached Jacob, but just as she discovered that his pulse had disappeared, someone looked up and spotted the shooter through the doors' windows. "Let's get him into better cover," the nurse told Pamela, and they carried Jacob inside another room. The aide pressed paper towels into the wound at the top of Jacob's thigh, and Angie began CPR. They used a scarf as a tourniquet, cinching it around his leg.

"We have a shooting at Townville Elementary," another school staffer who was in the room told a 911 dispatcher. "A little boy has been shot . . . He's bleeding horribly."

Meghan, who'd begun to sob, pleaded with Jacob to hold on as the woman on the phone with 911 explained that the boy's lips were turning blue. "We need EMS *badly*," she said. Someone noticed flecks of red along Meghan's jawline, where a minuscule piece of shrapnel had pierced her skin and lodged into her lip. Then they noticed the wound on her shoulder. "I'm fine, I'm fine," Meghan said, her voice quavering, as she insisted that everyone focus on Jacob. "Don't even worry about me . . . I can breathe, and I can talk."

Collin was soon carried into the same room because the dispatcher wanted paramedics to be able to treat everyone who'd been shot as quickly as possible. On the way, Collin noticed a puddle of blood spreading across the waxed gray tile floor in the hallway. Inside the room, as his foot was propped up and wrapped in more paper towels, he saw Jacob. He was the sweetest kid Collin knew, his "best best friend." They, too, liked to sit together on the green swings, where Collin sometimes called Jacob funny names—"Little J," mostly—because that would draw one of those cackles from him. But now the boy's eyes were closed, and Collin wondered if they would ever open again.

"Press, press, press," Collin heard the automated defibrillator repeat as the nurse continued to push on Jacob's chest, trying to keep him alive. "Give breath. Give breath."

"Look at me," a teacher urged Collin, but the boy couldn't stop staring at his friend.

FROM BEHIND A sign on a second-floor windowsill that read, DREAM, Principal Denise Fredericks peered down through a window at the shooter. She didn't know it then, but moments earlier, as he had shifted his aim from the green metal door to the playground, his .40-caliber pistol had jammed, ending the rampage twelve seconds after it began. Frustrated, he'd tossed the gun to the ground and walked to the building's edge, then around the corner, where the people treating Jacob in the first-floor hallway had seen him through the glass. Now Denise and a few of her staff members were watching him, hoping that help would arrive before he hurt anyone else. The shooter paced the sidewalk, a cell phone in his hand. Then he looked up.

A teacher gasped. "Oh my God," she said. "That's Jesse Osborne."

Jesse, who was fourteen, had attended Townville for seven years, from kindergarten through fifth grade, before he transferred and was later home-schooled. Not once had his behavior prompted concern. He was quiet but never a loner. He made good grades and had friends, and he participated in seemingly everything, playing baseball, joining an arts club for students who showed musical promise, representing his class in the spelling bee, becoming the top scorer on the archery team. "He was such a good kid," Denise would say later, and now, somehow, that same kid had returned with a gun, adding Townville Elementary to the long list of American schools fractured by a shooting.

Earlier, Jesse had called his grandmother, Patsy Osborne. He was screaming. She couldn't understand him. "Papa, come on," she told her husband, Thomas. "We've got to find Jesse."

The couple sped to the boy's house, where they discovered their son, Jesse's father, slumped on a couch, eyes still open. He'd been shot to death. And Jesse had disappeared. Then Thomas's phone rang. It was their grandson.

"Papa, I told him not to do it," he recalled the teenager saying. "I told him not to do that."

Thomas didn't know what "that" meant. He demanded to know where Jesse was.

"I'm behind the school," the teen said.

"You stay right there," Thomas told him.

Inside the building, three hundred children and teachers cowered in locked classrooms and storage closets. Siena later remembered someone covering up windows with paper. Karson remembered playing with markers and magnets. Ava remembered a teacher reading a book about sunflowers. They all remembered the sound of wailing.

Upstairs, in the corner of a fourth-grade classroom, a nine-year-old took the hands of two of his classmates and bowed his head, asking God to keep them safe. Down the hall from Jacob, twenty kindergarteners, including his four-year-old sister, Zoey, were packed into a locked bathroom no bigger than a single handicapped stall. Their teacher, Kerry Burriss, desperately trying to keep them calm, told a story about the time she stole pecans off her mother's Thanksgiving pie.

Twelve minutes after the first shot had been fired, with Jesse's grandfather racing to the scene, Townville fire chief Billy McAdams and Jamie Brock, a thirty-year volunteer firefighter, pulled up to the playground, parking behind the black pickup as they each drew their firearms. A teacher inside the school screamed that someone was bleeding badly and needed help. The two men looked at each other. They agreed that Billy, a paramedic, would go inside and that Jamie, armed with a nine-millimeter handgun, would search for the shooter. He walked along the back sidewalk, passing through the playground until he turned the corner and found Jesse.

"Freeze! Get on your knees!" Jamie shouted, and Jesse did what he was told. The firefighter, a thickset man with a horseshoe mustache, took him to the ground, pinning a knee against the back of the teen's neck.

"I'm sorry," Jesse said. "I'm sorry."

"Why did you do this?" Jamie asked, and Jesse told him he'd done it because he no longer believed in God.

Billy, meanwhile, had rushed through the first-grade door with the shot-out glass and past the multicolored rug stained red. Across the hallway, he found Jacob. Billy gave his pistol to a teacher and told her to watch the door. On his hands and knees, he helped the nurse give the boy CPR and applied a second tourniquet. As Billy struggled to find a vein for an IV, what color was left in Jacob's face vanished. Soon, SWAT officers carrying assault rifles descended on the rural campus, and a medical helicopter landed on the rec league fields. Eventually, Jacob was loaded onto a gurney and rushed out the door, and Collin would never see his friend's eyes open again.

"HE TRIED TO kill me," Ava, shaken and frantic, told her mother at Oakdale Baptist, where she'd been taken in a yellow bus shuttling kids from the school, four miles up the highway. It was a tense, tumultuous scene inside and outside the church. A large brick building topped with a lofty white cross and surrounded by farmland, it had often served as a central meeting place since its founding a century before, and now, for a new and unimaginable reason, it had become one again that afternoon. Rumors that two kids and a teacher had been killed only compounded the excruciating wait for dozens of parents desperately hoping their children were okay. A few minutes after Mary found Ava, a teacher brought over the girl's brother, Cameron, who was ten months younger and in the other first-grade class. He, too, had been on the playground during the shooting, and when he saw his mom, he swore to her that the man had pointed the gun right at him. Before they left, a detective got Mary's phone number, and a state trooper gave the kids stickers that looked like badges. In the car, Ava couldn't stop trembling.

"I didn't see Jacob," she said. "What happened to Jacob?"

The helicopter had flown the boy to Greenville, forty miles away, and when his mother, Renae, saw him for the first time in the hospital bed that afternoon, she passed out. His face was swollen, eyes rimmed in black. The bullet had sliced through her son's femoral artery, and in the immediate aftermath, he'd lost 75 percent of his blood. "When I looked at him," Renae said later, "I didn't see my baby boy."

Jacob's grandmother had come to the hospital with Zoey, a doll-size child with a round face and dark brown hair that matched her big, curious eyes. Perhaps because of the upheaval in their home life, Jacob, even at six, had often treated Zoey more like his daughter than his sister. He frequently checked in with his former kindergarten teacher, Kerry Burriss: "Did Zoey make good choices today?" he'd inquire. When he asked again one afternoon on the way to his grandmother's car, Kerry acknowledged the girl had gotten into trouble, and Jacob nodded. His face serious, he announced that he would "take care of it." Jacob also liked to dote on Zoey, though. He carried her food tray at lunch in the cafeteria and walked her into the school each morning, holding her hand until they reached her classroom. Now Zoey was at the hospital, trying to make sense of what had happened to the boy she called "Bubba" and who called her "Sissy." When Kerry arrived that night, the girl walked straight to her and looked up: "My brother is shot in the leg. He lost a lot of blood."

Kerry didn't know what to say, nor did hundreds of parents whose children were reeling from what they'd experienced, including Collin's. His mother, Stephanie Edwards, had beaten him to the hospital. When the ambulance pulled up, she climbed into the back and wrapped her arms around her son. On the way, he'd asked why his mom and dad weren't there, but by the time Stephanie reached him, shock had taken hold. Peering into her son's vacant eyes, she struggled to understand how such a thing could happen at a school like Townville Elementary.

In a community that was home to families that had farmed for decades, retirees with lake houses, college-educated professionals who commuted up the road to Clemson University, and hundreds of people in mobile homes living from one paycheck to the next, what connected almost all of them was the beloved redbrick school where generations of children had gathered to learn and play and grow up together. Now everything had changed.

Siena, the girl who had banged on the door to get back inside, almost immediately began to obsess over Jesse. She feared he'd somehow get out of jail, and that when he did, he'd come after her school again. When her parents tried to go next door the afternoon of the shooting to explain to her grandparents what had happened, she refused to let them leave her alone, even for a moment. Siena's mother lay beside the girl that night, listening to her daughter whimper until the sun came up.

Karson, who had leapt the fence, didn't know that Jacob had been shot until he heard it on the news the next day. Because the boys' mothers worked together at Subway, the two of them had been friends since they were toddlers. They'd bounced together for hours on a trampoline. They'd giggled together playing *Grand Theft Auto*, the video game with the bad words in it. At recess, they'd played tag, with Karson as the Joker and Jacob as Batman. Karson stopped eating after he learned that his friend was hurt, and asked about him constantly: "Mama, is Jacob getting better?" "Is Jacob going to get to come home?" "Is Jacob going to die?" Three days after the shooting, on Karson's seventh birthday, his family took him to celebrate at a Chuck E. Cheese. He tried to have fun, but his mind remained on Jacob, who should have been there munching pizza and collecting wads of tickets that they'd exchange for cheap candy. On the way home, Karson asked about him again. His mother had heard the news hours earlier but didn't want to tell him right way. Jacob, she finally acknowledged, had gone to heaven, and tears began to streak her son's cheeks.

It was an act of violence that few outside South Carolina remembered for long, a symptom of how numb Americans had grown to this crisis: almost no one pays attention to school shootings in which only a single child dies. And in a way, that made sense to me, until I traveled to Townville and immersed myself in the lives of children who, though they did not die or wear even a single scar from the shooting, had been shattered by it. That first trip to South Carolina made me realize that the vast majority of Americans, even those of us engaged on the issue of school shootings, fail to comprehend the devastation they truly leave behind. Seeing how much Ava, Siena, Karson, and the other young witnesses had unraveled was revelatory, but my real epiphany came during a conversation with Kyle Caudell, the pastor of a Baptist church near the school who counseled children for weeks after the attack. The kids who came to him were older, in fifth or sixth grade, which meant that none had seen any of the violence on the playground that day. Yet they, too, struggled with sleeplessness, nightmares, incessant fear that the gunman would return. One child, who had been locked away on the second floor throughout the attack, became convinced that Jesse was trying to kill him, personally.

To understand who those children represented, I spent weeks reviewing thousands of news stories dating to the Columbine High massacre in 1999. Steven Rich, my colleague at the *Post*, later joined me in that effort, and we found that the total number of students who have been on K–12 campuses during a shooting eclipsed 240,000— larger than the cities of Baton Rouge, Des Moines, or Birmingham. As dismaying as that figure is, it doesn't include hundreds of incidents of gun violence at after-school dances, sports games, and other gatherings, because I had no way to determine exactly how many children were present during those events. The true number is much higher, likely exceeding 350,000, if not a half million.

A meaningful percentage of those children will face significant struggles, according to mental health experts who described to me how a single moment of terror that lasts no more than a few minutes, or even seconds, can ripple through many more lives than most people realize. Samantha Haviland understands this as well as anyone. Now the director of counseling for Denver's public school system, she has spent almost her entire professional life treating traumatized kids. One day in 2008, she sat on the floor of a school library's back room, the lights off, the door locked. Crouched all around her were teenagers pretending that someone with a gun was trying to murder them. No one there knew that Samantha, then a counselor in her mid-twenties, had survived Columbine nine years earlier. On that day, April 20, 1999, Samantha ran from gunfire and heard some of it, too, but she didn't get shot or see a bullet strike anyone else. The shock and grief solidified her plan to become a counselor, though Samantha didn't get counseling herself. The nightmares, always of being chased, lingered for years, but she didn't think she deserved help, not when classmates had died or been maimed or had witnessed the carnage firsthand. Many others had suffered far more, Samantha decided. She would be okay. But now there she was, a decade later, sitting in the darkness, practicing once again to escape what so many of her friends had not. Then she heard footsteps. Then, beneath the door, she saw the shadow of an administrator who was checking the locks. Then her chest began to throb, and her body began to quake, and suddenly, Samantha knew she wasn't okay.

After the panic attack, she finally got therapy and made substantial progress. She forced herself to lead a normal life, going to movies and malls and political rallies. She told her story so often—of sprinting barefoot through the hallways, of losing one of her dearest friends—that telling it again didn't wreck her anymore. She earned a doctorate, becoming a leading expert in trauma and how to cope with it. She knew, though, that nothing could erase what was inside her. A few years ago, someone accidentally pressed a panic button in the school where she was working, signaling to police that a shooter remained in the building. Samantha wasn't there at the time, but she pulled up in her car just as the officers did. In front of her, she saw students streaming outside, their hands in the air, and she began to weep.

On a Wednesday morning in October 2016, Jacob lay inside a miniature gray casket topped with yellow chrysanthemums and a *Ninja Turtles* figurine. He was dressed in a Batman costume. Ava couldn't bear to look at him, so she sat on her mother's lap near the back of Oakdale Baptist and turned away. After the shooting, Ava discovered the note she'd written, the one with the invitation for Jacob to come to her house and play with her cats and get married. The girl realized that she'd forgotten to give it to him. Distraught, Ava crumpled it into a plastic bin in her bedroom. Now she was at his funeral.

"He's not really dead, is he?" Ava whispered to her mother.

"Yes," Mary told her. "He is."

Jacob's family had asked that people attending the service dress like superheroes because of the boy's infatuation with them. Ava wore a *Ninja Turtles* top with a purple cape. Collin, who'd begun to recover from the shock of what he witnessed but was still in a wheelchair because of the wound to his foot, dressed as Captain America, as did Siena. Karson had also come, his shirt displaying a *J* within a *Superman* logo. But he'd hesitated in the parking lot.

"Mama, that looks like that boy's truck. Is he here?" Karson had asked, motioning toward a dark pickup.

Kerry, the kindergarten teacher, had also needed a moment in her car at the visitation the day before, after she watched a deputy in a green shirt pass by. Famously unflappable, she had been a steadying force for many after the shooting, taking Zoey from the hospital that first night and caring for the girl at her own home in the days that followed. Kerry had thought she would be okay, but then there she was, chest pounding, palms slick, mind replaying that moment locked in the cramped bathroom when, as an officer knocked on the door, she wondered if he was actually the shooter. Still, she got out of the car at the visitation and did so again at the funeral. Like many of the other teachers there that day, she walked in wearing a handmade *Ninja Turtles* cape.

Dozens of people among the hundreds in attendance with her had favorite Jacob stories, but no one had more than Kerry. As part of the school's disciplinary system, all the kids at Townville Elementary were given small cards that displayed their names and photos, and on the back of the bathroom door in Kerry's room was a stoplight that went from white (for students on their best behavior) to red (their worst). Because Jacob was a devout follower of rules, his card had always been on white, until one day, in 4K, when Kerry caught him talking with classmates during a lesson. She told the boy to move his card. Dismayed, he stood up and put his hands on his hips.

"No ma'am. No ma'am. I can't move my card. I'll make better choices," he pleaded. When she wouldn't relent, he shook his head and stomped his feet on his way to move the card.

Outside of his talent show performance, Jacob was perhaps best known in kindergarten for the rattail that dangled below his shoulders, an object of fascination to his classmates, who liked to tug on it. Indignant after one such episode, he complained to Kerry, who couldn't resist video recording the exchange on her phone.

"Jacob, what happened?" Kerry asked, as he looked up at her, mouth agape, a pink beach ball dotted with flowers under his right arm.

"Chloe pulled my rattay-eeel!" he told her.

"Show me," she said.

"She pulled my rattail," he repeated.

"Is it still on there? Turn around and let me see," she said, and he turned his head to show her that it was, indeed, still there.

"Thank goodness," Kerry said. "And why did she do that?"

"I don't know," he said, pushing his too-large glasses up from the end of his button nose. As they called for Chloe to come back over, another child wandered up and, unable to resist, wrapped his fingers around the boy's famed threads of hair.

Jacob just made people feel good, normally through his presence alone, but often with intent, too. At recess, he would ignore his allergies in search of dandelions, yanking the flowering weeds out of the ground and arranging them in a bunch. Then he'd run up to Kerry and hand them to her as if it were a bouquet of red roses. "He was just one of the most genuinely loving children," said his mother. She knew of only one photo in which he wasn't smiling: when, after he'd had a fight with Zoey, Renae made them sit together on the couch.

From their seats at Oakdale Baptist, Jacob's classmates listened to the same pastor who had presided over the funeral for the shooter's father three days earlier. "I cannot understand what's transpired in Townville, in our community," the preacher said. "I can't make sense of it. I cannot." They heard about Jacob's devotion to God and what, in his family's view, he would have said about the teenager who killed him: "Forgive that boy and love him like Jesus loves him, because Jesus loves him." They watched as, midway through the service, his mom staggered to her son's casket and then collapsed to the floor. They stared as Jacob's body was wheeled up the center aisle at the end of the memorial.

Meghan, Jacob's teacher, watched all that, too. That morning, she'd put on a blue *Superman* shirt, grabbed a wad of tissues, and settled into a pew, despite the bullet hole in her shoulder and the post-traumatic stress that had already begun to bubble up. Afterward, she went to her first visit with a therapist, whom Meghan told about the guilt afflicting her. About all the things she imagined she could have done differently. About how, in her mind, she should have saved

Jacob. "It's not your fault," the therapist told her that day, as she would again and again in the months that followed.

Around the same time Meghan was hearing those words, Jacob's friends returned for the first time to the place he'd been shot. The school, scheduled to resume classes the same week, hosted an open house a few hours after his funeral. No one knew how the kids would react, but Denise, the principal, believed the small step of a brief return might help with the big step of a permanent one. In Townville, where nearly seven in ten of the school's students lived in poverty, it wasn't viable to construct a new building or bus the students elsewhere. They had to go back. And Denise's staff was doing all they could think of to make them feel safe again, planning a big welcome for that first morning of classes: uniformed officers, therapy dogs, volunteers in superhero costumes, more than twenty counselors, a line of signs—HAVE A GREAT DAY AT SCHOOL!—in the parking lot.

But first, the staff invited the kids back to the playground. Some even ventured onto it. Collin rolled out on his light-blue medical scooter. Siena climbed a jungle gym. Children who had screamed on that playground a week before were now, once again, laughing on it. Ava wasn't one of them, though. Her parents didn't know it yet, but the trauma that would eventually consume her mind had already begun to set in. Lingering behind with her mom, the girl couldn't forget what she had seen, and lost, here. "Please don't make me go out there again," Ava said, before they eased onto the sidewalk, holding hands. With each step, the girl's fingernails dug deeper into her mother's skin.

CHAPTER 3

"I CAN'T BELIEVE HE WENT THROUGH WITH IT"

Inside the Mind of a Teenage Gunman

In the weeks after Jesse Osborne executed his father and opened fire on Townville Elementary's playground, neighbors and teachers and family friends who had known the teen for years were convinced there must be a reasonable explanation. Jesse, after all, had attended that school, romping across the playground where his gun was found, walking the hallways he left smeared with blood. He had started at age four and was quiet then, never a troublemaker. He played catcher on the rec league baseball team. He had friends. "Smart, popular, funny, athletic, silly," said Kerry, who, years before teaching Jacob in kindergarten, had taught Jesse in it. He had stolen the scene at her daughter's ninth birthday party, toppling over a railing and "accidentally" pulling down his pants, which made all the kids, and the adults, laugh. He did well in class, too. One of his mother's favorite photos was of Jesse, at the end of fifth grade, with an award that recognized students who showed special academic talent. EXCELLENCE, the certificate read as a slight blond boy with wire-rimmed glasses and a sheepish smile held it up in front of the school's redbrick exterior.

There had, however, been one clear harbinger of the coming bloodshed. Less than two years before, Jesse's second school, West-Oak Middle, had expelled him for bringing a hatchet and a machete to school in his bag. That, though, didn't mean he was dangerous, said his mother, Tiffney, who had told and retold an uncorroborated story that made Jesse's decision sound more understandable. He had been bullied, she said, though not even that had made him do it. The tipping point came when his antagonists turned on a friend who had a disability. Jesse would never have used the weapons anyway, she claimed, and the people who had watched him grow up didn't doubt that. When Kerry's daughter, who went to a different middle school, came home saying she'd heard Jesse had gotten in trouble, his former teacher didn't believe it. "You quit saying that," she scolded. After the shooting, the principal, Denise Fredericks, called a guidance counselor and Jesse's old fifth-grade teacher, both of whom knew him well. The principal was overcome with worry that she or her staff had missed something, but no, both of them said, they hadn't. "That's our sweet Jesse," one told her.

Violence just wasn't in the boy's nature, insisted his paternal grandmother, Patsy, whose son Jesse had killed. She said he resisted working with his father in the family's chicken houses because he didn't like to break the bird's necks. Once, he rescued a wild rabbit from the jaws of a family dog, keeping the animal alive for five days in a cardboard box and nursing it with an eyedropper. His mother took pictures and recorded a video, admiring his compassion. One persistent rumor around town was that his dad, Jeffrey, a sometime heavy drinker, had killed another one of Jesse's rabbits, "Floppy"—or, at least, Jesse thought so, which had set him off. His grandmother contended that he had driven to the school only because he was suicidal over what he'd done to his dad and believed the police would end his life if he fired the gun on campus. Patsy knew that her grandson, who was intimately familiar with firearms, had shot a teacher in the shoulder, Jacob in the leg, and another student in the foot. "If Jesse had gone up to the school to kill someone, he would have killed them," she said. "Shot them right in the heart. That's how good a shot he was."

A reasonable explanation just had to exist, the people of Townville thought. Surely, this native son, this child they thought they knew, wouldn't do something so abhorrent if he hadn't lost his mind in a fit of anger or despair or illness. The people of Townville, though, didn't know Jesse Osborne.

Who he really was would shock his community, but the truth might have remained unknown, as it does in many of these cases, if not for the road map he left behind. Well more than half of the country's school shooters over the past two decades targeted specific people, and no one else. A few took their own lives, and about 10 percent fired the weapons accidentally. Just one in five, including Jesse, selected their victims at random. These were the would-be, or actual, mass killers, and they are the ones who frighten and confound us most.

In recent years, activists have pushed for journalists to ignore the shooters because it deprives them of the attention they crave and because it might prevent their narratives from inspiring other gunmen. It's a noble effort and one with which I and many other reporters have wrestled: how do we balance our duty as truth seekers with the potential dangers of promoting an evildoer's bad deeds and ideas? It's a difficult question to answer and one that we should take seriously, but in Jesse's case, there is, to me, a clear public good in exposing who he really was—and highlighting the many warning signs that those around him missed or ignored in the months before the shooting. Through texts, internet searches, Instagram messages, YouTube videos, and hours of conversation with investigators and doctors, Jesse Osborne has provided extraordinary insight into his own mind at a moment when this country is struggling like never before to understand how little boys who pose with education awards turn into teenagers who slaughter children.

—

"My plan is . . ." Jesse wrote in a private Instagram chat group on the night of September 22, 2016, six days before the shooting at Townville Elementary. He had been thinking for months, maybe years, about the words he would type next, but it was only in this dark, secluded corner of the internet that he felt free to share them. He had done his due diligence, run though the scenarios, and now Jesse knew how he would become the deadliest school shooter in American history.

Ninety-three seconds later, he continued: "shooting my dad getting his keys getting in his truck, driving to the elementary school 4 mins away, once there gear up, shoot out the bottom school class room windows, enter the building, shoot the first class which will be the 2d grade, grab teachers keys so I don't have to hasle to get through any doors then for all the other class rooms ima unlock the doors through my homemade pipe bombs into the class rooms then enter and kill the remaining students in each class room then get in a shootout with police then kill myself with my shotgun."

Jesse, a gangly six feet tall with a high-pitched voice that often cracked, had initially considered attacking his former middle school, but it was an hour away, and at least one resource officer worked there, he explained. He had also researched police response times to both campuses and found that it would take them much longer to reach the remote elementary school. At least fifteen minutes, he conjectured, maybe forty-five for SWAT.

"I think ill probably most likely kill around 50 or 60," he wrote. "If I get lucky maybe 150."

What led to that chilling declaration had begun two years earlier, with a song. Jesse, then twelve or thirteen, had heard a lyric about Columbine. He wanted to know what it meant, so he asked his dad, who told him two losers had shot up their high school, planting a seed in Jesse's mind that grew into an infatuation. He began to study it, and other incidents, obsessively. Before West-Oak expelled him, he produced what he called a documentary about the Colorado massacre that got him into trouble. Another time, after a student poked him in the chest, Jesse threatened to come back with a rifle and shoot the boy, who was terrified. His reaction thrilled Jesse.

He was home-schooled after the expulsion, which left him alone for hours in his room, on his computer. In that solitude, Jesse's fixation blossomed. He plunged into the "true crime community" on the website Tumblr, where fans of serial killers and mass murderers gather like groupies to share memes, essays, original artwork, and demented fantasies. "I finally found people to actually talk to me," he later told investigators. In the private chat group, which included users from other countries, they envisioned a simultaneous attack on schools around the world, referred to as "Project Rainbow," also the name a pair of teens used for an alleged plot (never executed) to attack a school in England a decade earlier.

No two names were more prominent in the chat group's conversations than those of Eric Harris and Dylan Klebold, the Littleton, Colorado, high school shooters who are worshipped in obscure corners of the internet by a group known as "Columbiners." Like Jesse, these are typically teenagers searching for identity. Many, including him, say they felt isolated and depressed, and in Harris and Klebold, who wrote prolifically about their own deranged interests, these young people see a reflection of themselves. Much of that, however, hinges on a misguided belief in a myth discredited by *Columbine* author Dave Cullen: that the shooters were bullied outcasts who therefore had some justifiable reason to kill their schoolmates.

"Most Columbiners have one thing in common: we have felt like outsiders or victims at some point in our lives," one person told researchers who interviewed twenty-two members of the internet subculture. "We have felt like absolutely NObody could understand how alone we have felt, and that experience is exactly what Eric and

Dylan lived. Knowing that there were even just two boys out there who felt the same way as we feel now gives us comfort."

The study identified four subgroups whose members often overlap: avid researchers, Columbiners, teen girls who have a romantic or sexual interest in the shooters, and copycats. The researchers concluded that even if someone had an intense interest in campus massacres, it didn't mean they were likely to pick up a gun, but those interviewed acknowledged that fellow members of their community could become, or already were, potential shooters.

These groups pose a challenge for law enforcement, in part because neither the FBI nor any local agency has the resources to monitor every dark corner of the internet, a fact that forces investigators to rely on the would-be gunman's friends, family, or teachers to intervene. Also, the First Amendment protects free speech, including even the most unsettling fantasies, and no one has developed a way to discern who is the merely obsessed and who is the actually violent person.

Always at the center of this depraved universe are Harris and Klebold, who have influenced at least forty-three school shooters over the past two decades, according to Peter Langman, a psychologist and one of the country's leading experts on campus gunmen. Why the Columbine killers have had such a lasting impact is complex, Langman suggested. Much of the drama they created was captured live by news cameras at a moment when both cable TV and the internet were exploding in popularity, immediately making Columbine a national, and international, event. Langman also suspects that the attackers' unachieved ambition—to kill as many as five hundred or six hundred—has impressed others who have studied them. Many subsequent shooters have become engrossed in Harris's writing.

"They can relate to his rage and his contempt and looking down on humanity as scum. People like that. They quote it. It's inspiring to them," Langman told me. "If you're a potential school shooter, you're looking for a role model. . . . Eric carried himself with a certain apparent coolness that appealed."

The pair's influence on Jesse Osborne was acute. His Instagram handle included "nbk," for the movie *Natural Born Killers*, and "kmfdm," for a German industrial band—a pair of pop culture references that appear frequently in the writings of the Columbine murderers. Comments Jesse left on YouTube videos betrayed his growing interest in weapons and violence. In reply to a question someone posted about needing a license to own a rifle, he wrote, "depends on your state. here in south carolina we dont need a lisense for anything except explosives or machine guns which are crazy expensive." He also studied school shooter training videos, perhaps to understand what he might someday encounter. On one, he added a comment and a laughing face: "someone f—ing threw a chair . . . savage." He watched a tutorial on how to make pipe grenades, writing, "were all flagged by the fbi cause we looked this up," followed by another laughing face. When someone replied, claiming to be a wanted criminal, Jesse asked, "wtf did you do . . . shot up 5 schools." And then: "columbine style?" As others jokingly bragged of the places they had attacked, Jesse joined in. "Bitch—i went into a school eith a minigun and killed 250 people hitler style."

Also, in stark contrast to the family's description of him as an animal lover, the teen began to delight in their torture. He ripped the legs off crickets and fed them to ants. He tore the wings off bees. He shot frogs with BB guns, then smashed them against concrete. He shot birds and fed them to the dogs, and he also shot at the dogs because their panicked reaction amused him. He watched and rewatched a video online of a man mutilating and killing two small kittens. Later, when a psychiatrist asked him what brought him pleasure, he recalled that scene.

What his family knew of those habits remains unclear, but all of them claimed that he hadn't gone through any especially alarming changes in the year before the killings. He went to a midnight showing of a *Hunger Games* movie with his mom and, she said, never stopped saying at the end of their phone calls that he loved her "to the moon and back." He continued to spend time with his grandparents, who lived on the property next door, watching the History Channel with his grandfather, Thomas, and *Frozen*, one of his favorites, with Patsy. But at the same time that his violent fantasies intensified, so, too, did his obsession with guns, which his family accommodated. He was enamored with Airsoft, a shooting sport in which combatants fire plastic orbs at one another with rifles that look almost exactly like the real things. His father, Jeffrey, worked long hours in the chicken houses, but when he was free, father and son liked to fire guns together at hay bales, as they did days before Jesse's attack on the school. In his room, he would play first-person shooters on some nights until sunrise, live-streaming games on a YouTube channel almost no one else watched. "Akbar—God is great," he said, giggling, early in one video, because that's what he thought killers did. In another, he looked into the camera and widened his manic blue eyes. "Look at this face," he said, wispy blond hair dangling across his forehead. "It's innocent."

JESSE HAD HANDLED guns since he was little, but so did lots of kids in Townville. His grandfather gave him a .410-bore shotgun for Christmas when he was eleven, figuring he was old enough to shoot squirrels. Guns were, perhaps, the thing that most bonded Jeffrey and his son, who had planned to hunt deer together for the first time that winter after the shooting.

As September arrived, and Jesse's scheme began to take shape, the teen knew he could get to the Springfield Armory .40-caliber handgun his dad kept in a nightstand beside his bed, but that's not the weapon Jesse wanted. If he was to become the deadliest school shooter ever, he decided, he'd need his dad's Ruger Mini-14, a semi-automatic rifle. That posed a problem, though, because Jeffrey kept it locked in a safe.

"Todays my lucky day," Jesse told his Instagram friends the night after he had laid out his plan. "I just seen my dad type in the code to the gun safe."

As Jeffrey punched the numbers in, Jesse tried to record them with his phone, pretending to text as he pointed the camera in his dad's direction. When he still couldn't open it, the teen turned to the internet for help. "How to unlock any digital gun safe," he searched, in various forms, many times that week. He even put dish soap on the keys and turned off the lights, believing the technique would reveal which ones his dad had pressed. None of that worked, either, so Jesse looked online at guns for sale, wondering if he could buy something in time. "South Carolina gun laws," he googled at one point, and he repeatedly visited Armslist, a Craigslist-like site that has been criticized because of the ease with which some users have procured weapons without undergoing background checks. Among many, Jesse looked up a Kel-Tec PLR-16, a semiautomatic handgun that comes with a ten-round magazine and a promise to deliver "rifle firepower." It was around then that his father took him to shoot an M16 rifle for the first time. "Fully automatic. Probably the funnest thing I ever done," he said later. The same day, Jeffrey told his son that he was, at last, the better marksman. That made Jesse happy.

He didn't buy a new weapon, but he wasn't deterred. His favorite gunman was Seung-Hui Cho, who in 2007 had killed thirty-two people at Virginia Tech with a pair of handguns. That inspired Jesse, whose focus on his goals sharpened as the day approached. His Google searches: "youngest mass murderer," "10 youngest murderers in history," "deadliest US mass shootings," "top 10 mass shooters." "I HAVE TO BEAT ADAM LAZA," he had written in the chat group once before, in a misspelled reference to the man who, in 2012, killed twenty-six people at Sandy Hook Elementary in Newtown, Connecticut.

"Tomorrows rainbow day for meh . . . im so excited," he wrote on the night of September 27, telling his friends to delete their messages in case the police or the FBI investigated them later—advice that Jesse himself failed to follow. The next morning, he loaded his dad's pistol, and at around eleven, he claimed online that he had already shot him, which wasn't true. Jesse also said he was waiting for Townville Elementary's lunch period to end so all the kids would be back in their classrooms. "I don't want any runners," he wrote, along with a smiley face. Around that same time, Jesse's grandmother stopped by to give him a hamburger, a bag of potato chips, and a Mountain Dew. He met her on the front porch. Patsy gave him his lunch and said she'd pick him up early that evening for youth group at church.

"You have a good day, Nana," he told her. "I love you."

The others in the chat group questioned whether he had really shot his father, asking for photographic proof. Jesse refused but swore that he would head to the school soon, after he finished his burger. One asked what he would do if his mom came home to find her husband's body. "Bang bang," Jesse responded.

At some point early that afternoon, Jesse went back upstairs to his parents' bedroom and retrieved the loaded pistol. When he came back down, his father was on the recliner. The boy approached him from behind and raised the weapon, then fired. He kept firing, he later told his mother, Tiffney, because his father moved after the first shot and Jesse didn't want him to suffer.

"Can someone motivate me real quick?" he wrote the group.

"You can do it . . ."

"Tell me how scumbag life is," Jesse asked.

"Life is s—."

"I'm about to go kill 8 year old kids."

His dad was dead, he wrote, and now he felt "so f—ing nervous." He said he would drink one last Mountain Dew, "then it's terminator time." He told the group he would join them on a Skype call once he reached the back of the school. It would take him about seven minutes to get there.

Jesse said good-bye to his dogs and gave his rabbit, Floppy, a kiss before slipping on a baseball cap and an Airsoft vest and packing it with more than a dozen extra rounds. He took his dad's black Dodge Ram pickup and headed up the dirt driveway, speeding by the bent green sign at its end: OSBORNE ROAD. He took a right and drove north, the same way he had been driven hundreds of times before to the place where he learned to read and write, to climb on monkey bars and scoot down slides. On his way, he passed his father's bright red chicken houses, fields smothered in corn stalks and soybean plants, pastures dotted with cows and goats and hay bales. On past the baseball field where he played catcher, by the windows pasted with cartoon drawings of children waving, up the driveway and around the corner, to the back of the building, where Ava and Jacob and the other first-graders had just come outside for recess.

"Now," Jesse wrote his friends. "I'm there."

They listened over Skype as he stepped out of the truck. *"Allahu akbar,"* he yelled, because that's what he thought killers did. "I hate my life," he also shouted, firing again and again. One round hit a window. One hit a teacher in the shoulder. One hit a boy in the foot. One hit the smallest first-grader at Townville in the leg. After twelve seconds, with his gun jammed, Jesse gave up and threw it to the ground.

"You heard gunshots," someone in the group wrote.

"He was screaming about going to hell."

"Are you guys still skyping?"

"I can't believe he went through with it."

ON A WEDNESDAY afternoon in February 2018, at the exact moment that Jesse was sitting in a South Carolina courtroom listening to a witness recall the time he warned a jail guard that he had put his own "dad in the f—ing ground," another angry teenager arrived on a high school campus in South Florida with an AR-15 packed in a duffel bag.

While Jesse remained in relative obscurity, Nikolas Cruz's name and photograph appeared in news stories around the world, prompting millions to wonder, yet again, who these school shooters really were. Despite the oft-referenced image of the brooding teen in a trench coat, there is no archetype. One of them, perhaps the youngest in history, was a six-year-old who, due to his age, couldn't even be charged with a crime after killing a classmate in Michigan because he didn't like her. Another was a fifteen-year-old girl in Arizona who murdered her former girlfriend, then herself, after a breakup. Another was a fifty-three-year-old who barged into his estranged wife's special-needs classroom in California, killing her and a student.

But it's the indiscriminate gunmen who kill at random, the Nikolas Cruzes and Jesse Osbornes, who most often leave people asking why and how and who. Of the more than forty school shooters who fit that profile over the past two decades, this is what we know about them: they were all male, their median age was sixteen, and among those whose race we've identified, nearly 80 percent were white. Here's what we also know: every one of them had access to firearms, despite the fact that many, if not most, waved bright red warning flags before they ever fired a shot.

"What is so tragic about school shootings is that in virtually every case, somebody knew something that in retrospect was a warning sign," said Langman, the psychologist who has spent years studying dozens of attackers. "This includes students who heard the perpetrators talking about committing an attack, teachers who received homework assignments that foreshadowed rampages, parents who knew their kids were building bombs or were obsessed with Columbine, or posting disturbing videos online, and law enforcement officers who received reports of potential violence but did not follow up sufficiently to prevent a shooting."

Cruz's case offered an infuriating number of examples. On the first day that the Marjory Stoneman Douglas High School Public Safety Commission gathered to review it, one of their investigators presented a slide breaking down nearly fifty instances of threatening behavior on Cruz's part that people knew about but didn't report or that authorities knew about and didn't act on. Instances in which he tortured or killed an animal: seven. Times he was seen with a bullet, knife, or firearm: nineteen. Declarations of hatred he made toward a group or person: eight. References he made about wanting to hurt or kill someone: eleven. Threats that he would shoot up a school: three.

Langman has catalogued many other cases as well. In 1997, before a teenager killed three girls at a school in Kentucky, he told other students that he was going to do it, calling the date of his attack "the day of reckoning." A year later, a boy at an Arkansas school stood on a table in the cafeteria and announced, "You're all going to die"; he and a friend later killed four students and a teacher. In 2006, a North Carolina teen who openly worshipped the Columbine shooters killed his father before wounding two students at a high school.

Even lesser-known shooters who intend to attack just one person almost never do it without warning. The six-year-old who killed a little girl had previously stabbed her with a pencil and struck other students. The fifteen-year-old who killed her ex-girlfriend had been noticeably depressed in the days before she persuaded a boy to get her a gun. The fifty-three-year-old who killed his wife and her student had a history of brutal violence toward his girlfriends.

And then there's Jesse, whose mother gave investigators a revealing interview just hours after the shooting, explaining how difficult he had become, something she had apparently blamed on puberty. One of her statements was read aloud during that weeklong hearing in February 2018, which was held to decide whether the teen would be tried as an adult. Tiffney and Jeffrey had once found online messages that unsettled them, and another time, she asked about the German industrial band included in Jesse's screen name. He talked his way out of it, she said, "but Jesse would also tell me and Jeff so many stories. You wouldn't know what was right. Sometimes I felt

like Jesse was just against me and Jeff. You know, we're the bad people. Like if he could get us in some trouble, it would be perfect."

These were the same parents who knew that their son had taken
a hatchet and a machete to school, who knew that he had an explosive temper, but who still provided him regular access to lethal
weapons. At one point during the hearing, Jesse's defense attorney
asked Danielle Atkinson, a clinical psychologist who had examined
him, how much his behavior might have been influenced by the violent video games he played. They probably should have been taken
from him, given his history, she said, but that wasn't what worried
her most.

"I don't think that the shooting video games have as a strong of
an influence," she said, "as actual shooting guns."

His plan failed, Jesse told investigators six and a half hours after
he had fired the last bullet, tossed the gun away, called his grandparents, and paced outside Townville Elementary until an armed
volunteer firefighter ordered him to surrender, which he did. "I was
thinking like twenty, thirty kids. I don't even know," Jesse acknowledged, though he was sure his first shot hit someone.

"I just seen red pop up, so I just assumed."

Had his gun not jammed, one of them asked him, what would
have happened?

"God knows," Jesse told them, but what the teen said *he* knew
was how different everything would have gone had he just gotten his
hands on that semiautomatic rifle locked in the safe. He sounded
disappointed, making virtually no effort to disguise his bloodlust
from investigators in an interview that was more a presentation than
an interrogation. Jesse never hesitated to answer questions, never
asked for his mom or a lawyer. He wanted to talk, though not just to
clear his mind or confess the truth. Jesse claimed that his father was
drunk when he shot him, and though a half-brother later testified
that Jeffrey could be abusive, a toxicology report showed no traces

of alcohol in the man's bloodstream at the time of his death. Jesse also claimed that he had attacked the kids in Townville because he had been bullied, but that, too, wasn't true. He might have experienced some mistreatment by kids at West-Oak, the investigators found, but they heard conflicting accounts about that from students who knew him—and even by own his admission, he certainly hadn't been bullied by the first-graders he terrorized.

Jesse suggested that what he really needed was treatment, telling the investigators that he was supposed to talk to a therapist after he was expelled but never had. "That might actually have stopped me from doing this," he said, and in the months that followed, Jesse tried to persuade the people involved in his case that he suffered from some condition beyond his control, which might mean he wasn't responsible for those heinous crimes. At the juvenile detention center, he researched signs of schizophrenia, autism, and major depression with psychotic features. He told at least three different experts hired to analyze his mental health that he was having wild hallucinations: blue figures with pointed limbs, faceless people, demon voices, Scooby-Doo.

All lies, the doctors said. They noted that he looked them in the eye, shook their hands, and was exceedingly polite, showing no signs of psychosis or any other mental illness. He failed at least three tests designed to determine whether the symptoms he claimed to have were real. On one of them, any total above a 14.5 indicated that he was faking. Jesse scored a 44.

"I think that Mr. Osborne started out as a really good kid," Mark Wagner, a clinical psychologist, testified during the 2018 hearing. "Early in the week, we saw lots of pictures of him at Townville Elementary. He was participating in a lot of activities. He looked like a really sweet boy, and he continues to be a really nice person, on the surface. He's polite. In the detention center, he's been cooperative. Repeatedly, people comment about his social behavior. That's in marked contrast to what was seen below the surface. And I frankly was shocked by the material that was retrieved by the FBI . . . particularly the internet searches, his fascination with shooting and death and guns. There's another side to him that's very dark and very concerning."

That side of Jesse proved hard for him to contain. When Jacob's autopsy findings were discussed in court, Dr. James Ballenger, a psychiatrist who interviewed Jesse for a total of nine hours, caught the teen giggling. "Now, he tried to hide it because he's learned that he's not supposed to do that," Ballenger testified. "But he had a real hard time hiding it."

"And you observed that personally this week?" a prosecutor asked.

"Again and again and again," Ballenger said, which was, in part, what led him to believe Jesse had a conduct disorder and was highly likely to develop antisocial personality disorder, which can't be diagnosed before age eighteen.

At some point after his arrest, I discovered, Jesse appeared to have gained access to his YouTube page, writing, "IM LOCKED UP AND THEY WONT LET ME OUT NOOOOOO. IM JESSE OSBORNE LET ME FREE. #RIPJ AND J"—an apparent reference to his father, Jeffrey, and to Jacob—"SORRY FOR THAT." Still, he didn't believe the shooting would have done any harm to the children inside the building, who didn't witness the gunfire. "But I'm pretty sure they're more aware of bullying now and what it could cause someone to do," he told Atkinson, speaking about children as young as four, some of whom cried, soiled themselves, had debilitating fear and nightmares for weeks. The kids on the playground, the kids like Ava and Karson and Siena—he guessed they might be more affected. "But they'll be able to get help for it," he said. "I try not to think about it."

Ballenger, a psychiatrist with more than forty years of experience, had already analyzed Dylann Roof, the white supremacist who killed nine African Americans in a Charleston, South Carolina, church in 2015, and Jared Lee Loughner, who killed six people and wounded Democratic representative Gabrielle Giffords in Arizona in 2011. Still, the doctor spotted things in Jesse that were uniquely disturbing. His cruelty to animals, for example, was the worst that Ballenger had ever seen. Jesse also showed a stunning lack of empathy, saying he had done Jacob a "favor" because he'd heard the boy's parents had struggled with drug addiction. Perhaps most chilling, though, was Jesse's central motivation.

"Now I have a life. Probably won't get a job, but I'll—I'll at least have a life," he told the investigators on that first night, and Ballenger had no doubt what that meant. He saw in Jesse a young man who killed not because of bullies or abuse or a fractured mind, but because he wanted to attain the status he'd envisioned.

"He was going to be famous, the best shooter ever," Ballenger told the judge, who ultimately decided, as expected, that Jesse would be tried as an adult. "He was going to be worshipped for a long time—worshipped."

"Did you see evidence of him looking at statistics of people to see how he lines up?" the prosecutor asked him.

Ballenger noted Jesse's Google searches for other mass shootings. "He actually confirmed that he would be one of the youngest, if not the youngest," the doctor said.

"And that was one of his goals?"

"That *was* his goal," Ballenger told the court. "To be the best shooter—to get fifty to sixty."

But Jesse didn't kill that many, not even close, depriving himself of the status he so badly craved. In his interview with interrogators, he couldn't stop wondering what might have been had he gotten his dad's Ruger Mini-14.

"You said you really wanted to use—" one of them started to ask.

"That, yeah," Jesse interrupted.

"What kind of gun is that?"

"To the media, it's called an assault rifle," he said.

"But you couldn't get that, you said?"

"No," Jesse told them. "It was locked up in the safe."

But he was wrong. Within hours of his arrest, police searched the family's home. In his parents' bedroom, investigators looked in a closet, just feet from where he had retrieved the pistol, and there, outside the safe, was the weapon Jesse coveted.

CHAPTER 4

"YOU HAVE TO SEPARATE THE GUNS FROM THE KIDS"

Children and the Firearm Safety Myth

Two years before Jesse Osborne walked into his father's bedroom in search of a gun, another boy a half hour from Townville, on the other side of Anderson County, did the same. On a Friday evening in July 2014, Tyler Paxton, who had celebrated his eleventh birthday with chicken nuggets and meatballs five days earlier, knew that the key to the gun safe was kept on top of it. His dad, Jonathan, had never hidden it from his only child because he didn't think the boy had given him reason to. So, as Tyler's parents watched TV in the living room, he reached up and took the key, opened the cabinet door, and pulled out a .357 magnum revolver with a snub nose. In a safe packed with rifles, it was the only loaded firearm. Tyler, gripping the pistol in his left hand, sat on the floor and faced a mirror. He raised the barrel to his temple. He pulled the trigger.

In the decade prior to that moment, the Paxtons' lives in West Pelzer, population nine hundred, revolved around their only child, who had never given them reason to believe he wanted to harm himself. Tyler's mere existence was, to them, something of a miracle. It had taken his mother, Olivia, seven years to conceive, and the pregnancy that followed proved no less fraught. A heavyset woman, she had only one kidney and high blood pressure, and after she carried him for four months, doctors told her that they didn't believe both mother and baby would survive. The next day, a 3-D ultrasound would determine whether the fetus was viable. Distraught, Olivia and Jonathan drove to Books-A-Million, where he bought her a baby name book. That night, after her husband fell asleep, she stayed up crying and praying. At 5:30 the next morning, Olivia reached for the book, opening it to a page that began with the name "Tyler" and a Bible verse, Matthew 21:22. "If you believe," she read, "you will receive whatever you ask for in prayer." At that day's appointment, the doctors told her their original assessment was wrong. Both she and the baby could survive, and they did.

Her son grew into a thoughtful, independent, and intensely curious child. At an age when most of his classmates were picking out storybooks from the library, he brought home encyclopedias. He became particularly interested in dinosaurs, memorizing the taxonomic names of dozens of them, though his favorite wasn't among the iconic carnivores that are typically the objects of adolescent fascination. He most liked the *Maiasaura*, an herbivore whose name meant "good mother reptile," which is what appealed to Tyler. This dinosaur took care of its children, and he appreciated that. His perspective was unusual for a boy his age, but his parents had gotten used to that, because he looked at many things differently from other kids. He decided, for example, to root for WWE wrestler "The Undertaker" not because of his sinister look or his patented piledriver; instead, Tyler admired that the man who played that character was an animal rights activist. "He's complex," said his father, whose son's observations often caught him off guard. Once, at a family barbecue, Jonathan's brother handed him a Sam Adams, and when Tyler noticed his dad holding the beer bottle, the boy confronted him. "It's bad for you. Why would you do something that's bad?" Tyler asked. "My heart sunk," Jonathan told me. He emptied the beer and never drank another one.

Tyler was serious about the things he deemed important, and he took nothing more seriously than karate, in which he earned a junior black belt at age ten, and church, which he attended almost every Sunday, even when his mother and father didn't. At school one year, he chose to write about Jesus for an assignment on heroes. "A hero is someone that does good things to help others, no matter how it hurts them," he wrote in neat print letters on notebook paper. Tyler brought his devotion home with him, too, requesting each night that he and his parents pray together before they went to sleep. "Dear Lord," he always began when his turn came, and sometimes it took four or five minutes for him to reach "Amen."

"An old soul," relatives often called the boy, who named his beagle "Johnny Cash." Still, Tyler was, in many ways, just a kid. He thought *SpongeBob SquarePants* was hilarious, and he could play *Minecraft* for hours. He didn't get in trouble often, but when he did, his parents confiscated his many electronics, because nothing irritated him more than that. In a letter to Olivia, he once tried to head off any potential punishment. "I love you mom. You are the best Mom ever," he wrote, signing it "Love Tyler," before adding, "P.S. I made a 61 on my math test. I'm sorry." A lanky kid who inherited his mother's green eyes and freckled skin, he liked to play with her long, curly brown hair and pretend that it had special powers. At bedtime, he often fell asleep to her rendition of "La La Lu," from Disney's *Lady and the Tramp*. As Tyler got older, he asked her not to tell anyone that he still liked it so much.

Tyler adored Olivia, who had been a stay-at-home mom since he was an infant, but the boy most wanted to be like his dad, a bearded, thick-armed U.S. Army veteran who worked as an operations manager at an asphalt plant. Jonathan taught him how to field and throw and hit a baseball, how to hook and clean a bass, and, as he got older, how to fire a gun. Jonathan, a competitive pistol shooter, had been enamored with firearms since childhood, and he wanted Tyler to be, too. He often suspected, though, that his boy acted interested only because *he* was. Tyler got bored sitting in the tree stand when they hunted deer, and he went to gun shops with Jonathan just to keep him company. When Tyler was ten, his dad bought him a .22-caliber rifle for Christmas, but the boy cared far more about his new Amazon Fire tablet.

As his eleventh birthday approached in 2014, Tyler seemed as content as he'd ever been. He had lots of friends and was excelling at karate. As in every other July, his parents took him to Isle of Palms, on South Carolina's Atlantic Coast. As usual, they went to Coconut Joe's, where he ordered fried shrimp and peeled off the breading before he ate them. He played in the ocean, ran the beach with Johnny Cash, his beagle. He smiled in every photo. On the Sunday before the shooting, he went back to church, standing up to share prayer requests for a family friend who was having heart surgery and for his grandmother, whose husband had taken his own life, with a gun, two years earlier. "She's still missing my Papa," he explained.

Then came the night of July 25. The Paxtons picked up food from Taco Bell and brought it home, and after Tyler finished his nachos, he headed to his parents' room. Sprawled on the bed in blue jean shorts and a greenish-yellow tank top, he scrolled through YouTube on his mom's phone until the battery ran down. He briefly came out to the living room and showed Olivia a funny video of an otter trying to dig a snack out of a tool box, then he plugged her phone into a charger.

"I'm gonna go watch cartoons," Tyler said, before he walked back to their bedroom.

To Jonathan, the source of the noise that soon followed didn't register right away. He'd heard gunshots thousands of times, but never in his home. Maybe a light bulb had popped, he thought. Worried that Tyler had shocked himself, his dad rushed down the hall and into the master bedroom. There, he found his son, who was still breathing, and screamed at his wife to call 911.

This was the sort of violence people seldom discussed in communities like Anderson County, where guns are held dear—where they're ubiquitous in closets, dresser drawers, and unsecured safes. And maybe, in some ways, that's because it's more frightening, and less explicable, than a school shooting carried out by a troubled teenager. In this case, the boy who took his dad's gun was a lot like everybody else's boys around here. He was kind and thoughtful and a devout believer in God. He was smart. He was obedient. And just like so many of those other children, he was educated on every aspect of what to do and what not to do with a gun. Yet, there he was, cradled in the arms of his father, the pistol by his side, his blood pooling on the floor.

THE CALLER INTO C-SPAN sounded angry. His name was Justin, from Maryland, and he loved his guns and wanted to make clear that the weapons, mere inanimate objects, should never be blamed for suicide, which account for around 60 percent of the firearm-related deaths in the United States each year. Any discussion of gun reform, he insisted, should ignore those shootings. On the receiving end of his tirade was David Hemenway, director of the Harvard Injury Control Research Center and one of the country's leading proponents of treating gun violence like a public health crisis.

"All your data, your research that you get, you include suicide. If someone is going to kill themselves, they're going to kill themselves regardless. Regardless if there's guns or whatever. So that should be obsolete," the man insisted, prompting Hemenway to sigh deeply, shake his head, and close his eyes. He'd been hearing this for years.

"You're entirely wrong about the suicide. The evidence is overwhelming. Everyone understands who has ever studied suicide that people go through bad patches. If the gun is in the home, it increases the risk of suicide—it increases it threefold," Hemenway explained.

"What that means, for example, for you is that instead of having a one percent chance that someone in your home will die of a suicide, you have a three percent chance. And you may think that's still not very large—most people with guns, nothing bad is going to happen. Most people who break the speed limit and go eighty miles an hour tomorrow—nothing bad is going to happen, but it increases your risk and it increases your risk substantially."

In fact, researchers have found that when people feeling suicidal are deprived of access to their preferred method, they often will not turn to another one—which means, contrary to Justin's pronouncement, that if those people don't have access to a gun during their moment of despair, they won't necessarily hang themselves or slit their wrists or jump off a bridge instead. The C-SPAN caller's argument is particularly misguided when it comes to children, a point demonstrated by a 2019 study that made a revelatory discovery: the single best predictor of a state's youth suicide rate is the proportion of homes in the state that contain a gun. Remarkably, one of the study's authors told me that single piece of data is a "far more accurate" indicator than the percentage of children who *attempt suicide*. "In other words," said Dr. Michael Siegel, a professor at Boston University School of Public Health, "if you had to guess the suicide rate in a state and could only ask one question, you would actually be better off asking for the percentage of gun households than for the percentage of youth who attempted suicide in that state."

A great many smart, well-intentioned gun owners—who, as Jonathan Paxton did, want nothing more than to protect their children from harm—believe that education ensures safety. Dr. Denise Dowd still remembers the first time she heard parents tell her that. It was 1991, just months into her fellowship at Children's Mercy Hospital in Kansas City. A boy, fifteen and from a rural community outside town, had learned that his girlfriend intended to break up with him. Stricken, he went to his room, pointed his .22-caliber mini rifle at his head, and fired, sending a round into one side and out the other. "We don't understand," the teen's parents told Dowd. He knew how to use firearms, they said. He kept his rifle safe, they said, always in his closet. He'd been educated on guns, they said, and now his mother and father wondered why that hadn't been enough. For Dowd, a physician and researcher who would go on to treat more than five hundred pediatric gunshot victims, the moment was formative.

"There's this mythical idea that you can teach kids not to want to handle a gun. . . . You can't train or educate curiosity out of a little kid, and teenagers are impulsive, and they act without any thought to the future," she said. "It's not even an issue of being educated about guns. Their brain is not developed. When it comes to guns, we seem to let that all go, which makes no sense, because it's lethal force."

Evidence suggests that in times when people are suicidal, they tend to turn to methods with which they're more familiar. Overall, men survive attempts at a lower rate than women in large part because men are six times more likely to kill themselves with a gun than women—unless those women have served in the military. "Female veterans are more comfortable with firearms," said Caitlin Thompson, the former director of suicide prevention at the U.S. Department of Veterans Affairs. "It's part of the culture." That reality raises a question: does training children how to use guns make them more likely, in times when they're suicidal, to pick up one of those rather than a rope or a knife or a bottle of pills, all of which are far less deadly? We don't know the answer to that question, but we should, because the stakes are extraordinarily high. A survey of 153 teenagers and young adults who survived suicide attempts found that a quarter of them tried to take their own lives within *five minutes* of deciding to, which, again, means that the method the young person chooses—or, better said, has the option to choose—is critical. Because of guns' extreme lethality, they're responsible for half the nation's suicide deaths. That number matters most because of another number: nine in ten who survive an attempt of any kind do not ultimately die by suicide.

"Whatever you think about guns, if a kid has unrestricted access to lethal force, that's a problem," Dowd said. "You have to separate the guns from the kids—the thing that does harm from the thing that's harmed."

Our country's repeated and ongoing failure to do that very thing has come at an immense cost, because if the only change we had made to America's gun culture over the past two decades was to prevent children from obtaining firearms, well more than half the school shootings since Columbine would not have happened; the hundreds of kids who accidentally shot themselves or each other every year would not have died or been maimed or suffered through the guilt of their mistake; and almost ten thousand children who, for at least a moment, felt an overwhelming urge to harm themselves, might still be alive, including a boy from South Carolina named Tyler.

Bob Maxwell knew how that night would end the moment he walked into the Paxtons' bedroom. Then one of only three police officers in all of West Pelzer, he had heard the "shots fired" call less than a minute earlier, and now he was standing over a father telling his boy how much he loved him. The smell of gunpowder still hung in the air.

"Bob, help my son," his friend pleaded.

"Jonathan," Maxwell said, "there's nothing I can do."

Jonathan had, up to that point, persuaded Olivia to stay out of the room, fearful that what Tyler looked like then would become the final, lasting image she had of her son. Her patience gone, she approached the doorway. "Do not let my wife come in this room," Jonathan told Maxwell, and the officer did as he asked. "Let me in there," Olivia demanded, but Maxwell wrapped his arms around her and held on, keeping her out until paramedics arrived and rushed past. Soon, she and her husband were headed to the same Greenville hospital where Jacob Hall would die twenty-six months later.

"God, don't take my son," Jonathan prayed, but what he didn't say aloud, to God or to anyone else, was that an overwhelming sense of shame had already begun to take hold. "How's my wife gonna ever look at me the same?" he wondered, because, to him, this was his fault. At the hospital, more than fifty people who knew Tyler from church, and had grown to delight in his presence there, prayed alongside his parents as they waited for an update. Then came the news. "We weren't able to save him," the doctor said, and the sound of wailing spread through the room. Jonathan braced for the blame. "I deserve it," he thought.

Police quickly separated the couple, interviewing each of them to ensure that their stories matched and raised no suspicions. With investigators satisfied, the coroner ruled Tyler's death a suicide, which his parents refused to accept. He had never acted depressed or been the victim of bullying, they said, and in a family that talked openly about feelings, they could not imagine that he wouldn't have spoken up if something was bothering him. His parents wondered if he knew the gun was loaded or if he didn't fully comprehend the finality of death or if a thought about his grandfather's suicide had suddenly made him curious. No one could convince them that Tyler understood the consequences of pulling that trigger, but to Olivia, why or how it happened didn't matter much anyway.

"I don't care what you write on that paper. It's not going to change anything for me," she said. "The only thing I know right now is that I'm never going to see my son again. I don't care about anything else. Nothing else to me matters, except how am I supposed to live now? What do I do now? He was my purpose. He's what I did, all the time, day and night."

The why and the how did matter to Jonathan, though, because he knew he could have stopped it. He'd gotten the revolver for Olivia back in 1997, at a time when he often worked late. She'd never liked guns, but Jonathan worried about her being alone at night without him, so he'd bought the pistol and kept it loaded, just in case. He hadn't once considered hiding it from Tyler because he always assumed his son knew better.

"It just never crossed my mind," he said. "It's just something I never thought about."

Not long after Tyler's death, Jonathan's brother, his hunting partner since they were kids, approached him with a question. "Don't get mad at me," he asked, "but can I take your guns out of the house?"

"I'm not gonna hurt myself," Jonathan said, though as the words left his mouth, he wasn't certain they were true. So he agreed. At the house, his brother went in without him, because Jonathan still couldn't bear to step through the front door. Afterward, he confessed that he had one more gun, a nine-millimeter pistol locked in his truck.

"You're telling me that because you want me to take it," his brother said.

"It's there," Jonathan responded. "Get it."

FOR DECADES, GUN control opponents have argued that they cannot support restrictions because they infringe on their constitutional right to bear arms. For just as long, their adversaries have argued that gun control opponents prioritize that right over human lives, particularly those of children. So often lost in this debate, however, is that the most obvious and urgent step that we, as a society, can take to protect kids from harm would do *nothing* to infringe on a person's right to buy or own a firearm. Demanding, by law, that a man with a dozen AR-15s must prevent his deadly weapons from falling into the hands of a child doesn't mean the man can't own those weapons, nor does it mean he can't go buy a dozen more. It simply means he must behave responsibly with the ones he has. And why shouldn't he be required to? If everyone in this country locked up all their firearms today, the number of gun-related accidental deaths and suicides among children and teens would drop by as much as a third.

And yet, a huge number of Americans don't take that simple step, either because of ignorance, in most cases, or negligence, in some. A survey of gun-owning families in the rural South found that a significant proportion of parents had no idea what their children knew about or had done with their firearms. Nearly 40 percent of parents who claimed that their kids didn't know where they stored their guns were wrong; the kids said they knew. More than 20 percent of parents who claimed that their kids had never handled one of those guns were also wrong; the kids said they had. Notably, children who'd been educated on gun safety were just as likely to say they'd played with the weapons. The findings are even more disturbing when you consider that, as of 2015, as many as 4.6 million children lived in homes with at least one loaded, unlocked firearm.

The Centers for Disease Control and Prevention didn't invest meaningful resources into the study of gun violence for more than two decades because, in 1996, Congress forbade the agency from using government funds to "advocate or promote gun control." Among an incalculable number of damaging repercussions, the limitations on research have made it exceedingly difficult to determine which gun safety measures are most effective. A comprehensive review of available studies by the RAND Corporation, however, found that no policy was backed by stronger evidence than child access prevention laws, the most robust of which allow prosecutors to criminally charge adults who negligently store firearms where children can reach them.

Just thirty states have adopted the law in some form, and among that group, only sixteen, along with the District of Columbia, have passed the most stringent versions. But even those statutes, researchers say, are often not enforced, are too limited, or carry weak penalties, rendering them far less effective than they could be. For a project at the *Post*, my colleague Steven Rich and I reviewed 145 school shootings committed by children in the two decades after Columbine and found that the weapon's source had been publicly identified in 105 cases. In total, we discovered that the guns those children used were taken from their own homes or those of relatives or friends 80 percent of the time, but in just four instances did the adult owners of the weapons face any criminal punishment for not having locked them up—and none of those prosecutions stemmed from negligent-storage laws.

An unanswerable question had inspired the project: had Jesse Osborne not killed his father, would Jeffrey Osborne have been charged for failing to safeguard his deadly weapon from a teenager with a history of violent, menacing tendencies? Some people in Townville did hold Jeffrey responsible for what they viewed as egregiously poor judgment, but many more didn't think much of it, in large part because guns were so embedded in the region's culture. In fact, Kevin Bryant, an NRA-supported Republican who represented Townville in the state senate at the time, said nothing in the shooting's aftermath about keeping guns from children and instead focused his efforts on legislation that would arm teachers (a bill that didn't become law and that was vehemently opposed by the district's superintendent and by Meghan Hollingsworth, the teacher who was shot). In Townville and similar rural communities across the country, most people I've talked to tended to blame the shooter—not the gun or its owner—because rifles, pistols, and shotguns are viewed much the same as shears, shovels, and rakes: essential tools that, on their own, can do no harm.

Bruce Brock, a South Carolina highway patrolman for twenty-seven years, had responded to the shooting at Townville Elementary, guiding teachers and students out of the building. His wife worked at the school. His younger brother subdued the teenage gunman. Bruce grasped the ramifications of that day better than most, but he also understood the community's reverence for the Second

Amendment. When I met him, he had just retired from law enforcement and taken a job at a local gun shop. He owned shotguns, rifles, and pistols and had been around them all his life, but he wasn't a member of the NRA or someone who instinctively opposed all new regulations. He supported universal background checks and thought anyone who wanted to buy a gun should have to undergo training beforehand. The vast majority of his friends, he told me, would agree. Still, he couldn't comprehend ever charging parents whose children used their guns to shoot themselves or someone else. After all, Bruce said, when he was an active-duty law enforcement officer, his son and daughter knew that he kept his service weapon in a gun belt near his bedroom window.

Two years after the Townville school shooting, another small, rural, gun-revering community faced the real-life question that I had pondered in South Carolina, about Jesse's dad being charged. A fifteen-year-old boy in western Kentucky had taken an unsecured Ruger nine-millimeter semiautomatic pistol from his stepfather's closet and used it to shoot sixteen schoolmates, killing two. Afterward, the local prosecutor, Commonwealth attorney Mark Blankenship, wondered if the stepfather should be held responsible. Blankenship understood why someone would want to keep a handgun nearby in case of a break-in, but when he researched gun safes online, he discovered more than a dozen for under $250 that had been designed to securely store pistols and be opened in less than three seconds. "That's when it really hit me that this was so easily preventable," he told me, reaching a conclusion that he knew could jeopardize his political future in such a conservative county. Because Kentucky's statutes provided few options to charge a parent in that scenario, Blankenship decided to wait to see whether the defense team's mental health expert found that the teen had psychological issues his parents could have or should have recognized. Before he got the results, Blankenship lost reelection, and he suspected his stance on that single issue may have cost him. "It wasn't popular," he said. No one understood why better than the owner of a local gun store, who told me what likely would have happened had Blankenship ever tried the case there: "Almost everybody sitting on that jury would be able to say, 'I have a gun at home. What if my kid takes it? What if my grandkid takes it? Should I go to jail for that?'"

It's that sort of thinking that Russ Hauge, another former prosecutor, believes a strong federal child access prevention law could transform. The need for such a statute became clear to him in 2012, when a third-grader in Washington State found a .45-caliber semi-automatic handgun in the home of his mother's boyfriend, Douglas Bauer, who kept firearms (loaded, unlocked, and in some cases cocked) throughout the home. The boy, then nine, put the weapon in his backpack and took it to school, where it accidentally fired, leaving a bullet lodged near the spine of an eight-year-old girl. It was a case of "gross, gross negligence," Hauge said, but when he tried to convict Bauer of third-degree assault, the state supreme court ruled that the law was too vague to sustain the charge. Hauge is a staunch supporter of the Second Amendment and owns several firearms, but at the end of that case—after he had to give Bauer his gun back—the prosecutor walked away certain that America had to do more to protect its children.

"We're looking at a class of crimes where deterrence might actually work," he told me. "If there was a clear law that says felony punishment will ensue if you don't handle your weapons safely, I think we could get some people's attention."

And getting people's attention on this issue is vital, the difference between life and death, because a significant but unknowable number of gun owners is under the false and dangerous impression that proper training will guarantee that their children don't make bad choices with guns. Even Bruce, the former police officer, told me he believed that.

"Education," he said, "is key."

Such misconceptions are not impossible to change. Once, for

example, most people didn't see the need to wear seat belts, and as recently as 1984, 65 percent of Americans opposed regulations that made them mandatory. But legislators ignored public opinion, and thanks to new laws, education, and technology, seat belt use in this country increased from 11 percent in 1981 to nearly 85 percent in 2010. That single device, and the relentless push to make people secure it across their waists, has saved more than 250,000 lives since the 1970s.

It's difficult to imagine a prosecutor ever going after a father like Jonathan Paxton, but what if the law Hauge described existed when Jonathan bought that revolver for his wife? What if the pistol came with a pamphlet that outlined the statute and the reasons for it? What if he saw government-sponsored ads that explained why his child's unfettered access to a loaded firearm dramatically increased the boy's chances of being harmed? What if he had heard one warning, one piece of data, one personal story, that led him to hide the key that opened the safe that held the gun?

EIGHT DAYS AFTER their son shot himself at their home, Jonathan and Olivia moved back into it, because they had to. It was Tyler's home, too, the place where their memories of him lived and always would. In every room, around every corner, Jonathan could see his son's face, spotted with that one freckle just above the left eye that he kissed each day. Night after night, Olivia's mind replayed the bedtime routine she shared with her son. "Mama loves you," she'd say. "Baby loves you," he'd say, and back and forth they'd go. On quiet evenings after he was gone, Olivia would recite both parts to herself.

The Paxtons left his bedroom just the way he had. They didn't touch the *Winnie-the-Pooh* wallpaper border they'd put up before their son was born and that he'd insisted they not take down. They didn't remove the martial arts trophy draped in medals, or the school project about polar bears, or the other one about a local farmer who let Tyler pet his goats and sit on his John Deere tractor. They didn't remove his assignment from first grade that began with "I am" next to a blank line. "A good boy and a fisherman," he answered. "I dream": "about cookies." "I say": "I believe in God." "I understand": "my Mom is so lovely." "I wonder": "what Heaven looks like." "I worry": "everyone that gets hurt."

In their own bedroom, Tyler's parents kept turning the pages of the calendar that featured a different photo of him for each month. Olivia's favorites were the ones that showed his beautifully imperfect smile, due to what she called a "pull," which had left one side of his bottom lip slightly higher than the other. At the end of each December, they'd start the calendar over in January. For the first two years after Tyler's death, they didn't travel back to Isle of Palms for his birthday. On the third, they went to another beach, in Florida, where Jonathan woke up one night with such extreme chest pain that he feared his heart was about to stop. They rushed to the emergency room, but the tests showed nothing. "You're just having an anxiety attack," the doctor told him.

The couple didn't let Tyler's death destroy their marriage, as Jonathan had feared it might. Instead, they leaned on each other, and on their faith, more than ever before. Jonathan became an ordained minister and began to preach at the church Tyler used to attend without them. Because they wanted people to remember his life, Olivia and Jonathan talked often of their son's empathy, his humor, his devotion to God and to his family. As painful as it was, they didn't shy away from talking about how he'd died, either. "If it can happen to me, it can happen to anybody," Jonathan would tell his friends. "You can never be too safe."

Bob Maxwell, the police officer who first responded to the scene, didn't need to hear that to be convinced. He'd followed the ambulance carrying Tyler to the hospital, and on the way, he called his ex-wife and asked that she put his two children on the phone. His daughter was just older than Tyler, his son just younger. "I love you," he told his kids, because he needed them to hear it. He stayed with

Tyler's body that night until the coroner arrived, and afterward, Maxwell returned to the Paxtons' home and helped clean up the scene. In their bedroom, he wiped blood from a pair of baby shoes. Maxwell had come upon gruesome sights before, but what he saw that night unmoored him. He had nightmares. The smell of gunpowder made him feel nauseated. After the funeral, he sat in his patrol car, holding a radar gun as tears cascaded down his cheeks. Eventually, therapy helped him work through the trauma, but the experience had permanently transformed him in at least one way. For years, Maxwell had returned home from work and left his gun, strapped to a service belt, on his bedroom floor. He had told his kids many times never to touch it, but he suddenly realized that wasn't good enough. So, Maxwell bought a gun safe, shared the code with no one, and locked every weapon he owned inside it.

CHAPTER 5

"I HOPE MY DADDY'S OKAY"

How Gun Violence Leads to More Trauma and Trauma Leads to More Gun Violence

Tyshaun McPhatter learned what it felt like to get shot at when he was six, skidding down a red plastic slide. He had gone with his father, Andrew, to visit friends at a notoriously troubled apartment project just up the street from their aging duplex in Southeast Washington's Congress Heights, a neighborhood long plagued by drugs, poverty, and violence. His dad stepped into a laundry room, and Tyshaun headed for a playground between buildings, and that's where he was when he heard the pops. Unsure of what to do, the boy took off toward the door his dad had walked through, but before Tyshaun made it, an older friend tackled him to the ground, covering his tiny body until the shooting stopped. Afterward, Andrew carried him home.

"I was scared," Tyshaun told his grandmother that evening in 2016 as she cleaned a bloody scrape on his palm with hydrogen peroxide and wrapped it in gauze. After that, Tyshaun seldom went outside at all when he came over for evening or weekend visits, but he didn't mind, because his favorite place in the world was Andrew's bedroom, and his favorite thing to do there was play the Xbox One.

Just miles from wealthy DC suburbs where parents discouraged their children from staring at video games because it kept them indoors too much, parents in neighborhoods like Andrew's did the opposite, because staying indoors often afforded their children the best chance to stay safe. And on a warm summer afternoon about a year after the shooting down the street, that's where Tyshaun was—in his dad's bedroom, playing *NBA 2K16*—when he heard a familiar sound from just outside the second-floor window. *Pow, pow, pow.* Andrew burst through the door, crouching. "Get down on the floor," he screamed, and Tyshaun knew what that meant: more gunshots.

Bullets could break glass and rip through skin and bone, he had learned by then, and not just because of his own experience. On his dad's dresser was that three-inch REST IN PEACE button for the family friend shot around the corner. Tyshaun didn't want to get hurt like that, so he dropped the Xbox controller and leapt down to the worn hardwood floor. Chest thudding, he hid behind the bed's footboard and covered his head with his hands. Tyshaun was afraid, but not as much as he had been the last time. Anyway, he figured all kids heard gunfire outside their homes, so he might as well learn to be brave, like his dad.

"I'm not scared of nothing," Tyshaun started telling himself, but his mother, Donna, knew that attitude wouldn't keep him safe. She had watched one brave young man after another lose his life to gun violence. In the three years prior, there had been 401 homicides in the District of Columbia, and among those, 54 percent of the victims were under age thirty, 75 percent were killed by bullets, 89 percent were men, and 91 percent were black. To Donna, identifying the root cause of all that bloodshed wasn't difficult. Decades of poverty and trauma in her community, and others like it across the country, had led to debilitating anger and hopelessness, feelings that had left many young girls and boys indifferent to the consequences of their choices. It wasn't money or drugs driving the vast majority of the killing; it was petty feuds between neighborhood cliques divided along arbitrary lines. The danger had become so acute that parents warned their sons not to brag about where they were from because something as simple as an address could get one of them killed. The neighborhood violence had already pushed Donna to move two miles away, to a quiet street just across the Maryland state line, but Andrew had remained at his mother's house, in Southeast. After the playground shooting, Donna had told Andrew that their son couldn't visit him anymore and that he needed to figure out another way to see him. Andrew refused to agree to that but swore he wouldn't take Tyshaun outside anymore, and he kept his word. Anyway, as much as Donna wanted to protect her son from danger, she couldn't deprive him of his father, because, in her experience, that's what was missing in the lives of so many of the girls who found no purpose or boys who ended up in graves. Around the same time as the gunfire outside Andrew's house, the twenty-two-year-old boyfriend of a woman Donna knew had been killed a half mile away, leaving behind an unborn daughter who would grow up never knowing her dad. As Donna had many times before, she shared her frustrations on Facebook, pleading for change.

"OPEN YOUR EYES YOUNG BLACK GUYS," she wrote, in all capital letters. "IT'LL BE NO BLACK FATHERS TO TAKE CARE OF OUR BLACK CHILDREN . . . IT'LL BE NO BLACK MEN FOR THESE YOUNG BLACK BOYS TO LOOK UP TO . . . IT'LL BE SINGLE BLACK MOTHERS WHO STRUGGLE . . . IT'LL BE NO BLACK MEN FOR OUR BLACK DAUGHTERS TO MARRY . . . IT'LL BE NO BLACK MEN AROUND TO HOLD THE BLACK WOMAN DOWN. . . . WHEN U TAKE EACH OTHER LIVES YOU TAKE AWAY FROM THE BLACK FAMILIES . . . THE BLACK COMMUNITY . . . AND ALSO OUR BLACK PEOPLE FUTURE."

She thought constantly about the plight of black men, both because of the one she was raising and because of the one who had raised her. In 1981, C. Kenneth Johnson heard someone at the door of his home in Southeast, and when he answered, a teenager outside shot him in the face. Johnson survived and recovered fully. Because of that, he realized he needed to do more with his life. He found that larger purpose three years later, when he attended a conference titled "What Are We Going to Do to Help Our Black Kids?" Inspired, Johnson, who served as a case worker at the DC Office of Paternity and Child Support Enforcement, went on to foster more than 140 children and adopt eight, including Donna. Single after two divorces, he ran errands, cooked meals, washed laundry, doled out advice, and ferried his children wherever they needed to go. He demanded a lot from them, too, insisting that they make good grades and stay off the streets that were devouring so many of their friends. To keep his children safe, he kept them busy. Donna took classes for ballet, tap dancing, and computers before discovering she was a natural at tennis, which her father had taught her how to play. She later earned a scholarship from Virginia State University, and at her graduation in 2010, Johnson wore a shirt with Donna's face on it and the words VSU DAD. Afterward, she got a job as a security officer at the U.S. State Department and, with money her dad had saved up for her since she was a kid, Donna bought her own home in Maryland. "The world's best father," she wrote on Facebook, and though she knew Andrew was not the same man Johnson had been, she also knew how much her son needed his dad, just like she had needed hers.

But as Tyshaun prepared to start second grade in the weeks after Andrew ordered him to get down on the floor, the violence around the two of them only crept closer. He arrived at his father's home one day to discover that a bullet had punched a dime-size hole in their steel front door, just below his eye level, before tearing into the back of the living room TV. In November of that year, five days before Tyshaun's eighth birthday, another of his dad's friends was shot to death on the street, and one more died just as 2017 began after being gunned down inside his car in the middle of the afternoon, five hundred feet from their house. Both men were targeted. The blood-shed intensified in late February, when four people were wounded one evening less than half a mile away and another was struck four nights later. Then, at 10:50 on the first morning in March, someone raised a gun a block from Tyshaun's home and a dozen steps from the front gate to his school, Eagle Academy Public Charter. But in-side, Tyshaun couldn't hear the five shots that would thrust the vio-lence circling him for years into the center of his life.

THE BOY WAS at lunch, trying to avoid the day's free serving of beef-a-roni, when he overheard a teacher mention that the campus had been locked down, which at Eagle meant no one could come or go from the building. The news didn't bother Tyshaun, because the school had called lockdowns many times before, including one just a week prior. Somebody was always causing trouble in the neighbor-hood, it seemed to him, so as class time approached, he headed out of the cafeteria, where a seven-foot-high red poster hung on the wall. THE CAT IN THE HAT, it declared, next to a smiling image of the char-acter, DOES NOT LIKE THAT VIOLENCE. Tyshaun didn't think much more about the commotion until he passed by Eagle's front lobby and, through an expansive glass window, noticed red and blue police lights flashing across the street.

I hope my daddy's okay, Tyshaun thought, because he knew his father's home was in that direction, just beyond all those officers.

They had last seen each other two days earlier, when Andrew dropped his son off at school after their weekend together. His par-ents had split years before, and sometimes didn't get along in those that followed, but Andrew, who worked construction, was always there for Tyshaun. Donna gave birth during college, and because Andrew wanted her to finish school, Tyshaun lived with his dad while she attended classes. As an infant, Tyshaun often cried late into the night, and many times, his grandmother came downstairs to find Andrew, then twenty, holding a bottle to his son's mouth, trying to rock him to sleep. When Tyshaun got older and started going to school, the staff at Eagle got to know Andrew better than Donna, because while she had to work, he picked Tyshaun up, met with teachers, went to football practices.

Andrew had three sons, but none looked or acted more like him than Tyshaun, who even cocked his head to the side in just the same way his father did. The boy used the look for everything: tongue out when he wanted a laugh, eyes pleading when he wanted a treat, lips pursed when he wanted to look like a teenager. Tyshaun respected his father, but Andrew left most of the discipline to Donna. During those evenings together in Andrew's bedroom, father taught son multiplication tables and son taught father the moves to the rap song "Juju on That Beat." Sometimes, his dad tried to rub his smelly feet on Tyshaun as the boy dodged and giggled until his eyes watered. They'd play on the Xbox deep into the night using Andrew's screen name, "lilandy," which Tyshaun thought was stupid because nothing about his five-foot-nine, thick-bearded father seemed little to him. Andrew would even let him play *Battlefield 4* and *Grand Theft Auto V*, the violent games Donna didn't like. About real-life violence, though, Andrew told Tyshaun the things Donna wanted him to: that you should never pick up a gun, but fight if you have to, because fighters live to fight again.

Now Tyshaun was back in his classroom contending with math problems, and the red and blue lights were still flashing outside, and he still didn't know why. He also didn't know why he'd been told that his mom was picking him up early, only to be told later that she wasn't. And he never did know that she had come, but that the moment Donna had seen him walking toward her down a hallway, she'd collapsed, unable to face him. That evening, Ashley Watkins, a social worker at Eagle, drove Tyshaun from school to a relative's home, and on the way, he talked about his aunt who was pregnant and his brother who was also eight years old, about how he was hungry but didn't like Burger King, about hoping that he would make good enough grades for his parents to buy him a new pair of Air Jordan sneakers.

Not until that evening did Tyshaun see his mother, and right away, he knew something was wrong. "Mom, are you okay?" he asked as they sat in the darkness in her gray Dodge Durango.

"Your dad was shot," she said, but he was still alive, and that gave Tyshaun hope. He returned to school the next day, and when a friend who knew about the shooting asked if he was all right, Tyshaun heard another classmate laugh. Furious, he shoved the boy.

From the moment his mom gave him the news, Tyshaun had started pressing to know what had happened, who had done it, where his dad was. He wanted to see him, desperately, but at Tyshaun's age, the hospital wouldn't allow it. So, he wrote a note.

"Dad I hope you are ok I wish that I can see you but I couldn't and I hope you are alright do you fill alright," Tyshaun scribbled in black ink, promising to "give up any thing on my body for you."

On Sunday, four days after the shooting, Tyshaun's mom picked her son up from the home of friends who'd invited him for a sleepover.

"All right, Ty. I'll see you next weekend," one of them said.

"No you're not. I'm going to be with my dad," Tyshaun replied, and he thought of their last weekend together. They had seen *The LEGO Batman Movie* and eaten chicken-flavored instant ramen noodles, Tyshaun's favorite. They had danced again to the rap song.

Six hours later, his mother got a call at home. When she hung up, she sat on the couch and held Tyshaun's hands as he stood in front of her. She looked him in the eyes. "Your father, he died today," she said, and without a word, Tyshaun slumped to the floor.

THE FLYERS HAD been arranged into three separate piles and stacked on a sign-in table near the entrance to Eagle's cafeteria, where dozens of frustrated neighbors, parents, and their children had all convened. At the top of each page, in white capital letters printed against a bright orange background, were two words: "HOMICIDE VIC-TIM." Below that, in bright red letters: "$25,000 Reward." Below that: the names and photos of three black men, all fatally wounded within a half mile of the school. The first, age twenty-three, in January. The next, age thirty, in February. The last, Andrew, age twenty-eight, in March. Now it was the day after his death, and an emergency meeting had been called at Eagle to address the most recent flurry of gun violence on Wheeler Road SE, which ran between Tyshaun's school and his dad's home. In seven days, six people had been shot.

For nearly two hours, the city leaders on the stage, bookended by drawings of pistols with red slashes through them, repeated the same talking points they had many times before, and would many times after, at similar gatherings in similar neighborhoods. Detectives, said the police chief, couldn't solve these crimes without help from the community. The community, said the council member who represented it, wasn't getting enough financial support from the city to grow jobs and offer kids support, noting how much cheaper it was to spend $75 a day for a child's after-school program than $300 a day to incarcerate him when he got older. Trivial disputes between rivals, said the chief, fueled most of the carnage. More than ninety times, said the council member, he had attended funerals for mur-dered constituents. The violence, both of them said, would lead to more trauma, and more trauma would lead to more violence.

Then, as the discussion neared its end, a little girl with braids and a bright-pink Shopkins backpack approached the microphone be-cause she had something new to say. Taylor Amoah, age six, was a year behind Tyshaun and didn't know him, but she cared about what had happened to her schoolmate's family—what was happening to all their families.

"Everybody's got to live," she said, her voice soft but her tone purposeful. "They won't be able to live. That's not fair."

The threat of gun violence had already shaped so much of Taylor's everyday life. Two years earlier, her mother, Myaa Amoah, had withdrawn the girl from a kindergarten program at another school in Southeast after realizing its playground was too exposed to the road. If one of Taylor's friends was having a birthday party outdoors, Amoah wouldn't allow her to go. When Taylor wanted to play outside, her mother drove her to parks in Maryland or Virginia rather than DC. Amoah also never took her daughter along when she got her nails done, because the woman had seen too many of those places get held up. And Taylor still remembered the moment at the shopping plaza in Southeast when, on their way to lunch at a Caribbean restaurant, gunfire erupted and her mother snatched her up and ran.

"People always shooting around this neighborhood," Taylor told the crowd in the cafeteria, which, by then, had gone quiet. "We want everybody to live."

The first-grader didn't know what the word *trauma* meant, but she understood what it looked and sounded and felt like, because just four miles from the U.S. Capitol, epicenter of the world's wealthiest and most powerful nation, the signs of trauma in Taylor's elementary school appeared everywhere. To her right, a question typed on a sheet of paper had been stapled to the wall. "What makes you sad in your neighborhood?" it asked, and around it were sixteen pictures that students at Eagle had drawn in response.

"Bang, bang," an eight-year-old had printed next to a man, beneath a dark sky, firing three bullets toward another man with his hands up, shouting, "NO!"

"Bang, bang. Bang, bang. Bang, bang," a second eight-year-old had written next to three people shooting at three other people down the street from a police car. In the background, a child watched from an apartment window.

"Bang, bang, bang," a six-year-old had scrawled next to two stick figures smeared in red marker and lying near a set of gravestones inscribed with "RIP."

None of those images, Eagle's staff knew, had come from TV shows or video games. Almost every one of their seven hundred students, who ranged in age from three to nine, had personally witnessed violence or its aftermath. There were the half dozen who had needed counseling because they'd passed a corpse near their bus stop. There was the kindergartner who told teachers how sad his father's killing on Halloween night made him feel. There was the third-grader who broke down crying in class the day after a cousin was shot outside his front door. There was the second-grader who saw his uncle's body and subsequently began to explode in class, punching and picking on his friends without warning. There was the girl in pre-K whose dad survived being shot in front of her only to be shot again, fatally, a year later.

What hundreds of thousands of black children in urban environments perpetually contend with, however, seldom generates the same attention or demand for change as rarer school shootings that impact white children in more affluent neighborhoods. That's due at least in part, experts say, to the outside world's perception of kids who grow up in these high-crime communities.

"Often, we have this notion that, 'Oh, they're used to it'—and that's BS," said Steven Berkowitz, former director of the Penn Center for Youth and Family Trauma Response and Recovery in Philadelphia. "They're not used to it."

ShotSpotter, a company that's developed a high-tech gunshot detection system, found that for every homicide in urban neighborhoods, the system identified between 125 and 150 illegal incidents of gunfire, according to David Chipman, who worked at ShotSpotter after serving twenty-five years as a special agent with the Bureau of Alcohol, Tobacco, Firearms and Explosives (ATF). In a separate review of a single school year, the firm discovered that between the hours of 7 a.m. and 7 p.m., guns had been fired within one thousand feet of *66 percent* of DC's public and charter schools. For Chipman, the findings called to mind the DC sniper case he worked on in

2002. In the Washington region, ten people were killed and three wounded in a series of seemingly random shootings that terrorized the community.

"What that sniper invoked was a fear level amongst white, sub-urban communities that I would say is ever-present in Southeast," he told me, noting how differently law enforcement responded to those attacks, investing millions of dollars and hundreds of investigators, than it does to similar bursts of gun violence in poorer, minority neighborhoods.

Such chronic exposure can disrupt a child's brain development and inflict profound mental and emotional harm that, in some cases, clings to them for decades. Years of research show that kids in these environments are more likely to experience depression, anxiety, sleeplessness, and uncontrollable anger. For more than two decades, Berkowitz, a psychiatrist, has treated inner-city children contending with those symptoms, finding that some students in parts of Philadelphia felt such constant fear that they instinctively kept their backs to the wall at school all the time, and often couldn't explain why. Many were in states of hypervigilance, he said, which meant they perceived danger even when none existed, not unlike combat veterans with post-traumatic stress disorder. When kids in that mindset, who mistakenly believe they need to defend themselves, lash out and harm someone else, they often face severe discipline, including criminal punishment, only exacerbating the underlying problem.

Even school shootings, so often thought of as a problem exclusive to white, suburban campuses, affect minorities at a much higher rate. In fact, more than 60 percent of students exposed to on-campus gun violence since 1999 were children of color, but because nearly all incidents at predominantly minority schools were either accidental discharges or targeted assaults that typically harmed just one or two people, they received far less attention than the indiscriminate attacks.

"I think these mass school shootings are absolutely horrific,"

Berkowitz said, but "it's much more insidious and potentially really life altering to have this ongoing danger. . . . It's not different than kids living in chronic war zones."

That phrase, "war zone," was the same one Dawne Wilson used to describe the world in which her pre-K class of four-and five-year-olds had to grow up. When she first started at Eagle, she would take her kids, nicknamed "Wilson's Wonders," outside the campus's eight-foot-high black steel fence for walks around the block, because she'd learned that exploring led to learning. Then the corner store across the street got robbed, and the walks ended. About four months before Tyshaun's dad was killed, Dawne and her students were outside for recess when they heard gunshots.

"Wilson's!" she called, and the kids knew that meant they should run to her.

"Let's play a game," she calmly told them, determined to disguise her fear. "Everybody get down."

Like many of her colleagues, Dawne, then an educator for twenty-nine years, didn't work at Eagle just to teach lessons from books. Its founders had opened the pre-K–third grade public charter in 2012 *because* of the struggles in Congress Heights, not in spite of them.

"Some of these children," Dawne told me, "have been through more in their young lives than I've been through in my adult life."

Tyshaun was so young that what he went through was, at first, too much to accept. He imagined creating a potion that would make his dad come back to life, and he obsessed over building a time machine, traveling back, and whispering in his father's ear before he got into the car that morning: "Don't go nowhere, Dad." Donna told her son that wasn't possible, that he would never see his father alive again in this life, and eventually, he believed her. Then, one after another, questions she didn't know how to answer began to tumble out.

"Did my daddy do something to deserve this?"

"Where was he shot at?"

"Where do guns come from?"

"Did they catch the person?"

"Is the person going to try to come and get me?"

TYSHAUN WAS SITTING with his grandmother on her bed, sifting through old family photos, when he came upon one taken just before his father's eighth-grade prom. Tyshaun stared at Andrew, in his black suit and matching vest and his long hair done in twists for the first time. "That's my daddy," he said, smiling because the boy had never seen him dressed up before. Tyshaun decided he wanted to look just like that at his father's funeral, so Donna went to Kids for Less, and when she brought an outfit home, Tyshaun arranged it atop the Marvel superheroes bedsheet on his lower bunk and insisted no one touch it. For three days, no one did.

Then came that cold, gray Friday morning in the middle of March. Standing just inside the door of his bedroom, I watched him get ready. The boy slipped on his black shirt and buttoned it up. He then donned a silver vest, black pants, black socks, and size-three-and-a-half black shoes. He reached next for his silver clip-on tie. Tyshaun looked at it, then up at me. The boy didn't know how to put one on because his dad had never shown him, so he asked for help. I paused for a moment, because I had spent a career working to stay out of these scenes, to never influence moments, but here, at the precipice of one of his life's worst days, was an eight-year-old whose father couldn't show him how to do anything ever again. I tucked my notebook under my arm and leaned over, guiding him to fasten his top button and slide the metal clip behind it. He snapped it on, then stuffed a matching handkerchief in the vest pocket. His ensemble complete, Tyshaun glanced down, contemplating why he had to wear what he was wearing.

"Whoever invented guns needs to stop," he told me.

For twelve days, Tyshaun had vacillated between grief and bitterness, the latter of which had been fueled, in part, by his doubt that detectives would ever catch the person who killed his dad. "Police only stay for one week," he'd told his mom. "They never find out who did it." At a candlelight vigil for Andrew, held on a frigid evening at the intersection where he was shot, Tyshaun felt so overwhelmed with despair that he could barely speak, but still, the boy took the microphone and stood in front of the local TV cameras and told three dozen people how much he loved his dad, because he thought that was the right thing to do. In the car later that night, though, Donna overheard him tell his half-brother that he wanted someone to get the shooter—to pay the person back. It unsettled her. That was God's job, she told him, then, to make sure he heard her, she told him a second time.

Now, all dressed for the funeral, he picked up a video game controller and walked over to his dresser, standing on his toes so he could turn on his father's old Xbox One. "Where's my daddy's shirt?" he suddenly asked himself, whipping around to see that the purple Hugo Boss sweatshirt was on the bottom bunk. He had taken that from Andrew's closet and slept with it every night since, demanding that his mom not wash it because he didn't want to forget his father's scent.

Tyshaun stood on the bed so he could peer over the dresser's edge. On the TV, his character, a soldier armed with a machine gun, sprinted through a big-city downtown. In an instant, blood spattered across the screen. "Ah, they sniped me," he said, before his character was reborn for another firefight.

"Stop playin' with me," he continued. "Killed y'all."

Then he died again, and the leaderboard popped up. Tyshaun noticed his dad's screen name, "lilandy."

"I miss him," he mumbled.

Donna tried to teach Tyshaun to respect the danger of firearms and, in fact, carried one in her job at the State Department, but she hated the video games. When she was a kid, her father wouldn't even allow his children to play with Nerf or water guns, and she knew he'd never have let them stare into a TV screen as they simulated acts of violence that so resembled the real ones happening just beyond the walls of their home. Donna sometimes wondered if she should have insisted that Andrew not allow their son to play the games with him, but it was too late now. She understood that they kept Tyshaun connected to his father, and she couldn't deprive him of that. Any time the issue came up, her son had an answer. "It's not real," he told me. "It looks like cartoon pictures." Asked about actual guns, he'd say that he would run if he saw one and that only the military should have them. He'd also begun to parrot the mantra of community meetings: "Too many black people is dying."

Now it was almost time to leave for the funeral, but Tyshaun wanted to switch games. He hopped down from the bed and, reaching up toward the console, knocked over a photo he'd posed in with his dad years earlier. It was his favorite. The night before, he'd fallen asleep staring at the image. He picked it up and carefully put it back before his attention returned to the next game, *Grand Theft Auto*. On the screen, his new character, a man with cornrows and a tan trench coat, jogged down the street, shooting at passing cars.

"We got to be leaving," a relative yelled from downstairs, but Tyshaun kept playing. On the TV, he heard approaching sirens.

"People always got to call the police," he complained.

"Tyshaun!" someone shouted. He didn't answer, firing off a few more rounds at a truck.

"We're leaving!"

"Coming," Tyshaun shouted back.

Red and blue lights flashed across the screen. At a street corner, three armed policemen raised their guns. Tyshaun blew up the first one with a rocket launcher and killed the second with a machine gun. The third shot him, and as the camera zoomed out, his character crumpled onto the pavement. A word appeared on the screen in red letters: "Wasted."

Tyshaun leapt down to the worn gray carpet and turned off the game, then remembered his black T-shirt, a custom-made one that on the back read, REST IN PEACE DADDY. He picked it up and rushed downstairs.

TYSHAUN AND HIS mother waited in a long line inside East Washington Heights Baptist Church as late-morning sunlight, pouring in through the sanctuary's tall, narrow windows, flashed against his silver vest. The boy didn't know what they were headed toward until, at last, he rounded the final pew and his father's body came into view. He stopped. His mouth fell open, and his eyes widened. He shook his head. "I don't want to see that," Tyshaun said, retreating up the center aisle. His mom followed.

"You can be strong," she said, leaning down and peering at him from behind her wide-brimmed black hat and matching sunglasses.

"I don't want to."

She held his right arm with both hands, easing her son back toward the glossy, gray casket adorned with a bouquet of fuchsia carnations and milk-white lilies. He stared at a face that, to him, looked nothing like his father's. "I can't touch him," he whispered. "I can't touch him." Tyshaun stepped past and took a seat in the front row, where his half-brother, Zah'Kyi Bynum, joined him.

"You know they put makeup on him?" Tyshaun asked, and Zah'Kyi, also eight, nodded. Their younger half-brother, Andrew "AJ" McPhatter II, who was two, waddled toward them. The boys hoisted him onto their laps. "You okay?" Tyshaun asked the toddler, who was dressed in a pink button-down and black jacket. He didn't respond, instead grinning as he whacked at his older brothers. And they let him.

Almost everyone had sat down when an older woman in a black cap passed by the front row. "Family," she said, "last viewing before closing."

Tyshaun rubbed his watery eyes and looked at Zah'Kyi. They whispered. From their pockets, the boys both removed handkerchiefs.

"You want to do it?" Tyshaun asked.

"Yeah," Zah'Kyi responded.

"Come on."

The brothers stood, then approached the casket. Just before the lid was closed, they laid the squares of cloth atop their father's body. "So he would remember us," Tyshaun told me later.

The service began, and the choir sang. A deacon read letters from Andrew's friends, and an organist played "Great Is Thy Faithfulness." When the pastor asked the crowd for a round of applause in honor of Andrew's life, Zah'Kyi clapped, but Tyshaun just stared ahead. He'd stopped listening. He skimmed through a Bible and opened a program, searching for the photos that showed the boys with their father: wrestling with him on the couch, sitting atop his lap during a *Batman*-themed birthday party, laughing next to him at a Chuck E. Cheese, falling asleep on his shoulder. Then the choir returned, and each brother opened a hymnal. Number 313, Zah'Kyi told him. "I've got a feeling everything's gonna be all right," the people on the stage sang, and Tyshaun mouthed along until, midway through, he shut the book and his lips stopped moving.

"We've got to put violence to the side," one speaker said from the pulpit. "I'm begging."

"We need men, not cowards," said another. "I'm sick and tired of doing these funerals and vigils."

Tyshaun didn't hear any of that. Instead, he tried tossing a pencil into its holder in front of him, the wood clacking against the tile floor each time he missed. About then, his cousins, ages six and nine, walked to the front to read "God's Garden."

"Come on. We about to go up there," Tyshaun suddenly whispered to his brother, and they did, joining the girls behind the lectern. Each child read a section of the poem.

"He knew that you were suffering," Tyshaun said into the microphone. "He knew that you were in pain."

As the service, and the pleas for peace, continued, the boys moved to a pew toward the back, fidgeting and whispering about video games. Tyshaun took off his tie and hung the metal clip from his bottom lip. A youth pastor, Kevin McGill, who had attended the same high school as Tyshaun's dad, addressed the audience last. He, too, demanded change, describing his years of violence on the street. "Same drugs. Same guns. Same beefs," McGill said, but he also said that things could get better, that people could make different choices. They must, he told the crowd, because the cost not to was too great.

"Twenty-three of my friends been killed," McGill said, and now Tyshaun, his arm around his brother's shoulder, was staring at the pulpit, listening to every word.

"Why would you take this?" Tyshaun's mother asked him, having just discovered in her Durango a blue sticky toy that he'd won over the weekend at a Dave and Buster's. They were on their way to school, his first time back since his father's casket was lowered into the ground three days earlier, and already, Donna could see what lay ahead.

"Mom," he said, "I'm going to play with it at recess."

"That's just something that's going to get you in trouble for no reason," she told him.

"Mommmyyy," he cried, but she didn't budge. On many Mondays, Andrew had dropped his son off at school, and both Tyshaun and Donna knew he likely would have won this argument with his dad. Now, though, he had just one parent, and in her prayers, she'd promised Andrew to do the best she could. She understood that some people would treat Tyshaun differently, that pity would push them to let him get away with bad choices, but Donna decided she couldn't be one of those people. She knew where enough bad choices could lead him, and now, as much as ever, his mother believed he needed discipline.

"Make sure you come back with all of your homework, or it's

going to be no TV or games," she continued. Tyshaun stared out the window, ignoring her as they departed their quiet residential neighborhood and headed into Southeast, past unkempt empty lots, a rundown strip mall, a row of aging housing complexes.

"I hate coming up this way. Go to my daddy's house side," he told her, suggesting a detour that bypassed the crime scene. His mother took a left, then a right. She thought about what had become of her old community. Gun violence wasn't new to Congress Heights, not at all, but to her, it felt different. The shooters seemed younger, their motivations less comprehensible. When Donna was a kid, she and her friends found refuge in the local recreation center, but that had closed years ago, she said, leaving teenagers with nothing to do, nowhere to feel safe.

"That's when everything got worse," she said, pulling over to a curb just across from Eagle's campus. As Tyshaun hopped out, she realized he still had the toy.

"Ty, I'm not playing with you," she said. "Come on, before you late."

"Ugh," he groaned, handing it to her and slamming the door behind him. His eyes welled as he stomped across the street.

"You all right, man? Who you mad at?" the crossing guard asked, but Tyshaun didn't answer.

He joined his classmates in the cafeteria, and soon they were in a line, on their way to class. Lingering in the back, Tyshaun dragged his feet and ran his hand across the wall. His teacher, Nikki Lee, put her arm around him, and when she did, he rolled his head back, gazing up into the overhead fluorescence. "You're getting frustrated again," she said as they walked, because none of this was new. Sensitive and quick-tempered, Tyshaun had struggled with managing his exasperation before, but he'd improved in second grade. Nikki tracked her students' progress on a five-panel chart hung from the wall. The ratings went from "Spreading wings," the worst, to "Off the charts," the best. Tyshaun's name, written on a clothespin, was clipped to the panel in the middle, "Keep it up." In his electric-orange Adidas backpack was a sheet, meant for the children's parents, that Nikki used to rate behavior from 0 to 6. "Great job," she had written below a 5 a week before the shooting. Tyshaun got a smiley face below another 5 two days before it, and another 5 on the day it happened.

Nikki didn't know whether his mood that morning was related to his father's death, in part because he had never discussed it with her, but she understood how what her kids endured in their homes and neighborhoods could stymie their ability to succeed in school. Nikki wanted them to excel at math and reading, but it was ludicrous, in her mind, to believe that test scores were their greatest concern. Throughout the school were boys who hit girls, because that was what they saw at home, and girls who got hit but said nothing, because that, too, was what they saw at home. When Nikki's students reached her third-floor classroom that morning, all of them were given a bowl of Cinnamon Chex, a cheese stick, and an orange. With so many of Eagle's students living in poverty, each one received three free meals a day. "Have perseverance," she would tell them time and again, and they needed to hear it. By that afternoon, she would manage a girl who rushed out in tears, a boy who hurled his chair against the floor, and another who purposefully and repeatedly knocked his head against a desk as he muttered, "I'm going to hurt myself."

That morning, Tyshaun did little more than lay his cheek against his forearm until the clock neared eleven, lunchtime. Nikki asked if he could open the door, his official classroom job. "Are you ready to fix it?" she asked, referring to his behavior, and Tyshaun nodded that he was. He held the door open, and the class marched down the hall, where he held another door. A girl approached him. "Did your father die?" she asked, and he sensed a trap.

"Shut up," he snapped. Another boy laughed and motioned in his direction. Tyshaun's fingers tightened into a fist.

"I'm going to smack you," he said, but before he could, Nikki intervened. She called the other child over as Tyshaun explained what had happened.

"Tyshaun thinks you were laughing at his situation," she said.

"I didn't laugh at him," the boy said, but Tyshaun didn't believe that.

Seething when he arrived at the cafeteria, he asked a woman at the door if he could see Mr. Murray, his favorite teacher. She told him he needed to eat first. Tyshaun's jaw clenched. He walked away, then turned back and shrieked. A woman in the kitchen spotted him. "You look like you need a minute," she said, placing her hand on his head. When he'd had one, she allowed him to leave. He walked down the hall and into a classroom, where he got a high-five from Curtis Murray, an assistant teacher in the special-education program. Tyshaun sank into a miniature blue couch in the corner, opening a ninja game on an iPad and reaching into a bag of Goldfish. His shoulders relaxed. His eyes calmed.

He hadn't talked about his dad's death with any schoolmates, and Curtis was just one of a couple adults at Eagle in whom he'd confided. Tyshaun had asked another, Ashley Watkins, the social worker, to explain the difference between heaven and hell, because he wanted to make sure his dad had gone to the right one. It worried her that neither she nor Curtis had ever seen Tyshaun break down over the killing, which he'd begun to call a "murder." In a week or two, she knew, someone else would get shot, and what if the world around him moved on to that loss, then the next and the next, before he'd dealt with his own?

"My fear for him is that because he's so kind of emotionally guarded, he will eventually internalize it," said Ashley, who didn't know how all that held-in grief and shame and rage might someday spill out.

Tyshaun left Curtis's room and returned to class, but his mind remained elsewhere, ignoring most of what Nikki asked him to do. "Tyshaun, you're not trying at all," she scolded, as his friends studied how to read clocks. "Not even a little bit." At one point, when his teacher turned away, he drew a picture of his father, a smiley face with dreadlocks, before furiously scratching it out because he thought it looked ugly. That afternoon, Nikki told him he had to write an apology letter if he wanted to join his classmates for recess. "This is your opportunity to fix it," she told him, and he listened, sitting at a picnic table with a pencil and a sheet of paper.

"I am sorry for beanig disrespectful and I will not do it again and I am sorry," he scrawled, and when Nikki told him he could go, Tyshaun played football with his friends in the dirt and the grass, and it took four other boys to tackle him. At gym, he noticed a classmate sitting alone on the floor by the wall, rubbing his eyes. Tyshaun sat down next to him. "You okay?" he asked, but before the boy could answer, a staff member led him out. Tyshaun looked disappointed. "I was trying to make him feel better," he said.

That afternoon, Nikki gave him his behavior sheet back. "Trouble following directions," she'd written beneath his score, a 2. When she wasn't looking, he crumpled up the paper and dropped it on the floor so he wouldn't have to show it to his mom. At the end of the day, Donna waited for him in the lobby, smiling as he approached. Behind her was the expansive glass window, and there, across the street, a mobile police camera now stood on the corner next to where his father had been shot five times. On top of it, red and blue lights flashed.

CHAPTER 6

"IT'S NOTHING TO GET A GUN"

The Plague of Illegal Firearms

In 1988, the year Tyshaun's father, Andrew McPhatter, was born, the number of homicides in Washington, DC, reached 369, a record. The next year's total, 434, easily surpassed that mark, and the figure continued to grow until it peaked at 482 in 1991. Not until the year Andrew turned sixteen did annual homicides in his hometown, the only place he'd ever lived, dip below 200. Fueled by the crack epidemic that decimated many black neighborhoods in DC, the violence prompted journalists to brand the city "America's murder capital."

This was the backdrop to Andrew's childhood, a period of violence much worse than what his three sons would experience years later. For most of the boy's youth, his mother, Jessica Jackson, insisted that he and his siblings, an older sister and younger brother, stay inside, away from the perpetual gunfire. Like every other kid in the neighborhood, Andrew often heard about friends of friends and cousins of neighbors who'd been shot to death on the blocks he walked each day. To keep her children safe, Jessica sent them nearly every summer to stay with relatives in North Carolina, and when

Andrew was around ten, she moved the family from their home in Northeast Washington to the redbrick duplex in Southeast, hoping it would be safer there. It wasn't.

"The staggering body counts back then created a culture or mindset on the streets in which killing was practically normalized for a lot of young people," said Paul Duggan, who's worked for the *Post* since 1987 and covered the turbulence of that era extensively. "Teenagers started gunning down other teenagers over the pettiest of insults and slights. Murder became almost casual."

It was a time of unprecedented existential turmoil in DC. Entire neighborhoods fell below the poverty line, the school system struggled to provide even a basic education to its students, and the city was so poorly run that Congress appointed a financial control board in 1995 to oversee its management. The combined failures deprived blacks throughout the city of quality learning environments and proper mental health care, both things research has shown dramatically decrease the odds that someone will commit a crime. Though many middle-class African Americans fled Washington for the security of the Maryland suburbs, Andrew's family couldn't afford to leave.

His father went to prison when Andrew was about seven, disappearing from his life, Jessica said. To provide, she worked double shifts as a caretaker for the elderly, sometimes leaving her kids by themselves for long stretches. Andrew, a quiet kid who mostly stayed out of trouble, didn't hesitate to speak up or fight for his siblings, always acting like the oldest even though he wasn't. His mother admired his decency. As a little boy, Andrew and his sister once brought home a pair of Rottweiler puppies they'd found covered in fleas. The kids gave them baths and picked the bugs off, and they wanted to care for the animals until a neighbor said they were his and took them back. Andrew cried when the dogs had to go.

Not until he started junior high did he meet the guys who became his closest friends, many of whom would eventually join Trenton

Park, one of the city's neighborhood "crews." The crews—too dis-organized to qualify as legitimate gangs, though the police some-times call them that—are groups of young men, brought together most often by geography rather than money or drugs, who carry on trivial feuds, sometimes decades old, with other crews separated by mere blocks. As Duggan once wrote, they are "a loose collection of street acquaintances, some of them varsity-level felons, some junior varsity, some just adolescent wannabe gangstas." Andrew's mother would later deny that her son belonged to Trenton Park, despite the police's conclusion that he did. He might have been involved, and even sold drugs, during his teens, the family said, but he'd backed off those habits years before he was shot. Police had arrested him on a handful of minor charges (marijuana possession, unlawful entry), but prosecutors never pursued a case against him. He had no history of violence or criminal convictions on his record, and he even tried to join the military but couldn't because, a recruiter told him, he hadn't graduated from high school.

Fatherhood changed him, his family told me. He wanted to be the dad he never had, and that's what he was. He spent all those hours in his room with the boys, playing video games and wrestling on the bed, telling silly jokes and, now and then, doling out advice. To save money to pay for birthday presents and after-school pro-grams, he bought his suits at thrift stores. When his mother once noticed him wearing a pair of old, tattered sneakers and asked him why he hadn't gotten new ones, he told her he needed to save up.

"I gotta take care of my kids," he said.

To better do that, Andrew tried to improve his professional life, finding work in construction and attending night classes to earn his GED and new certifications for his job. Even with the duty to help raise three kids, though, he refused to abandon the people he'd grown up with, the guys who'd played ball and talked to girls with him, who'd thrown punches alongside him. To Andrew, it didn't matter that they'd remained on the streets—or that their feud with a nearby crew, Wahler Place, had led to an explosion of gun violence that he knew could jeopardize his own safety.

"He just felt like he couldn't turn his back," said Benica Mc-Manus, the mother of his youngest son, AJ. "That's ultimately what got him killed."

Researchers who have analyzed similar community gun violence have discovered that it spreads like an infectious disease. A study spanning an eight-year period in Chicago, for example, found that nearly two-thirds of the shootings were connected—the result of "social contagion." What that means, essentially, is that the more contact people had with someone who'd been shot, the more likely they were also to get shot. In Andrew's neighborhood, such contact was inevitable.

His mother first learned that he feared for his life when she gave him a hug one day and felt something in his pants. He wouldn't tell her what it was at first, but when she pressed him, he admitted that he'd started carrying a pistol. Furious, Jessica told him she didn't want a gun in the house, but he said he had no choice, that he needed it to keep himself and the family safe.

"From what?" she asked.

"From the world, Ma," he told her.

In mid-February, Andrew pulled his green Buick Regal into a parking lot two blocks from his duplex. When he got out, a man in a car that had followed him emerged in a ski mask and began firing, wounding a friend of Andrew's as he tried to flee. Panicked, Jessica asked her son to stay for a few weeks with his sister in Maryland, offering to Uber him to and from his construction jobs and the classes he attended at night, but Andrew didn't want his mom paying even more to support him. Besides that, and a feeling of responsibility to protect his family and friends, he was too proud to run away.

"There's nothing more important than your life," Jessica insisted, begging her son to leave. But he refused to go.

—

DEREK TURNER, THE man police say murdered Tyshaun's father, first tried to kill someone at the age of seventeen. His intended victim, Delonte Grimes, was just fourteen, the sibling of a man against whom Turner held a grudge. The brother had been arrested for robbery, though, and in his absence, Turner decided to target the boy. In August 2008, three months before a newborn Tyshaun was brought home from the hospital to grow up in this same Southeast neighborhood, Turner spotted Grimes walking down the street and pointed a gun at him. The boy turned and ran as bullets zipped past, one of them nicking his arm. Turner, nicknamed "Fatz," attacked him twice more, once smashing his face with a revolver and later chasing him into an apartment building. Inside, Turner opened fire, blowing five holes through Grimes's front door. One round struck him in the leg.

It wasn't Turner's first experience with the criminal justice system. As a juvenile, he'd been convicted of making felony threats, and just three months before the attacks on Grimes, a jury couldn't decide whether he'd committed armed robbery. "Regardless of any opinion about the Defendant's guilt or innocence in that case, the Defendant did not make any kind of major changes in his lifestyle even after several months of incarceration," prosecutors told the court before Turner's sentencing in the Grimes case. They argued that he showed an "absolute disregard for human life when indiscriminately firing through the front door of the Grimes household," where the boy's grandmother and a number of other children could also have been shot. The damage to Grimes's mental health, prosecutors wrote in a court memo, was "substantial," explaining that the terror he had suffered would haunt him "for the rest of his life." The judge sentenced Turner to seven years in prison, two fewer than prosecutors requested.

Almost immediately after his release in late May 2015, Turner resumed his life of violence, according to investigators. That summer, police searching an abandoned home found seven handguns, including one that held traces of Turner's DNA. Weeks later, Turner took off running when he saw officers approaching, and though they found a loaded .45-caliber handgun along the path he took, he again avoided a criminal conviction.

Soon after that, in 2016, he became increasingly involved in a turf dispute between Trenton Park, the crew Andrew allegedly belonged to, and Wahler Place, of which Turner was a member. An eruption of bloodshed that led to more than a half-dozen shootings would leave two young men dead and Turner wounded before Andrew and his friend were attacked in the parking lot. The next shooting in the feud—the one that ended Andrew's life—came seven days later, on March 1.

A week after the ambush, and three days after Andrew's death at the hospital, two people sought revenge on Turner, firing at him from a passing SUV as he walked to his white Lexus sedan. When police searched his damaged car, they found seven shooting targets, six of which were pocked with bullet holes; they were later tracked to a gun range he'd visited in North Carolina. In the locked glove compartment, investigators found a Glock 29 that they quickly identified as the one used in each of the prior shootings. Soon after, police arrested Turner at a hotel room in DC, and inside his rental car, they recovered another Glock.

In the months that followed, as police collected more evidence and the breadth of Turner's alleged brutality went public, the community reacted with disgust and indignation. Inevitably, the focus in the aftermath of such shocking acts of gun violence, whether committed in a single massacre or a series of targeted shootings, falls on the gunman and those responsible for stopping him. Why would someone behave with such malice? What had all that terror achieved? Did anyone know how dangerous he was and neglect to warn police? Could detectives have caught him sooner? But as is almost always the case, too few people asked one of the most important questions of all: how does someone as violent as Derek Turner get a gun in the first place?

DAVID CHIPMAN HAS heard gun lobbyists make the same argument for years, and it's always some variation on this: firearms regulations must not work because cities with some of the toughest laws (New York, Chicago, and DC, for example) often can't stop criminals, such as Derek Turner, from obtaining weapons and shooting people. To Chipman, that claim is nonsense, and gun lobbyists probably know it is because, as their assertions go, it's among the easiest to refute.

"If the gun laws in New York didn't work, criminals from New York would not drive on I-95 all the way to Georgia . . . but they're forced to do that to acquire their guns," said Chipman, the former special agent at the ATF. He was referring to what's become known as the Iron Pipeline, a span of interstate that traffickers use to move weapons from states with weak laws to states with strong ones.

The numbers back Chipman up. Of the more than 5,100 illegal guns recovered in New York State in 2018 and traced back to their origin, just one in four came from somewhere within the state, less than half the proportion brought in from the South. The trend was even more dramatic in the nation's capital, home to perhaps the strictest firearms laws in the country. Police haven't announced how or where Turner acquired his gun (investigators seldom reveal this information) but it's easy to speculate. In DC, only *3 percent* of the guns traced in 2018 originated in the city—while neighboring Virginia, a state that has earned a D rating for its firearms regulations from the Giffords Law Center to Prevent Gun Violence—accounted for *fourteen* times that amount, illustrating how much one jurisdiction's effort to prevent gun violence can be crippled by another's unwillingness to do the same.

"It's nothing to get a gun," a former drug dealer from Southeast told me, noting that he once bought a pair of assault rifles—an

AR-15 and an AK-47—that were both illegal to own in the District. "All that stuff was easy to get." Some people he knew broke into cars outside bars and nightclubs because they knew reckless partygoers tended to leave their pistols in the glove boxes, but he said that a huge number of the firearms that circulated on DC's streets came from gun shows in Virginia, where it took little effort to buy weapons from private dealers, who weren't obligated to run background checks.

In 2016, the U.S. Department of Justice surveyed thousands of prison inmates about where they had obtained the guns they used in their crimes, and just 10 percent had bought theirs directly from a retailer; nearly half had obtained them from an underground market or off the street. Generally, firearms go from being legal to illegal in two different ways. At least a quarter of a million guns are stolen each year, according to the Department of Justice, but because the owners aren't obligated to report them missing, and often don't, that number is almost certainly much larger—perhaps even double the government's estimate. A huge proportion of those weapons are then resold, providing a consistent stream of firepower to would-be criminals across the country. Although tens of thousands of guns are taken directly from dealers, few states require stores to maintain specific security standards to ensure that their deadly merchandise is kept safe. And despite, in one recent survey, nearly half of gun owners saying they would buy a "smart gun" (a fingerprint-activated pistol, for example, that could be fired only by the owner, rendering its theft pointless), the industry hasn't developed the technology thanks to a blend of poor legislation, NRA opposition, and lack of interest among major firearms manufacturers.

The second avenue by which guns inundate the illegal market is through what's known as "straw" purchases. Put simply, person A buys a gun from a shop, an online seller, or a dealer at a gun show on behalf of person B, who transports the weapon somewhere else and sells it at a higher price. Prolific traffickers travel to places such as

Georgia or Virginia and enlist dozens of "straws" to buy them hundreds of weapons that they then peddle for much higher prices elsewhere. To the frustration of firearm safety activists, we as a country have known for years how to subvert the black market, and thereby save thousands of lives, but Congress has never been willing to take action.

"Universal background checks, on day one, would be the most effective way to absolutely upend firearms trafficking, because there would be no incentive to leave your state," Chipman said, explaining that the would-be buyer in Georgia would suddenly face the same restrictions as the one in New York. Traffickers would still try to use straw purchasers with clean records to get around the law, but, Chipman noted, there's a solution for that, too. "In my experience, if you're required to get a license and the gun is registered in your name, you're less likely, then, to want to have that gun in someone's hands you don't know, because it'll come back on you, just like you wouldn't loan your buddy your car for a bank robbery or for a bombing."

Chipman, an intense, square-jawed man with short, graying hair, knows how controversial background checks and, especially, firearms licensing are, at least in the eyes of the gun lobby, though he's no extremist. He owns firearms and has a concealed handgun permit in Virginia, but after a career on the front lines of the gun violence epidemic, he knows as well as anyone that the United States must evolve.

"I have no problem if getting a gun is inconvenient if the trade-off is that public safety is enhanced," said Chipman, now a senior policy adviser at Giffords. "You won't ever see me in line at DCA [Washington's national airport] waiting for a plane bitching because of TSA, because, like, I know why I'm doing that: because we don't want planes flying into towers. And, sure, we could debate, is there a better way to do it? But today, with guns, you know, it's like having two lines at the airport. Law-abiding people stand and go through security, and then we let criminals take this private-sale loophole and circumvent the whole system. It's ridiculous."

To Chipman, nothing better illustrates Congress's indifference toward gun violence than the menial support it provides his previous employer, ATF, the agency most responsible for addressing the issue. Its annual budget, about $1.3 billion, costs the federal government one-tenth what it spent on one of the military's latest aircraft carriers, the USS *Gerald Ford*—a single weapons system. The Broward County Sheriff's Office in South Florida employs more deputies (2,800) than the ATF employs special agents (2,600). Meanwhile, the agency's 800 or so industry operations investigators are tasked with overseeing *more than 60,000* licensed gun dealers, which means, Chipman said, that most sellers undergo an inspection only about once a decade.

"There is no way that we can, with a straight face, Democrats or Republicans, look in the mirror and say that we're serious about gun violence when the agency who is in charge of enforcing the gun laws and regulating the entire industry has that type of budget and those types of resources," said Chipman, who emphasized how important it is to understand that none of this, not the gaping holes in policy or the lack of funding for ATF, has happened by accident. America's leaders know how to make things better but choose not to, he said, because too few of them are willing to defy the NRA.

In fact, legislators haven't even created a law that specifically bans gun trafficking. For decades, prosecutors have been forced to charge people with dealing in firearms without a license; whether the person has illegally sold ten guns or ten thousand, they face the same count. "It's like saying 'El Chapo' Guzman and your corner street drug dealer are accountable for the same crime," one investigator told me, noting that even the most egregious offenders face relatively light punishments.

One of them is Bobby Perkins Jr., a drug dealer who bought more than two hundred guns in Virginia and sold many of them in DC, including to feuding street rivals in neighborhoods where he'd grown up. At least ninety-four of the weapons he sold, prosecutors said, were recovered at crime scenes, some as far away as New Jersey and Pennsylvania. Investigators linked five of his guns to three separate homicides, including two in the District. Among the victims was an eighteen-year-old who stopped by a dice game during a walk to the store from his family's apartment. A passing gunman opened fire and hit four people. One round struck the teen in the chest, killing him. His name was Bryan Perkins. He was the trafficker's cousin.

Bobby Perkins knew, investigators found, that he was selling his deadly weapons to felons. He also understood what they intended to do with them, but that didn't stop him. Nevertheless, for a crime that would lead to bloodshed all along the East Coast, that would cost three lives and devastate his own family, Perkins pleaded guilty to a single count of dealing without a license and received the maximum sentence allowed by the statute: ten years in prison.

Peter Newsham, chief of DC's Metropolitan Police Department, has also argued that traffickers should face more severe consequences because, he maintains, the primary cause of violence in his city is easy access to guns, but he contends, too, that people who commit crimes with those guns should face harsher penalties. His office analyzed homicides over a twenty-four-month period and found that, in one year, 49 percent of those responsible had a prior gun arrest; in the other, it reached 52 percent. The vast majority of the time, he said, someone caught with an illegal firearm in the city faces less than a year of incarceration, if any, a result that Newsham believes only encourages other people to take the same risks. At minimum, he said, those convicted should face three years behind bars.

"You will still have gun-related crime in the city, but there's going be a whole category of folks out there that says, 'I'm not taking that gun out to the club tonight. I'm not, because if I get caught, I'm not doing three years," he told me. "There's going to be that group of people that feels that way. I'm convinced of it. Right now, they're like, 'You know, I'm not going to do any time, why don't I take my gun?'

"We want to be compassionate to a person who's lived a very difficult life, who's grown up in very bad circumstances. We all do want to be compassionate about those things, but we also have to take into consideration that the other side of the issue is this person could go out and shoot or kill somebody else. And in my mind, that always outweighs my compassion for an individual and their circumstance," Newsham said. He's attended enough children's funerals to know that the consequences of gun violence in DC, a problem driven almost exclusively by illegal firearms, extend well beyond disputes among gang members.

Between 2014 and 2019, more than three hundred children were shot in the District. Among those, at least twenty-eight died in homicides. These included Taiyania Aaliyah Thompson, struck in the head at age sixteen, one year younger than her father at the time he was shot to death. Steve Slaughter, fourteen, was walking to 7-Eleven with his friends to pick up chips, candy, and a Sprite when someone shot him three times in a botched robbery. There was also Karon Brown, eleven, a football player and practical joker killed outside a McDonald's in Southeast; and his friend Makiyah Wilson, a vibrant ten-year-old struck in the chest as she headed to an ice-cream truck. Another young victim, Ahkii Washington-Scruggs, who was gunned down along with his father inside their apartment, wrote a poem titled "I'm from . . ." just weeks before he died. In it, he bemoaned the perception that black kids like him would amount to nothing but drug addicts, and he complained of the way tourists claimed his hometown was such a wonderful place but never saw the part of it he struggled to survive in every day.

"I'm from a city full of hate. In D.C., it's nothing but people trying take your life away," he wrote. "I'm from a city where it's a blessing to see the age 20."

On the day he died, Ahkii was seventeen.

TYSHAUN WAS GROWING restless. At a park a half mile from the site of his dad's shooting, Andrew's family and friends had organized a cookout in his memory, and Tyshaun hung out in the hot afternoon sun for more than an hour, devouring a snow cone and munching on Takis Fuego tortilla chips, bobbing to a Migos song, winning a balloon sword fight with Tayvonne, his best friend from Eagle Academy. Now, tired of sweating, he wanted to go to a pool up the street, so the boy told his mom good-bye and headed off with his friend. As they walked, the kids talked about *The Lion King* and about their least-favorite teachers, before Tyshaun recalled a recent interaction with a campus security guard, and that brought them back to a topic seldom far from their minds.

"Security don't even have guns," Tyshaun said. Tayvonne, a husky kid with thick shoulders and a short haircut, told him he thought they should.

"'Cause you never know if bad people coming," he said, but Tyshaun, dressed in a sleeveless white T-shirt, cargo shorts, and brown high-top Nikes, wasn't so sure.

"What if they get mad at a kid and shoot them?" Tyshaun asked, and that made the boys think of all the massacres at schools they'd been hearing about. Both worried something like that could happen to them, too.

"'Cause it's a lot of gangs, and they want to kill people," Tyshaun said. "I don't know why they think killing people is cool."

"I know," Tayvonne added.

All this reminded Tyshaun of another of his father's friends who'd recently been shot. "He died," Tyshaun said. He'd heard that the person responsible was the victim's roommate, who had killed him because he wanted the guy to move out.

"That's disrespectful," Tayvonne said.

"That's stupid," Tyshaun replied. Both boys said they were tired of all the killing in their neighborhoods.

"I don't like when people be shooting around places where you live," Tayvonne said, recalling the time his cousin was killed. "He was sitting on a car and he got shot by a person. And then the person who shot him, he died, too."

"How did the guy that shot him die?" Tyshaun asked.

"Shot, with a gun."

"Did your cousin shoot him back?"

"No."

"Then how did the guy who shot him die?"

"Because there was another person who had a gun behind him that shot him. That killed him," Tayvonne explained. Then the two elementary-schoolers recounted the times they'd seen guns in person.

"At my father's house," Tyshaun told Tayvonne. He'd seen the pistol once before the time he spotted it in a dresser drawer. "My dad told me it was a water gun, so, I was like, I started playing with it. I didn't shoot it. My dad walked in the room. He say, 'What are you doing!?' Then I said, 'It's a water gun.' He said, 'Put it down!'"

Tayvonne didn't understand why adults thought they could keep stuff hidden from their kids. "We're little monsters. We can get around anything," he said, but Tyshaun told him he knew why his dad kept a gun close by.

"It was for protection," he said.

"You don't need a gun to have protection," Tayvonne responded.

"No, but other people started shooting and coming around, 'cause they know where my dad lived and stuff," said Tyshaun, whose father, he insisted, seldom hung out in the area where the neighborhood gang members did. Tyshaun still couldn't fathom why anyone would want to hurt his dad.

"Probably 'cause they thought he was probably in another gang, because he had a gun," Tayvonne suggested, but Tyshaun didn't see what else his father could have done.

"They pulled up again at nighttime and started shooting again," he said, recalling one of the incidents just before his dad's death.

"At your house?"

"That's how that hole got in the wall," Tyshaun explained, and for a few minutes after that, the boys fantasized about how they would one day escape all the violence around them. Tyshaun considered moving to Texas because he'd heard it had big houses. Then Tayvonne brought up Japan, and Tyshaun learned that wherever that place was, almost no one owned guns, so the boy decided he wanted to live there when he grew up. At last, they arrived at the pool, and their conversation reached its end. Rushing across the deck, Tyshaun stripped off his shirt and leapt into the water, where Tayvonne soon joined him. Beneath a blue sky dappled with puffs of white, the boys splashed and wrestled and laughed.

CHAPTER 7

"CAN YOU STOP VIOLENCE?"

The NRA's Faltering War on Common Sense

My drive begins at the home where Tyshaun shared a bedroom with his father, the place that the boy once played with a gun he didn't know could kill him and later hid from the sound of shots fired by another he feared would. I head to the end of the street and take a left, less than a block from the mural for a fifteen-year-old honor student named Maurice Scott, gunned down on a Sunday morning a few weeks earlier outside a market where Tyshaun had gone dozens of times to pick up Takis chips and root beer. Then I go north, over the spot at which Andrew was shot five times in his car, and keep going, past the Eagle Academy lobby from where Tyshaun peered out at the flashing police lights and hoped his daddy was okay. I turn onto the avenue named for Martin Luther King Jr., killed in 1968 with a rifle, and then onto the one named for Malcolm X, killed in 1965 with a sawed-off shotgun. I cross the river and travel west, past the U.S. Capitol Building, where Senate Republicans are refusing to consider a bill requiring background checks for all firearm sales, a measure supported by more than 90 percent of the country. I continue on past the White House, inhabited by a man whom gun lobbyists spent more than $30 million to get elected in 2016. I cross another bridge, this one taking me into Northern Virginia, and pass Arlington National Cemetery. Four hundred thousand dead military veterans and their family members have been buried there over the last century and a half, a sobering total that still falls more than two hundred thousand graves shy of the number of Americans killed by guns in only the last twenty years. I exit one interstate and merge onto another, heading through some of the nation's most affluent suburbs. Then I take a final turn, into the parking lot of a three-hundred-thousand-square-foot, six-story building encased in reflective glass. Outside, an American flag flaps from a tall white pole beside another flag, flying at the same height, inscribed with NATIONAL RIFLE ASSOCIATION OF AMERICA. This is the headquarters of an organization with immense influence over Washington that, both behind the scenes and in plain view of the American public, has strangled this country's repeated efforts to strengthen its gun laws. Inside the building, I arrive at an exhibition titled, *A Child's Room*, but that doesn't entirely capture it. Before me is an idealized version of a child's room as envisioned by the NRA's National Firearms Museum. A light blue paper decorated with illustrated saddles, boots, and gun holsters coats the walls. Above a shelf holding a Slinky and a globe and a pair of *Hardy Boys* books hangs a gun rack that displays a Harrington and Richardson twenty-gauge shotgun, a Stevens Arms .22-caliber rifle, and another .22-caliber rifle equipped with a scope. On a shelf just below it, cartoon images of police officers adorn a bright red box for a Smith and Wesson model 34 revolver. On the bed, beneath a coonskin cap hanging on the wall, is a third .22-caliber rifle, this one lying amid a half-dozen comic books and a BOY SCOUTS OF AMERICA pennant. The child's room is just on the other side of a wall from an exhibit for the AR-pattern assault rifle, a weapon that's been used time and again to slaughter dozens of children in their classrooms and hallways. AMERICA'S RIFLE, reads a sign written in red letters above the display.

In a single half-hour drive, I'd traversed the landscape of this country's relationship with guns—from a community ravaged by them for decades, among the seats of power where so little had been done to stem the bloodshed they cause, to the center of a universe where they were so beloved, and so profitable, that a shrine had been erected in their honor.

Much of this country expected the status quo to change dramatically after the Sandy Hook massacre in 2012, when a young man killed twenty first-graders and six adults with a pair of guns, including one of "America's rifles." For the first time since taking office, then-President Barack Obama fought for sweeping gun reform, but four months after the killings, the measures he supported—an expansion of background checks, a prohibition on high-capacity magazines, and a ban on assault weapons—all failed, largely, but not entirely, because of Republican opposition. The president called it a "shameful day for Washington," a feeling shared by millions of Americans and one that only grew after similar inaction following the mass shootings at the Washington Navy Yard in 2013; the San Bernardino holiday party, Roseburg community college, and Charleston church in 2015; the Orlando nightclub in 2016; the Las Vegas country music festival and Sutherland Springs church in 2017; the Pittsburgh synagogue, Thousand Oaks bar, and the Santa Fe and Parkland high schools in 2018; and the Virginia Beach city building in 2019.

That collective embarrassment further intensified when New Zealand responded decisively to the slaughter of fifty people at a pair of Christchurch mosques in early 2019. Less than a month after the attack, lawmakers passed a gun reform bill by a vote of 119 to 1. "There have been very few occasions when I have seen parliament come together in this way, and I can't imagine circumstances when it is more necessary," Prime Minister Jacinda Ardern said. Within hours, cable news producers in the United States were sending requests to reporters like me, asking us to explain how another country's leaders had accomplished something in a matter of weeks that our own had tried and failed to do for years. The answers were both simple and complex. Most obviously, gun rights are enshrined in the U.S. Constitution, obligating the country's courts to protect them. Our system of government also gives rural voters disproportionate influence: states that are fiercely protective of their guns, such as Idaho (population 1.8 million), have as much authority in the U.S. Senate as states that back strict gun legislation, such as New York (population 19.5 million). Also, unlike America, New Zealand, Britain, and Australia require licenses for the purchase of firearms, regulations that, in some cases, were shaped by mass shootings. Of course, America is also home to the NRA, the world's most forceful gun lobbyist.

Regardless of the reasons, one more nation's commonsense reaction to a mass execution prompted a fresh round of fatalism in ours, where many had given up hope that reform would ever happen. "If Sandy Hook and Parkland didn't change things, nothing will," people asserted in a refrain I have heard hundreds of times, but here's the problem with that claim: Sandy Hook and Parkland *did* change things.

Much of America has forgotten that many Democratic lawmakers once supported the NRA and that the party's presidential nominees, who've led the campaign for gun control in recent years, essentially ignored it *for more than a decade* before the Newtown school shooting. "After Al Gore's 2000 defeat, Democrats decided, rightly or wrongly, that the gun issue was a poison pill for them, so they all but abandoned it," explained Robert Spitzer, a political scientist at SUNY Cortland and one of the nation's foremost experts on gun policy. "This left the national gun debate mostly in the hands of the gun-friendly Bush administration and gun rights supporters. That one-sided national debate turned public attitudes more strongly in favor of gun rights." The debate's one-sidedness ended with Sandy Hook, which also led to the creation of a number of grassroots activist groups that have since gained national prominence, including Moms Demand Action for Gun Sense in America. "It's unfortunate it took so long, but what we realized was that we had to build a political movement to be equal in power to the special interests, just like Americans did with the alcohol lobby around drunk driving," said Shannon Watts, who launched the nonprofit from her kitchen table after the killings in Newtown. "There had to be a grassroots movement that could go toe-to-toe with the gun lobby, and that doesn't happen overnight. It takes a lot of money. It takes the unglamorous heavy lifting of grassroots activism, which women in this country are well acquainted with. And it took building political power."

Around the same time that the NRA began to show existential fissures—multimillion-dollar shortfalls; allegations of cronyism, corruption, and exorbitant spending by its leaders; an investigation by the New York State attorney general into its tax-exempt status—the lobbyist's political enemies were gaining substantial momentum. During the 2018 midterm elections, gun safety groups for the first time spent more money on national races than did the NRA (which declined my repeated requests for an interview). One exit poll found that Democratic voters considered gun policy the second-most-important issue to them, and among all voters, it consistently ranked third or fourth. Giffords, the group cofounded by former congresswoman Gabrielle Giffords, claimed widespread victory after Election Day, saying that 81 percent of the 307 candidates it endorsed won their races.

"The results indicated that the gun issue was helpful . . . at least to the Democrats that embraced it, and there was a large number of them compared to past elections," Spitzer told me, noting how many candidates who ran for the 2020 Democratic nomination had made gun reform a central tenet of their campaign. "They're no longer scared to talk about it, including in toss-up districts and toss-up states, so it's not just traditional liberal bastions."

There's a reason for that: Americans disagree about guns far less than they think they do. A survey by Johns Hopkins University found overwhelming consensus on everything from universal background checks to stricter regulations of gun dealers to barring domestic abusers from owning firearms to enacting higher safety training standards for concealed-carry permit holders. A separate poll revealed that nearly 80 percent of Americans supported red-flag laws that would allow family members to ask a judge to temporarily take guns away from someone deemed a threat.

"I often get into conversations with NRA members who have approached me in Connecticut with a furious look on their face. And then, as soon as I start talking to them about background checks, we're on the same page," said Senator Chris Murphy, a Democrat from Connecticut and a relentless proponent of gun reform. "What I think you're seeing is an awakening of parents across this country. Parents that are conservative and parents that are liberal because, you know, these parents are listening to their kids coming home and telling stories of lockdown drills, and all of a sudden, they decide to elevate that question of a candidate's position on guns in their evaluation."

If that's true, and America is closer than ever to the opportunity for meaningful change, that raises two questions: what needs to happen for the United States to reach the point at which things will tip, and if they do, what changes to our laws will make the most significant difference? The path to answering both questions, in my view, begins with something simple: research. Despite the NRA's denials, gun violence is, unequivocally, a public health crisis and one that's especially harmful to our children, a point illustrated by dozens of studies, including a recent one showing that nearly 39,000 young people ages five to eighteen were killed by bullets between 1999 and 2017. "Mortality from firearms in U.S. schoolchildren is increasing at alarming rates, especially among blacks and those aged

15–18 years," the authors concluded in the *American Journal of Medicine*. "We believe that combatting the epidemic of mortality from firearms among U.S. schoolchildren without addressing firearms is analogous to combatting the epidemic of mortality from lung cancer from cigarettes without addressing cigarettes." But how did this country learn, in the face of tobacco lobbyists' denials, that cigarettes did indeed cause cancer and, later, how to effectively combat the disease? Using the same thing we must have now: research so compelling that neither the product's manufacturers nor its lobbyists nor its supporters in Congress nor its consumers can refute the truth.

While researchers from the DC-based Children's National Hospital have found that kids are killed by guns at a lower rate in states with stricter firearms laws, the RAND Corporation, a nonpartisan think tank, set out to understand which specific restrictions make a difference and which don't, reviewing eighteen different classes of gun policy. In their effort, the researchers discovered a dearth of reliable data. Besides finding strong evidence that child access prevention laws save lives, they also discovered that background checks likely prevent violent crime, that keeping guns from people with mental illness does the same, and that stand-your-ground laws may, in fact, increase violent crime. What they couldn't determine was whether a half-dozen other policies (including establishing gun-free zones, mandating firearm licenses, and requiring people to report lost or stolen weapons) made a real difference.

"This does not mean that these policies are ineffective; they might well be quite effective. Instead, it partly reflects shortcomings in the contributions that scientific study can currently offer to policy debates in these areas," RAND concluded, meaning, in essence, that America hasn't done nearly enough research into what will save people from being shot to death. There is, of course, a reason for that, and its origin dates back to a three-minute speech delivered in the U.S. Capitol one afternoon during the summer of 1996.

—

IN THE EARLY 1990s, three years before the vote that would cripple the country's ability to understand gun violence, the *New England Journal of Medicine* published a study funded by the CDC that reached a simple conclusion: "Rather than confer protection, guns kept in the home are associated with an increase in the risk of homicide by a family member or intimate acquaintance." This discovery infuriated the NRA, which argued that the government agency was using taxpayer money to advance a political agenda. The lobbyist tapped one of its proudest members, U.S. representative Jay Dickey, of Arkansas, to help, and he eagerly agreed, becoming the organization's self-described "point person" on the issue.

What happened next stemmed from an NRA plan that dated back to the 1970s. "The strategy was either that you can do the research or you can keep your guns, but you can't do both," said Dr. Mark Rosenberg, former director of the CDC's National Center for Injury Prevention and Control (NCIPC). "They knew it wasn't true, but it was an all-or-nothing dichotomous approach . . . It was a brilliant strategy for the NRA, but for our country, it was devastating."

Rosenberg met Dickey, who'd been persuaded by the NRA's argument, at an April 1996 hearing held by a House Appropriations subcommittee where the doctor, there to testify, tried to explain what had motivated his center to study gun violence. "In part, our difficulty in this area has been that the field has been so polarized that science hadn't been used, that people hadn't agreed on definitions," Rosenberg told the lawmakers. "They hadn't even agreed on how to view the problem, let alone how to start solving the problem. What we're trying to do is share that science."

"The problem you're talking about is gun-related activities?" Dickey responded. "Is that what you're saying the problem is?"

"No. The problem is violence in our society and the problem is that people, especially young people in increasing numbers, are being murdered and are committing suicide," Rosenberg said. "I think it is so important for us to remember that the problem is the problem; it is the problem of premature deaths of our young people that we're trying to focus on."

"Can you stop violence?" Dickey asked. "You can't stop violence unless you stop people from committing it, can you? How can you stop violence by attacking the gun?"

"We're not trying to attack the gun, sir. We're trying to understand the problem," Rosenberg said. "And absolutely yes, we can prevent violence. I think the way to do it is by first trying to understand it."

Unconvinced, Dickey took to the House floor three months later, delivering his speech on the afternoon of July 11, 1996. "This is an issue of federally funded political advocacy," he began. "We have here an attempt by the CDC, through the NCIPC, a disease control agency of the federal government, to bring about gun control advocacy all over the United States." Congress went on to cut the CDC's budget by $2.6 million—the exact amount it had spent on gun violence research the year before—and at Dickey's prodding, lawmakers included a provision in the next spending bill that forbade that any money "be used, in whole or in part, to advocate or promote gun control." The language, though vague, had such a chilling effect that it halted almost all federal and most private research on the issue. Rosenberg continued to fight for funding, and because of that, the doctor said, he was fired three years later.

Nearly two decades after that, researchers revealed the enormous consequences of the provision, which came to be known as the "Dickey Amendment." In a study published in *JAMA*, they identified the top thirty causes of death in the United States from 2004 to 2014, then compared the mortality rates with the funding for research devoted to each of them. In theory, the investments should have been proportional with the death rates (e.g., cause A kills 100 people per 100,000, so it receives $100 in research; cause B kills 20, so it gets $20). Causes including HIV, viral hepatitis, Parkinson's disease, and anemia—each of which killed fewer people than guns do—had all received more than $1 billion apiece in funding, which implied that gun violence should have, too. Instead, the study found, it got just $22 million, which equated to *1.6 percent* of the logically predicted amount.

"In relation to mortality rates," the *JAMA* paper concluded, "gun violence research was the least-researched cause of death."

In the years after the passage of Dickey's namesake amendment, he came to regret it, and that was due in large part to Rosenberg. The two had met in Dickey's office after their confrontation. Dickey had always been interested in people who disagreed with him, so he invited Rosenberg to chat. They talked mostly about their kids at first, and after Dickey offered to give Rosenberg's son and his class a tour of the building, a relationship developed. Eventually, they addressed the issue that made them enemies, with Dickey, a Deep South conservative Christian who cherished his shotguns, explaining to his friend what the Second Amendment meant to people like him, and with Rosenberg, a Harvard-educated Jew from the Northeast who believed in the power of science, explaining to his friend that good research could save lives without robbing law-abiding citizens of their weapons.

Just as the mounting number of mass shootings began to wear on Dickey's conscience, he made a discovery in an entirely unrelated field—car safety—that convinced him he'd been wrong about what the research into gun safety could achieve. "They had a goal of eliminating head-on collisions in our interstate system. And they never— they didn't come out and say, 'We're going to eliminate the cars,'" Dickey once explained. "And they spent the time and the money for science and developed these 4-foot barricades that now you can see on the highways between the lanes of the interstate. And the results have been remarkable, as far as eliminating head-on collisions. And I thought, *Well, we could do the same thing.*"

He and Rosenberg called for Congress to fund new research in a pair of *Washington Post* op-eds they coauthored, one in 2012 and the other in 2015. Each piece revealed just how much the doctor's perspective had also shifted. Because Rosenberg understood that what the CDC needed in order to proceed was bipartisan support from Congress, he decided that the Dickey Amendment should remain in place because it provided cover to Republicans who wanted to back new research. In 2019, Rosenberg made this case to another House Appropriations subcommittee, this time through testimony he co-authored with Dickey's former wife, Betty. "Jay died in 2017," they wrote. "But if Jay were alive, he would want to appear as a witness at this hearing to tell you in his own words that Congress should appropriate funding for this important research that has the potential to save lives and reduce disability." Within weeks, the House had passed a budget that included language clarifying the Dickey Amendment, stating that the "CDC has the authority to conduct research on the causes of gun violence." Lawmakers also included $50 million for it, a gesture that Rosenberg considered mostly symbolic because of the staunch gun rights Republicans in the Senate. In the end, they allocated $25 million, "a tiny, tiny fraction of what's needed," Rosenberg said, to make a real difference. To him and other activists, though, it was at least a start.

Before Dickey's death at the age of seventy-seven, he and Rosenberg liked to give interviews together because they thought their friendship—how it began and evolved—could serve as a model for others at odds over firearms. They had been bitter adversaries at the outset, but remarkably, through mutual respect and hours of thoughtful discussion, they'd come to agree on what was best for the country. In one of those interviews, a reporter asked if they had taken their joint recommendations to the NRA, the organization whose cause Dickey had fought so hard for that it defined his political legacy.

"I've made phone calls," he replied. "But I haven't gotten a return call."

—

"SIX MINUTES AND twenty seconds with an AR-15," said Emma Gonzalez, as she stood on a stage before a crowd of hundreds of thousands stretching for blocks along Pennsylvania Avenue in the nation's capital. She wore a MARCH FOR OUR LIVES T-shirt, the name of the March 2018 event, and a dark green jacket adorned with buttons and patches. WE CALL BS, read one, referencing a line Emma had repeatedly delivered during a speech the month before, about the dismissive arguments made by the NRA and its supporters after mass shootings. From the stage, she continued: "My friend Carmen would never complain to me about piano practice. Aaron Feis would never call Kyra 'Miss Sunshine.' Alex Schachter would never walk into school with his brother Ryan. Scott Beigel would never joke around with Cameron at camp," Gonzalez said, and on she went, naming each of the seventeen killed at Stoneman Douglas. When the girl had finished, she went silent until an alarm sounded six minutes and twenty seconds after she'd taken the stage, signaling the time it had taken the gunman to forever change her school.

It was the most memorable moment of a day on which children from all over the country walked up on that stage to share their experiences with gun violence, including Mya Middleton, a sixteen-year-old from Chicago who, as a high school freshman, witnessed a store being robbed before the gunman approached her, pointed a pistol at her face, and said, "If you say anything, I will find you." Edna Chavez, seventeen, from Los Angeles, asked the crowd to chant the name of her brother, Ricardo, and recounted how he died: "Sunset going down on South Central. You hear pops, thinking they're fireworks. They weren't pops. You see the melanin in your brother's skin turn gray." Samantha Fuentes, her face bruised and leg still recovering from a bullet wound suffered at Stoneman Douglas, threw up during her speech, but kept going. "Either you can join us or be on the side of history who prioritized their guns over the lives of others." Zion Kelly, seventeen, announced that he was there to represent every child who feared being shot on their way to and from school each day. He told the crowd about his twin, Zaire, shot to death the year before during a botched robbery less than three miles from the Capitol as he walked home from a college prep course. Then, in nine words, he summed up the feeling at the rally and in much of the country on that day: "Just like all of you, I have had enough."

That simple motivation—of having had enough, of being unwilling to continue to do nothing—has driven a huge number of people to dive into the fray in recent years. In 2012, it's what led Gabrielle Giffords, shot in the head the year before, to launch an organization that spent nearly $7 million during the 2018 election cycle to go after NRA-backed candidates. It's what led two parents who each lost a child in the Newtown shooting, Nicole Hockley and Mark Barden, to cofound Sandy Hook Promise, which has received commitments from more than 4.5 million people to join them in the fight. It's what led Ed Stack, chief executive and chairman of Dick's Sporting Goods, to stop selling assault-style weapons in his stores. It's what led Dr. Joseph Sakran, a surgeon who'd been shot as a teenager, to inspire other doctors to speak out with the ThisIsOurLane movement after an NRA tweet alleged that "self-important anti-gun doctors" were promoting gun control and should "stay in their lane." It's what led thousands to offer support for Moms Demand after Parkland, when the nonprofit tripled the size of its volunteer base.

What the gun safety movement's leaders have learned, though, is that viral tweets, massive rallies, and impassioned speeches don't matter unless they lead to tangible change that can be achieved only through politics. Dr. Deborah Greenhouse, a little-known activist five hundred miles from DC, understands that reality as well as anyone because she's contended with it for years in Ava's home state of South Carolina, one of many places where the debate over guns often feels intractable. Greenhouse, a pediatrician, also responded to the NRA's directive to doctors, tweeting that during a checkup with a six-year-old, she asked the boy what he would do if he ever found a gun. "He said he'd grab it and play with it," she wrote. "His mom was shocked. I wasn't. It was the most important thing I talked about at his well visit. #ThisisMyLane." Greenhouse had long embraced what she views as an essential part of her duty in the effort, which started in her office with her asking questions about guns in the home as often as about healthy diets. Some parents—exclusively dads, she said—objected, insisting that it was none of her business, so Greenhouse told them her job was to keep their children safe and that guns, especially when they were unsecured, could pose a lethal threat. Sometimes that changed minds, and sometimes it didn't, but Greenhouse kept asking because she knew how lofty the stakes were. She once saw a sixteen-year-old who was showing signs of depression but denied feeling suicidal. Greenhouse turned to his parents and asked if they kept a gun at home. They said they did. "Please get that out of the house," she told them, and a few days later, the teen called her. "Thank you," he said, before explaining that he'd lied to her before—the teen had intended to kill himself after his doctor's visit but changed his mind when his parents removed the gun.

That exchange, like the one with the little boy, demonstrate the unique role doctors can play in changing parents' minds about gun safety, but even as some of the most trusted voices in their patients' lives, they can reach only one family a time. That's why Greenhouse, who lives in the state capital of Columbia, has also worked as a member of the legislative arm of the American Academy of Pediatrics to change the minds of lawmakers. After more than a decade of advocating for kids' needs, she began to campaign for new gun laws in 2015, after a white supremacist killed nine people at Emanuel African Methodist Episcopal Church in Charleston. Greenhouse had already helped push through legislation on everything from vaccines to child passenger safety, but on firearms, she said, her efforts went "absolutely nowhere." And it wasn't hard to see why. All three branches of government were controlled by Republicans, who governed a state where the NRA wielded enormous influence. Greenhouse's years of lobbying experience had taught her that although many South Carolina legislators understood that both their state and country faced a catastrophic problem, such knowledge wasn't enough to make them do anything about it.

"Everyone really knows when it comes down to brass tacks that gun violence is a huge issue. It's all the politics that create the barrier. It's all people trying to be sure that they're protecting their ability to get reelected," she said. "Anyone who sticks their neck out on this issue has to do it knowing it may cost them their political career."

It was the day after Parkland, February 15, 2018, and the first lawmaker to address the South Carolina Senate chamber on that Thursday had already brought up the massacre, framing it in the same way that other massacres had been framed time and again in this century-old room of dark mahogany and polished brass. He didn't mention the word *gun*, instead referring to the shooting simply as "violence." The state senate, he suggested, would have to discuss its "duty" at some point in the future. "Today is not that day. Today is a day to pray," he concluded, before asking his fellow lawmakers to stand for a moment of silence. They did, and after sixteen seconds, they sat back down. Another senator, a Republican from rural Lancaster County, then approached the lectern, holding his reading glasses in one hand and, in the other, a notepad on which he'd been jotting down thoughts at his desk until just moments earlier.

A deep-thinking native of South Carolina with the pronounced accent to prove it, Greg Gregory hadn't addressed the entire senate often during his two-decade career, seldom more than once or twice a year, so when he did speak, his colleagues paid attention. On this day, none of them knew what he was about to say. He hadn't told a single person, not even his wife, that he was on the verge of taking perhaps the biggest risk of his life in public office.

"This issue has been on my mind, is weighing heavily on me," said Gregory, fifty-four, dressed in a crisp blue sport coat and a matching checkered button-down shirt and bow tie. He set his notebook down, removed his glasses. He placed both hands on the lectern. "This issue of mass shootings in our country, and here in our state. Tragically, it's a sadistic fad that has been sweeping our country with increasing frequency, and we talk about it, but we really don't come up with any solutions, and it's time, I think, for us to do that.

"You know, the biggest threat to the safety of children in our country and people in general is not Muslims. It's not 'Mexican rapists,'" Gregory said, using air quotes as he referenced Trump's attack on Hispanic immigrants. "It's punks with a gun and a grudge, and this keeps going on, time and time again. And you know, the response, especially from Republicans whenever this occurs"—he put his hand on his chest, because he was one of them—"the response is typically 'thoughts and prayers.' And thoughts and prayers are not doing any good. God is not listening."

Gregory had been around guns all his life, and as a kid, was infatuated with them. He learned to fire shotguns and rifles. He hunted dove and deer. When he had first joined the senate in the early 1990s, he'd helped push through legislation that allowed South Carolina residents to discreetly carry firearms in public, citing a desire for his constituents to protect themselves from "young criminals." Gregory, who'd earned both an endorsement and an A rating from the NRA, had never given up his guns, but as time passed and the body count mounted, he realized that his belief in the Second Amendment didn't preclude him and other conservatives in power from doing whatever they could to save lives. The gradual shift in perspective had been expedited by the murder of a man Gregory had shared a desk with in the senate chamber for years, Clementa Pinckney, who was among those slaughtered in the Charleston church. Then a teenager in Townville killed a first-grader, then a maniac in Las Vegas killed fifty-eight people at a country music concert, and now a young man in Florida had killed seventeen people at a school.

"The first thing we need to do, in my opinion, with regard to gun violence in our country, is quit rationalizing it," Gregory continued on the senate floor. "We need to quit rationalizing gun violence and talking about—anytime one of these incidents happens—that this is 'the price of freedom.' That's a load of malarkey . . . Nowhere else in the developed world is this going on. Not even in the uncivilized world—this is not happening. But we've got, in my opinion, again, a misguided debate over guns. The debate that we tend to have about guns here, especially in South Carolina, is whether or not we're going to let somebody go to Walmart, buy a gun, and carry it around loaded *without* a permit. We're debating the issue way over here," he said, motioning his arms far to one side. "We need to be debating it in the center."

Gregory recalled the first editorial he'd ever read, around age ten or twelve in the mid-1970s. A writer in *Sports Afield* magazine had written a piece saying that he so feared the government coming for his guns that he'd buried them. That same unfounded paranoia, Gregory said, continued to poison gun owners' minds, making rational discussions all the more difficult. He'd gone to a sporting goods store a week after Sandy Hook, in 2012, and overheard a young woman who worked at the store telling a coworker that she wanted to buy an AR-15 but couldn't afford it. By the time she could, she suspected they would be outlawed. Maybe, he said, she wanted the semiautomatic rifle for sport shooting, but he doubted it.

"I think she probably just wanted a gun for the reason that most everybody else wants these guns. It's because it brings them some false sense of security that having these weapons is going to somehow protect them when the government comes to overthrow them or do something of that nature. Some far-fetched fantasy," he said. "Our country is awash in military-grade weapons designed to do one thing: *kill people.* Not hunt animals or shoot targets . . . We've got to get past this mentality that we all have to possess these military-grade weapons with these high-capacity magazines. And anytime I hear a debate over this, they talk about 'Well, you can't really define what an assault weapon is.' Well, I can define what a *weapon of terror* is. That's a weapon that's got a big clip on it, holding thirty rounds of ammunition, because you can go in there and kill as many people—just like it was designed for in the military—you can kill as many people as you can in a short amount of time. That is a weapon of terror."

Gregory then told his fellow lawmakers that what he found particularly striking, and infuriating, was that the epidemic of gun violence had touched all of them in a personal way. Pinckney—"Perhaps the most genteel, well-liked, nonthreatening person to have ever served in this body"—had been gunned down in a church "like an animal," he reminded them. Gregory motioned over his right shoulder, pointing to the portrait of Pinckney that looked over them. He paused, hoping the silence would remind them of how, in his view, they had failed to honor the man's life or his death.

"What's happened here since then?" he asked. "Nothing."

Gregory returned to his desk, aware that he might have just set in motion the end of his tenure in the senate. In 2016, Donald Trump had won Gregory's decisively conservative county by 25 points, far outpacing the state average. To many people there, guns were sacrosanct, a point made clear by a moment at a public meeting in 2018 between the region's U.S. representative, Ralph Norman, and his constituents. After a few of them brought up gun safety issues, Norman, in an apparent attempt to prove that firearms were dangerous only in criminal hands, pulled out a loaded .38-caliber Smith and Wesson and placed it on the table. "I'm not going to be a Gabby Giffords," he said afterward.

"Greg lives in rural South Carolina, where this kind of stuff is not only tolerated, but probably helps," state senator Vincent Sheheen, a

Democrat who represents an adjacent district, said of Representative Norman's audacity.

South Carolina lawmakers had paid steep prices for positions like Gregory's. Larry Martin, a Republican, represented a county near Townville for more than thirty-five years, eventually becoming one of the state's most powerful senators as chair of the judiciary committee. After the church shooting, lawmakers proposed legislation that would close a loophole in the law that allowed people to purchase firearms before their federal background checks were processed. The law, which would have given the FBI more time to investigate, was written to deprive criminals of one avenue they could use to buy guns. Martin, a staunch supporter of the Second Amendment, killed the bill, not even allowing it to be debated in a hearing. "I don't support any of that," he told a reporter at the time. Not long after, though, Martin surprised many of his colleagues when he backed legislation that would dispossess domestic abusers of their firearms and opposed another bill, proposed by fellow Republicans, that would allow people to carry a concealed handgun without a permit. In an op-ed defending both positions, Martin wrote that he was "not one of those types who believe that any common sense approach to solving a problem is always trumped by the Second Amendment." A fanatical gun rights group in the state labeled him an "Obama-loving gun grabber," and in 2016 he lost reelection. Martin told me he didn't regret his decisions—"I wouldn't go back and undo any of it"—but he knew what an ominous message his loss sent to other Republicans. "There's no question I'm being used as the poster child for anybody who might be on the fence," he told me. "They're saying, 'Look, you want to be like Larry Martin?'"

Gregory heard that message as well, but it didn't stop him, nor did the universal silence from fellow Senate Republicans after his speech. Instead, he went further, writing a widely shared op-ed that detailed his stance.

"I've been a state senator a long time, some will say too long. One thing I know from experience, though, is that good and lasting policy is crafted from the center, not the extremes. In order to create effective policy enhancing gun safety, most Republicans must move past doing nothing other than allowing increasing access to guns," he wrote. "Most of all we need to meet, talk, consider all reasonable remedies, and take action. There's certainly a need for 'thoughts and prayers,' but as we're told in James 2:17, 'faith, if it does not have works, is dead.' Without action, many more will be dead before year end. Now is the time to act."

He did act, too, pushing for legislation that, again, would give federal agents a longer period to check backgrounds, that would shorten the amount of time courts had to give a federal database the names of people deemed mentally ill, that would ban bump stocks and high-capacity magazines. The blowback, as he expected, was intense. "This is completely unacceptable!" one of the state's influential gun rights groups posted on its Facebook page, where Gregory was lambasted in a cascade of online outrage. "He better get out of South Carolina If he is Trying to Take Away our 2nd Amendment. WE WILL NOT ALLOW THAT," one wrote. "Greg Gregory I hope you are voted out of office and move from our town," added another. The group created an image that included a photo of Gregory; his partner on the legislation, Democrat Marlon Kimpson; and the former mayor of New York, Michael Bloomberg. "NO GUN CONTROL," it read, in black and red letters. In his own district, the lawmaker heard from people who told him he was "dead" to them.

Gregory, a stoic, introspective man who seldom raised his voice, ignored the threats and responded to the questions with facts. He had never shied from taking controversial positions in his public life, because that's the way he'd long been in his personal life, even as a boy. He and his wife, Sherri, met in high school, and she was immediately drawn to his independence on issues both large and small. As an avid tennis player back then, he dressed in polo shirts almost every day, then trends changed, and his friends began to dress in them as well. "He stopped immediately and started wearing T-shirts," Sherri recalled. As an adult, he added bow ties to his wardrobe, mostly because he liked the look of them, but also because he'd once seen a sign that said they were "a symbol of obstinance."

Gregory, who ran his family's successful building supply company, had grown up in a home with a deep-rooted sense of Southern pride, and when he started in the senate in the early 1990s, he vehemently defended South Carolina's practice of flying the Confederate flag over the statehouse. Then he learned that the flag had not, in fact, flown there without interruption since the Civil War but, instead, had been raised again a century later in 1961, amid the civil rights movement. "As I listened to the debate, it became apparent to me that that wasn't an appropriate place for the Battle Flag," said Gregory, who was the first senate Republican to argue publicly for it be moved to another spot. After Charleston two decades later, he supported its removal entirely, a position that once would have been unimaginable to him. He'd bucked his own party on other measures, too, including controversial taxes on gas and cigarettes, and when his neighboring Democratic senator, Sheheen, unsuccessfully ran for governor, Gregory gave him an endorsement and a donation. During Gregory's next campaign, one of his opponents blew up an image of the check he had written and mounted it to the back of a pickup that was driven around the county. "Greg never backed down. Never flinched," Sheheen said. Gregory still won the election.

On guns, it had taken years for his thinking to progress, but Gregory felt certain that he'd arrived at the right place. He'd seen the determination in parents, the furious rise of Moms Demand, and realized that intransigent Republicans would one day have no say in the matter. Gregory, who knew that the percentage of American households with a gun had plummeted to less than a third, recognized a slippery slope, just not the one so often cited by the NRA and its supporters. "Suburban mothers are not going to put up with these mass shootings," he told me. "If it continues, eventually the tide will be so strong that it's just going to sweep away the Second Amendment."

He didn't support all gun regulations, but the ones he'd proposed made sense to him. Eighty percent of the state supported lengthening the period for background checks to be completed, so why shouldn't the legislature listen? South Carolina had already barred the mentally ill from purchasing guns, so why not force the courts to supply their names to the federal government more quickly? No one needed an extended magazine or a bump stock to kill a deer or a home invader, so why allow them to be sold at all?

In March 2018, with the long-term ramifications of his momentous speech still uncertain, Gregory returned to the chamber lectern, now flanked by Kimpson. It had been exactly one month since the Parkland shooting, and students across the country were walking out of their classrooms in protest of gun violence, an act that South Carolina's governor would describe as "shameful." Gregory disagreed. "We certainly are in support of that," he told the senate. "I'd encourage students out there that are allowed to do it to be rebels with a cause, regardless of what anybody's saying about it, criticizing them." It was for those children, after all, that he and Kimpson were standing there arguing for bills that Gregory suspected would fail—and they did.

Two years after that, in 2020, Gregory decided not to seek reelection so he could focus more on the family business, but he knows he'll likely run for public office again one day. Winning his seat back is far from assured. Gregory understands what he's risked. The NRA would almost certainly strip him of its endorsement and back an opponent in the primary. Maybe he'd get beaten, too, but that threat didn't deter him, which is why he'd continued to push for gun legislation in 2019 and, when it failed once more, did it again during his final session, in 2020. Gregory planned to keep fighting for reform after he left office and to do the same when he tried to return.

The Confederate flag had flown outside that chamber for more than half a century before it came down, but it did, in the end, come down, and he'd helped make that happen. If his mind could change on that issue or, especially, on guns, so could the minds of others. Sometimes, he understood, all that change required was time and persistence, and whether his continued stand cost him a desk in the state senate, Gregory decided he could live with the result, because what he couldn't live with was learning that one more child had been shot to death and knowing that he'd done nothing to stop it.

CHAPTER 8

"ONE DAY HAS RUINED EVERYTHING SHE DOES"

The Agony of a School Shooting Survivor

"I don't want to go," Ava shouted from the backseat of the car. "Why are you forcing me to go?"

"So you can talk to her and—" her mother, Mary, tried to explain.

"I don't want to talk to her!" Ava interjected. "You always want me to talk to her, and you know the answer is going to be no."

"You want to tell her about skating?" her mom asked.

"No."

Her voice measured, Mary tried to distract her daughter. "What kind of candy do you think she'll have this time?"

"I don't want any candy," Ava snapped, before falling silent. For sixteen seconds, she stared ahead, thinking. "This is so"—the girl paused, searching for the right word—"hard."

Everything about Ava's life was hard now, which was why, on this sweltering summer afternoon in upstate South Carolina, they were once again headed to meet with her psychiatrist. It was June 2018, and this day had been much like many others since the playground shooting more than a year and a half earlier. The morning began with doses of Abilify, an antipsychotic, and Zoloft, an antidepressant, and after each pill, Mary shone a flashlight into the eight-year-old's mouth to ensure that she had swallowed them. When the time came for them to leave and she and her parents walked outside, Ava took off, sprinting across the front yard. Poking out from atop her pink-and-gray sneakers, the girl's baby-blue socks, adorned with cat faces, flashed across the green grass. After Mary guided her back, her dad, David, a police officer, picked his daughter up and carried her to their rusting 2001 Dodge Neon. MY CHILD IS A TERRIFIC KID, read an old bumper sticker on the trunk. TOWNVILLE ELEMENTARY.

Ava's parents buckled her into a booster seat, and her mother sat next to her, as she always did, and off they went, past #TOWN-VILLESTRONG, painted in yellow on the front window of the lone café near the interstate, past the green road sign next to their exit: JACOB L. HALL MEMORIAL INTERCHANGE.

Ava had been seeing the psychiatrist for six months because Mary believed that the medication helped, though in moments like this one, it was impossible to tell. Ava hated going, and because of that, her parents always worried what she would do when they arrived. She'd had an outburst during their last visit and seemed even more agitated this time.

"Why do I have to go to this place?" she asked again, as they continued northeast through a corridor of pine trees and billboards toward Greenville, about forty-five minutes from their house. "Why are you forcing me to go?"

"So you can tell her how you feel," said Mary, who had already promised her daughter a banana split after the appointment.

"I don't want to tell her how I feel," Ava responded. "She already hasn't helped me at all."

Ava had never been an extrovert, but before the shooting, she was exceedingly polite and, when she got to know people, could talk to adults as if she were one of them. She liked her friends in first grade and revered her teacher, Meghan Hollingsworth, the woman who was shot alongside Jacob. After his death, Ava, like many of her classmates, was reluctant to go back to school, but she did, and at times seemed fine. She was deeply introspective, though, even before the attack, and as the weeks passed, the girl's fixation on her fear and loss mushroomed. She alternated between long stretches of quiet anguish and bursts of rage, sometimes slapping herself and jerking out her eyelashes and, once, clawing her nails so sharply into her elbow that it caused an infection. Ava no longer talked of wanting to become a cheerleader and instead began to repeat what the shooter, Jesse Osborne, had screamed on the playground: "I hate my life."

She stopped watching *Frozen* because Elsa's parents die in it. She erupted when her mother didn't wear the necklace with the vial of Jacob's ashes his family had given them. She couldn't stand to see her father's service pistol, so he had to lock it in his cruiser each night. She stopped attending gymnastics practice because of the noise. She sat on the lap of a man dressed as Santa Claus and told him the only thing she wanted for Christmas was her friend to come back. She snipped glittery green and red stickers into tiny pieces, then used them to cover up scary words in her copy of *Little House on the Prairie*: *gun, fire, blood, kill.*

"It's my fault," Ava would tell her mom and dad, inexplicably convinced that she should have saved Jacob's life. A shooting that had lasted just twelve seconds was now consuming every single one of Ava's, and her parents didn't know what to do about it, in part because her brother, Cameron, just ten months younger, had also been on the playground during the gunfire but been far less affected by it.

Five months after Jacob's funeral, in February 2017, Mary took Ava to the doctor's office, where she sat on an exam room table, her eyes on the floor. In front of the girl, her pediatrician kept asking questions. Did she still feel scared a lot? "Yes," Ava's mother recalled her answering. Did she feel safe at school? "No." What did she not like about school? Ava, clutching a stuffed Ninja Turtle that had once belonged to Jacob, didn't answer. Three weeks later, the doctor filled out a state form recommending that she be home-schooled.

"Severe PTSD/depression, exacerbated by school attendance . . . unable to concentrate, complete work, interact effectively w/ teachers & peers," he wrote, adding that she needed "intensive psychologic & psychiatric care."

After Ava withdrew from Townville Elementary and Mary began teaching her at home, the little girl seldom left their house. Even trips to the grocery store or restaurants became fraught as her parents struggled to anticipate what would lead to another tantrum, which could sometimes be violent. As Ava's world shrank, she chronicled her torment in a leopard-print notebook.

"Today I feel mad . . . I miss Jacob," she wrote in neat block letters in March 2017 below a drawing of a face with a deep frown.

"I am mad. I don't want to go to counseling this week," she wrote in April. "No one ever listens to me. They don't help me ever. I hate it."

"Today I planted my garden," she wrote in May. "I miss Jacob a lot today."

"I hate guns," she wrote in June.

"Today I heard a popping noise," she wrote in July. "Mom said it was fireworks, but it made me think about the bad day!"

"I miss Jacob today," she wrote in August. "I miss how he would smell my hair. I wonder if he would like my new lavender shampoo."

"I hate this day," she wrote in September, on the first anniversary of that afternoon she saw the teenager with a gun. "I hate him."

"Cameron went to his school carnival," she wrote in October. "I was worried that he was not safe. Kids aren't ever safe at school! But he won a pumpkin cake."

"Today Cameron got me angry and I broke a vase," she wrote in November.

"I am mad. I will not talk to her they will not make me go!" she wrote in December, before her first appointment with the psychiatrist. "I will run away if they trie."

During a brief stretch early that year, her parents thought she was making progress. Then, on the day before Easter, she and her brother went outside to play "boat" in the bed of their dad's Chevrolet pickup. Suddenly, Cameron frightened her, and she pushed him. He fell backward, hitting his head against a stone well. Blood trickled down the back of his neck.

"Oh my God," Ava screamed. Their parents loaded the kids into the car and rushed to the emergency room. "I don't want to die," Cameron cried. Then Ava, fearing what she'd done to him, said, "I'm just like Jesse."

BY THE TIME her dad pulled past the UPSTATE PSYCHIATRY sign and into a parking spot, Ava had quieted. She unbuckled her seat belt and stepped out, taking her mom's hand. In the other, she held the Ninja Turtle, Mikey, and a stuffed polar bear, which she had named Bowers after the sheriff's deputy who'd given it to her. He had come to her house one night months earlier because, after an especially intense outburst, Ava had run outside into the frigid darkness. With her husband at work, Mary panicked, ordering Cameron, then seven, to call 911 while she searched for the girl, whom she quickly retrieved. Ava had so appreciated how nice the man was to her that she seldom left home without her bear.

Now she was headed down a hallway, into an office, and onto a couch where her sneakers dangled off the edge. The doctor, Hope Cromer, asked how she'd been, Mary recalled later, and Ava said a bit better, though that wasn't really true. Ava mentioned that she'd made a friend at ice-skating practice, which had become the activity she looked forward to most each week. Mary told Cromer that the sport had provided her daughter with more peace and confidence than anything else, including months of sporadic counseling. They discussed her medication, and her mother asked again about Ava's apparent tendency to "disassociate," a condition that can cause someone who has experienced trauma to periodically detach from their thoughts and emotions. Cromer, Mary told me, had previously suggested that might explain Ava's insistence after her most severe eruptions that she had no memory of them. "Just contain her. Be her foundation," Cromer said this time, and soon, she arrived at the main reason for the Olsens' visit and wrote new prescriptions for the Zoloft and Abilify as well as clonidine, meant to help Ava sleep, and hydroxyzine, for her anxiety.

Ava emerged from the office with a cherry Charms Blow Pop and went with Mary back down the hallway, where they waited for David to check out. When Cromer walked past, I watched the girl approach her and reach one arm up for a hug. "Good-bye," Ava said. Smiling, Cromer leaned down and returned the hug. "Oh, good-bye, sweet Ava," the doctor said, turning to her parents. "She was wonderful." During Ava's last visit, she had been so volatile that David was forced to restrain her, but this time it felt as though that side of his daughter didn't exist. She sat quietly with Mary in the lobby until her dad finished up, and then the family returned to the car. Ava looked forward to her treat. "We'll share the banana split," she told her mom.

On the way to the restaurant, Ava pulled on her wireless purple headphones, which she often wore outside the house to guard against loud, sudden noises that might startle her. She turned on her favorite singer, YouTube personality JoJo Siwa, and when they arrived, she took Mikey and Bowers and went inside, sliding into a booth while David placed their orders. When he returned with her dessert, Ava's brows rose and her eyes widened. She swiped her finger across a glob of chocolate syrup dripping off the cup's edge and licked it off before nabbing the two cherries on top. Comfortable and content, she immersed herself in a game on her tablet as Mary, David, and I sat with her at the booth, and for the first time in a long while, the Olsens looked at ease.

David thought back to how he used to judge the mothers and fathers of unruly children, how he swore that it could never happen to him. *I wouldn't let my child do that*, David recalled thinking, but he'd learned how misguided that was. "You have no idea what you would do. . . . Unless you've lived with it, you have no earthly idea."

Increasingly, he and Mary had detected that same judgment directed at them, and not just because of the couple's inability to control their daughter. They understood, too, that many people in their community and beyond would condemn their decision to so heavily medicate Ava, but they trusted Cromer (who declined to speak with me), and each of them sensed that the drugs had helped. Anyway, with David making less than $40,000 a year as a police officer and his insurance offering them only so many options, they couldn't afford to take their daughter to a leading specialist on childhood trauma in some faraway big city, a problem faced by thousands of parents whose children have been forever changed by gunfire. That constraint had contributed to their decision, along with the families of several other children, to sue the school district and, despite David's discomfort with targeting fellow law enforcement, the sheriff's department. The first of the lawsuits, all initiated by the same Anderson County firm, had been filed in the name of Jacob's estate, which many Townville residents resented because the boy's parents had already received more than $125,000 in online donations. Though people here had questioned why it took officers more than twelve minutes to arrive on scene after the shooting began, most in the community seemed to believe that school staff had handled the incident with aplomb, both in the immediate and long-term aftermath. When word spread that language such as "reckless" and "grossly negligent" and "unsafe school environment" appeared in the court filings (much of which focused on the attorneys' claim that Townville Elementary should have been equipped with tourniquets), parents, teachers, and their neighbors were furious.

"People think it's about money," Mary said in the restaurant. "They hear 'lawyer,' and then—"

"You really think we want our kid acting like that and destroying the house?" David added. "Absolutely not."

"Choking her brother out and calling the police," Mary continued. "I mean, that's embarrassing."

They had concluded that even if Ava did improve, she would need a lifetime of therapy, if not medication. And what might that cost, stretched across several decades? Six figures? Seven? They suspected it would well exceed David's income, even after he reached his late fifties and started receiving his military retirement pay from the twenty-three years combined he'd spent in the U.S. Navy, Navy Reserve, and Army National Guard. Regardless, the couple asked, why should they or their daughter be responsible for paying to manage the harm done to her by a shooting at the school she attended? The lawyers said they intended to go after the Osborne family as well, but everyone understood that the potential payout wouldn't come close to the amount they might receive from the school district or sheriff's department.

"I want her to be set up," Mary said of Ava, because that was the future they'd begun to plan for, one that looked nothing like what the couple had envisioned in the beginning.

Mary and David met in 2008 on Christian Mingle, an online dating site, and quickly recognized how alike they were. Both had moved around a lot as kids, she the daughter of a Presbyterian minister and he the son of an Air Force master sergeant. They shared a similar sense of humor, and David appreciated that, at five feet tall, Mary was seven inches shorter than he was. They also worked in the same field. When the pair started dating, he was serving as a cop in South Carolina, and she'd just left her first job as an officer in North Carolina and had begun looking for a new one. Mary soon got pregnant with Ava, and the couple eloped in 2009, deciding to settle close to David's parents, near Townville. At the baby shower, Mary wore a tiara and posed in a photo with her husband, whose baseball cap read PROUD DAD. Their daughter was easy to care for as an infant, seldom fussy and a sound sleeper. Less than a year later, Mary had Cameron, and with his addition, they considered their family complete. Few of the good times that followed went undocumented on the couple's Facebook pages.

For the kids' first Halloween together, they dressed Cameron as a hot dog and Ava as a witch, complete with a towering orange-and-black pointed hat. They picked out pumpkins together and gawked at giraffes at the zoo, went camping in summer and played with snow in winter. When Ava was three, she colored on the walls, and after she got caught, her parents took a photo of her. Grinning, she had streaks of blue all over her arms and legs. "She is completely innocent," her dad wrote. Later, Mary shared a photo of Cameron, his lips smeared red and eyebrows blotched purple, along with a caption: "What happens when big sister gives her little brother a makeover." Like many younger siblings, Cameron often annoyed Ava, but she also liked to nurture him, brushing his teeth, cleaning his face, sneaking him snacks.

"How the time has flown!" David posted on his daughter's fourth birthday, writing that Ava had "made our lives so awesome and you are loved so much." She celebrated at a Chuck E. Cheese with a *My Little Pony* cake decorated in pink frosting. One day in 2014, a photographer spotted Ava's grandfather Norman Olsen pushing her on a park swing. The next morning, their picture ran in the local paper, Ava beaming in a *Superman* shirt and Norman laughing behind her.

At age five, Ava's personality blossomed. She started karate, and in a video captured by her mother during a lesson, she hopped around on one foot to practice kicking before unleashing a flurry of adorable punches, all while in a pink *gi*, head guard, and gloves. At a bookstore one day, Mary turned around to find that, as a joke, Ava had put a rubber horse mask over her head. Another time, at home, she dressed a three-foot Darth Vader figurine in a fuchsia dress accessorized with a *Little Mermaid* purse.

"Just registered the kids for school! I'm excited for them, and also kind of sad they are growing up so fast," Mary posted in 2015, along with a frowny face. "Parents can't even go in when we drop them off on their first day. It's for the best, but . . ." She trailed off, adding four crying emojis. A day later, Ava discovered her first loose tooth. "She's such a big girl now," Mary wrote, wistful but also thrilled with the modest, contented life the four of them had begun to build. She intended to get another job in law enforcement once the kids reached second or third grade, but with her and David about to buy the family's first house, she wanted to be as present as possible for a while. She hadn't ever been close to her own mother, who divorced her dad when Mary was about twelve, so she worked hard to be the mom, and provide the home, that she'd never had. And here it was. On their wall, Mary had hung a painted wooden plaque depicting a solitary house in the serenity of rolling hills and evergreens. She'd picked it up at a local shop because its message so aptly described how she felt: IF YOU ARE LUCKY ENOUGH TO LIVE IN TOWNVILLE . . . YOU ARE LUCKY ENOUGH.

On their first day of kindergarten, Ava, who wore pink Velcro sneakers that matched her backpack, smiled in every photo. "They love it, but are very sleepy," Mary wrote at the end of the day. For that year's talent show, Ava wore the pink *gi* and showed off her karate skills. A month later, she won Townville Elementary's "Super Leader" award and, not long after that, joined the Daisy Scouts and sold cookies. She sang in the school recital and enjoyed it so much that her parents planned to get her lessons when they could afford it. After kindergarten graduation, the kids gorged on ice cream.

The year had been a joy for Ava, who looked forward to first grade even more. A few of her closest friends were assigned to the other class, but she didn't mind too much because she'd gotten Mrs. Hollingsworth, the teacher she most wanted, and, of course, there was Jacob. Then, on that September afternoon just over a month into the school year, everything changed, and soon the Olsens' Facebook posts about their daughter dwindled, because what was there to say? She'd become a child they hardly understood, whose moods they couldn't predict, whose agony they couldn't fathom.

One day, after Ava had quit school and karate and the Daisy Scouts, after she'd started taking antidepressants, after she'd stopped smiling for photos, I sat beside her at the Olsens' kitchen table, watching her sew together two pieces of orange felt cut in the outline of a cat. She seemed relaxed, even gleeful, until, during a break, something across the living room caught her attention. Her eyes narrowed. She walked to the far wall and stood on her tiptoes, reaching up toward the painted plaque Mary had bought years earlier. Ava pulled it down, walked back to the kitchen, and shoved it in a trash can. After she sat back down, I asked why she'd done that.

"It says you're lucky to live in Townville," she told me. "So, not true."

AVA HAD FINISHED her banana split and gotten back in the family's Dodge Neon, where she took off the purple headphones and quietly enjoyed the ride home. David turned down their dirt driveway, and Ava peered out the window at the expansive grass field that abutted their property. "There's the horses!" she said. "The baby is trying to catch up." She hopped out, bounding toward the fence in her blue shin-length summer dress. "Look," she said, pointing at them. "They're running!"

Inside the house, Ava, still buoyant, gave me a tour of her room, which had been updated since my last visit. "You're not allowed in there," she told Charlie, her chunky, brown tabby. "He'll chew my dresses and stuff." On her dresser, she pointed out a pair of personalized plastic soda bottles she'd found, a Diet Coke that featured her middle name, "Rose," and a Cherry Coke that included "Jacob." Memories of him appeared in all directions. Next to the closet, she'd tacked up a pillowcase that everyone in her kindergarten class had signed, including the boy she loved, in dark blue. On another wall hung their class photo, in which she, in the second row, is looking over at him, in the first. Beneath it, she had arranged her dolls around a miniature toy table, as if at a picnic. The blonde Barbie, she told me, was Ava, and the Ken doll in a plaid shirt and glasses was Jacob. She also showed off her jewelry box and her tub of pink Play-Doh. "When I get a little stressed, I just squeeze it," she said. Down the hall, in the game room, where her brother kept his Hot Wheels collection and a mini basketball hoop, she complained that he didn't like to play dolls with her. "All he wants to play is city, and I'm like . . ." she said, dramatically rolling her eyes.

While her mom prepared dinner, Ava sat at the kitchen table and opened an American Girl box that on the front read, GRACE'S 2-IN-1 DAY IN PARIS, which included LEGO-like blocks to build a French market promenade. "Paris or Italy are two places I would like to go," Ava said, even though she suspected she'd have to wear headphones most of the time. "But I heard they have very, very fancy things there, and I like fancy. Like fancy dresses and fancy foods."

"Have a good job to pay for your trip first," Mary said.

As Ava completed a miniature sign, LA CREPERIE, she thought she heard her dad walking across the back deck, about to come inside. "I'm going to let him in, so he doesn't beat on the door," Ava said, because he did that sometimes when it was locked, and the noise always bothered her. She checked, but it was only wind, so she returned to the table and her thoughts about Paris. I asked if she expected to always need headphones. "I think I'll always need them in places like that, because there's a lot of people," Ava said. About then, she smelled her mother's macaroni and cheese, which Mary made fresh, just the way her daughter liked it. "I'm not the biggest fan of boxed kind, because it's not creamy," she said.

"It's that refined palate," Mary suggested, as Ava kept working on her craft.

"I did the doors! All by myself. And they're perfect," she said, just before Mary opened a bottle of Dr Pepper, and the sudden hiss made Ava flinch.

"Sorry," Mary said, and her daughter shrugged it off.

Still snapping pieces together, she brought up her past counselors, and one guy she particularly didn't like. "He would just stare at you," she recalled, stroking an imaginary beard. Had she liked any of her counselors? Ava shook her head. "I wish they would listen," she said. "I feel like they don't listen." Out on the porch, she heard another noise, no louder than the groan of a wood plank beneath a footfall. She made it to the door just before her dad opened it.

"That wind is really picking up," he said, and Ava fixed her eyes on the kitchen window. She could see the skies darkening.

Mary noticed. "We can go in my room?" she suggested, and Ava nodded.

"I'm going in the closet," the girl said, retreating to her parents' bathroom, where she kept blankets, toys, and a giant teddy bear, also named Jacob.

"To me, it feels safer," she said of the closet. Her mother soon followed. "What game do you want to play, Mama?" Ava asked.

"Do you want to do the 'Go Charlie'?" Mary suggested, referring to a version of Go Fish that they played with cards featuring their cat's photo on the back. Ava said yes.

"Here, let's get this liquid," Mary said, reaching for a bottle of cherry-flavored Equate Children's Allergy Relief. Mary used it as a substitute for hydroxyzine until they picked up the new prescription. It helped Ava sleep, her mother said. Ava took a shot and sat down on the floor, and they played the game until the storm had passed and the beef had finished cooking. At the kitchen table, she folded her hands and bowed her head.

"Thank you, God, for this wonderful food," she prayed. "And thank you for this wonderful day."

She ate a bite of meat and her salad with Caesar dressing and croutons, but mostly she wanted the mac and cheese and the kale bites. "Watch, I can eat these and I won't make a face," she said, before eating a glob of the cheesy baked green and not making a face, which she'd come to understand was quite a feat for an eight-year-old. "Very much the gourmet," Mary said, and she wasn't exaggerating.

Ava explained that her favorite food was gnocchi soup, which she pronounced "noshee," and said she wanted to become a vegan, but only after trying sushi first. After dinner, she took her paper plate and her mother's and threw them away before tracking down her other cat, Autumn, and bringing it out into the living room to play. Sitting on the floor, she zipped a string on a stick back and forth across the faux hardwood.

Nothing in that scene suggested that she or her family was different than anyone else, but she was and they were, and all of them knew it, and Mary, especially, couldn't stop thinking about it, even then. Absent from the table that night was Cameron, who, as on many nights now, had spent that one at his grandparents' home. As David silently checked his phone and Ava kept playing in the living room a few feet away, Mary, in the kitchen, said without prompting that she worried her son had begun to internalize the chaos, and she didn't know what to do about it. She said that skating had helped Ava, but that her daughter had few opportunities to make friends. She said Ava had recently snarled at a child in Walgreen's, prompting Mary to restrain her. "I can't have her attacking another kid," she explained.

Her daughter acknowledged none of this, and Autumn kept chasing the string, but after a minute or two, Ava stopped. The girl grabbed a blanket and wrapped the cat in it, picking her up and squeezing tighter than she normally would. Then, as the pitch of her voice shifted a touch higher, she stood on the couch. Mary asked her not to. What I saw then, in Ava, was a little girl feeling tired and punchy after a long, trying day, like any kid might. But that's not what her parents saw. They had witnessed the switch flipped dozens of times, and not just when Ava heard the neighbors firing their rifles or after Cameron let slip news of another school shooting. Sometimes, it seemed to Mary and David, the episodes began for no reason at all, and now, on this night, they sensed what was coming.

Ava, her body tensing, looked at the front door, then darted toward it. Mary cut her off, so Ava turned and ran down the hallway, into her brother's empty bedroom. David followed, and before Ava could reach Cameron's window, he wrapped his arms around her from behind and hoisted her onto Cameron's child-size bed, its frame creaking beneath their weight. Mary, meanwhile, had gone to retrieve a clonidine.

"Stop sitting on me," Ava screamed at her father.

"I'm not sitting on you," he said, as she squirmed in his arms before slapping him on the side of the head.

"Quit," he said. "Quit."

"Let go!" she demanded. "I can't take medicine like this, you know."

"Well, when she gets back you can sit up," David told her, and when Mary walked in, Ava slid down to the floor and lunged toward the closet.

"You're not going in there," David said, grabbing her again as Mary sat on the floor and pressed her back against the closet door.

"I don't want you holding me," she said. "I'm not taking it until he lets me go."

"No," said her mother, holding a *Ninja Turtles* squeeze bottle filled with water that she hoped her daughter would take a drink from before she swallowed the pill. Mary held the bottle up to Ava. She took a sip and spat it at David.

"Now, that *that* didn't work," he said, exasperated. "If you don't drink it, I'm going to force, okay? You understand?"

"Quit. Let me go," she said, grabbing the bottle and spraying it on her parents. Her breath quickened. "It's what you deserve." His face wet, David picked her up and moved her back to the bed. "Lay down," he said, calmly. "Lay down."

"Get off of me," she screamed again, nearing a falsetto.

"Nah, we're going to lay right here," David said, holding her as she tried turning her head to spit on him again. Mary walked around to the other side of the bed and knelt beside her daughter's head. "Hey," she whispered. "Hey."

"What we going to do tomorrow?" her father asked, attempting to shift Ava's focus.

"What restaurant you want to go to tomorrow?" her mother asked, and again Ava tried to spit. "Are you Ava?" her mother asked, but the girl ignored her. "Are you Ava?" she repeated.

"Nooooo. I'm nobody," Ava said, and it was hard not to believe she meant it. Her eyes appeared dilated, and her voice, now laced with a high-pitched rage, sounded unrecognizable, as though it had been digitally altered and sped up. Ava asked for something to squeeze, and her dad offered his hand, but she didn't want that, instead reaching toward Cameron's toy bin in the corner of the room.

"No, we're not going to throw an action figure," Mary said. They continued to struggle until Ava began to spit at them again, and her mother held a shirt up to the girl's mouth.

"F—ing get this thing off of me," Ava shouted.

"Quit spitting," her dad repeated, and at last they guided her back down the hallway, where she again dashed toward the door. Together, they picked her up and laid her facedown across their laps on the couch, David holding her arms and Mary her legs. When they sat her up between them, she swung at her mom, who was nearing tears, and jerked her head back around to spit at David. When Mary covered her mouth, she dug her fingernails into her mother's hand. Ava, whose hair was now a wild mess across her face, demanded that her parents let her go as they told her, time after time, that they couldn't. Mary briefly tried to restrain Ava by herself, holding the girl from behind until she slammed the back of her head into her mom's face. David picked his daughter up again and leaned back onto the couch, wrapping both arms around her torso and his legs around her knees.

"You made me do that," she screamed at her mom, who rubbed

the side of her face, then shifted over and placed a hand on her daughter's head, gently stroking the girl's hair. Ava spat at her mother again, then jabbed her fingers up to her own neck. Mary lunged toward the girl, grabbing her hands.

"No, you're not going to claw yourself—no," she said, before Ava's frustration turned back to her father, who still had her pinned. She told him he didn't pay enough attention to her, that he spent too much time on his phone.

"I hate you so much," Ava shrieked, and on and on this went.

"We're going to stay until you quit spitting and you quit fighting," her father said.

"I'm trying to," she screamed, "but I can't."

Ava writhed in his grasp, looking back at her mother. "You aren't helping me, Mommy," she said. "I would expect you would help me, but you don't because you hate me."

"No, Mommy loves you," Mary said, but she told her daughter that she couldn't let her go because she might hurt herself.

"You don't understand! You don't understand!" Ava screamed, and finally, when they sensed that their daughter had exhausted herself and that the tempest would soon pass, Mary took the girl back into her arms and David went to the freezer to retrieve a flat, pink ice pack that looked like a cartoon pig. He brought it back and handed it to Ava, who was slumping onto the end of the couch.

"We're not trying to hurt you," David said. "We don't hate you, okay?"

Her parents stroked her hair as Ava, sweaty and breathless, rubbed the ice pack over her tomato-red face. She stared at it, and Mary saw an opening. "She's got a bow," her mother said, pointing to the pig's face. "What color are her eyes? Are they brown, like yours?" she asked, and her daughter looked closer, then nodded. "And she's got eyelashes?" Mary continued. "Uh-huh," Ava said, noticing that the pig had white ears but should have pink ones.

With that, thirty-four minutes after the unraveling had begun, it was over. Ava walked to the kitchen table and sat down. Her mom followed, giving her a hug before retrieving an Odwalla strawberry protein shake from the fridge.

"Is that your favorite flavor?" David asked as she sipped it.

"I've never had any other flavor," she said, her breathing normal, her voice composed. "It sort of tastes like strawberry milk."

"You want lavender oil in your bath?" her mom asked, and Ava nodded.

"Does your head hurt, baby?" Mary asked, and Ava nodded.

"Are you okay, baby?" David asked, and Ava nodded.

"I'm excited to see you ice-skate tomorrow, baby," David said, and this time, for a fleeting moment, his daughter smiled.

IN MORE THAN a decade of reporting, I had never witnessed anything more unsettling than what happened that day. I barely slept the night of, and for months after, the incident replayed in my mind. The pitch of her screams, the intensity of her fury—it was like nothing I'd ever seen. Reporters are taught not to intervene or influence a scene in any way, but I admit, at the start of a similar episode later that week, I so desperately wanted Ava to be spared from it that I spoke to her as she stood on the couch, her parents braced for the imminent explosion. I hoped that hearing my voice and acknowledging my presence might derail what was to come, but when she turned her head, it was as if she were looking right through me, as if I weren't there at all.

Ava's parents and grandfather told me she had never suffered any abuse or other notable trauma, and others who knew her said that, before the shooting, she was a normal, happy, well-mannered child. So, in the weeks that followed, a question lingered in my mind: how could what was, seemingly, a lone experience—the brief moment of trauma that caused the death of a beloved friend—lead to such extreme behavior in an eight-year-old girl?

"The thing that people tend to not appreciate is that when there's a single intense, overwhelming event, particularly if it involves unexpected traumatic death, that's not really one event," explained Bruce D. Perry, the nationally renowned psychiatrist who worked with families from Columbine and Sandy Hook after those shootings. "What happens is your brain revisits that thousands of times, and so it becomes thousands of little events, all of which are able to activate your stress response . . . For many people, the deceiving thing is that when you look at an event and you go, in a really concrete way, 'This was a five-minute-long experience,' and they think, 'How in the world can a five-minute experience twenty years later or five years later result in paranoia, explosive behaviors, inattention, and so forth? . . . The systems in your brain and body that are involved with dealing with stress are able to influence every aspect of your thinking, feeling, perceiving, your motor movements, the physiology of your heart, the physiology of your pancreas. Literally, those systems control every aspect of your existence. And so, when those systems become abnormally sensitive, when they become oversensitive and overly reactive, you'll have a cascade of physical health risks, mental health risks, that can persist for a very, very long time."

Ava, of course, was constantly reminded of what she'd experienced. From sirens and loud noises to scary words in books and in conversation, from the class photo that included Jacob to the Ken doll named for him, from the daily journal entries obsessing over her memories to her mother's tendency to rehash Ava's meltdowns in front of her, from the stuffed Ninja Turtle the boy once owned to Mary's necklace with the vial containing his ashes—the girl could almost never escape her past, even for a moment.

As intense as Ava's reaction had been, though, it wasn't unique. Holly French, who would become Ava's counselor months later, had treated a number of other kids who had displayed similar symptoms as the result of similar experiences. French once worked with a middle school girl whose family had lost a close friend to a self-inflicted gunshot. The girl, who'd viewed the dead man as a father figure, later went into the house where he'd killed himself, but she didn't witness the suicide or see the body. Still, the pain of his loss, combined with the fear of how it had happened, overwhelmed the girl, leaving her with severe PTSD. She became depressed and volatile, and at times, she hallucinated. Still, though her home life wasn't perfect, she, like Ava, had two parents and other family members who loved her.

That reality, French said, speaks to another misconception about PTSD: children don't have to experience years of hardship to exhibit acute symptoms, and in fact, in the short term, kids from stable environments can sometimes be more susceptible. Children who come from safe, loving homes, she said, may be more at risk of extreme reactions because they haven't built the same foundation of resilience as children from difficult upbringings. While prolonged childhood adversity will almost certainly have a more profound effect over time, kids in those situations may initially view a single bad experience, even as severe as a school shooting, as just "another scary thing."

In Ava's case, her therapist told me, the girl's symptoms persisted for months because something deep inside continued to signal to her mind that she remained in jeopardy. "That normal, natural response to a trauma is the body's fight-or-flight response. It is the signal 'I'm unsafe.' And if it doesn't get the message back that it is safe again, that danger is no longer present, that's what causes it to carry on," French said. "The longer we avoid putting those pieces back together, or the longer it takes to train the brain that it's safe again, the worse the symptoms can get."

CAMERON CALLED THEM Ava's "episodes," those terrifying stretches like the one I witnessed that summer night, when his sister became a person he didn't know. They were why he had gradually seen less of his dad and even less of his mom, whose every waking minute, it seemed to him, was devoured by Ava's needs. Mary had stopped dropping her son off at school because Ava would explode as they pulled up, and that embarrassed Cameron. It got so bad that David had to quit a better-paying job in security and return to law enforcement because he needed to work hours that allowed him to drive his son each morning.

Cameron had nightmares, and never stopped watching suspicious cars that passed his school, but the pain and shock of that day didn't overwhelm him as it had his sister. He'd finished first grade at Townville Elementary before transferring to another school, where he excelled. He made lots of friends and just as many As, winning his way into a regional math competition in Atlanta. He earned a dozen badges in the Cub Scouts, sang a duet at a school recital, started learning to play the piano, and fantasized about competing as an Olympic gymnast one day. Through the lens of his parents' Facebook pages, he looked entirely unaffected by the tumult in his home, but that façade masked a much more troubling reality, and Mary and David knew it.

At the end of another difficult week for Ava during that same summer, Cameron stayed for a few days with his grandparents who lived in Seneca, about twenty minutes north. Their home had become a refuge for him, despite the worsening dementia in his grandmother, who required near-constant care from Norman, then in his mid-seventies. Cameron didn't mind spending time alone, though. The couple had a dog he liked to play with, Delilah, and a computer he used to watch hours of gymnastics routines on YouTube. He also found peace there, something he'd grown to crave because of its absence in his own home. Like his sister, Cameron could be remarkably contemplative, and also like her, he had an uncommon gift for a second-grader to articulate his view of the world around him. One morning that weekend, soon after his eighth birthday, I visited Cameron at his grandparents' place, and we sat together at a kitchen table draped in a gingham cloth. He ate McDonald's biscuits and drank a tall glass of milk and explained, in vivid detail, what the school shooting that devastated his sister had also done to him.

Her episodes made him feel "really nervous, especially since sometimes she'll really hurt herself, she'll bang her head into the wall . . . I'm starting to get sick and tired of barricading myself in the room, in my room . . . When I come out of my room, usually when she's finished, I cry now because it's really heartbreaking to know that I have to stay in my room to hide from someone I shouldn't hide from, my own sister."

I asked him what he thought caused her outbursts.

"You know, we can't see her mind, and she can randomly have them, and we don't know," he said. "She'll do anything to stop it, but she can't control herself.

"I can't believe that one day has ruined everything she does."

What did he remember about having to call the police?

"My mom was screaming, 'Get the phone, get the phone,' and Ava was screaming, 'No, no, no,'" Cameron told me. "I shouldn't even be dialing nine-one-one."

"They asked me if she was on drugs or anything. I said, 'No, she's only seven.'"

Cameron knew she couldn't help it, but the angry words Ava yelled at their parents upset him. "I always feel really bad for my mother and my father when they have to be called stuff like that and they don't deserve to be called that."

He'd also begun to resent how much less time they spent with him than they used to.

"I usually just try not to think about her getting all of the attention. It's kind of hard to do that, though," he said, explaining what he planned to do when he got older. "I'm moving to another state when I grow up . . . I have to wait nine years to finally get out of the house. When I'm seventeen to eighteen, I can probably get out."

He would miss Ava then, but so much of the sister he once knew was gone now anyway.

"We would always play in the snow together. Can't do that anymore. We would always walk Charlie. Can't do that anymore," he recalled. "We can't go to the fair anymore. We can't go swimming anymore. We can't go bowling anymore, although we only did that like once or twice. We can't do interactive stuff where you have to interact with people you don't know. I think those are the things that Ava just can't handle."

But what Cameron missed most about his sister, the boy told me, had nothing to do with him.

"I miss her being happy."

AVA'S PARENTS MISSED that, too, and in an effort to help their daughter feel the way she used to, they had taken her to five different therapists, none of whom had worked out. There was the man Ava pantomimed, with his beard and tendency to stare, and another therapist who felt so intimidated, Mary said, that she told them her office wasn't "equipped to handle violence." Another billed them $170 on the first visit, far more than they could afford out of pocket, and one man, an unlicensed faith-based counselor, focused only on his belief that Ava needed to forgive the person who hurt her if she ever wanted to recover. To her parents, the closest she had come to the girl she'd once been was in the presence of Breigh-Anna Bennett, an ice-skating coach who, at age nineteen, had no formal training in child psychology and charged just $20 per session.

And now, on a Tuesday a few weeks after that violent meltdown at their home, Ava and her mother were again riding to the Greenville rink, this time with Norman in his Chevrolet pickup. What would have been a benign trip for most children had, for Ava, proved taxing. When a police car on the interstate buzzed by, sirens wailing, she put her head between her legs. When she recalled how funny it was that her dad blew salt off his potato chips, and her mother explained it was because of his "high blood pressure," Ava flinched. "Sorry,"

Mary said. When Norman told a story about an injection for his dog and used the word *shots*, Ava, sitting just behind him, covered her ears. Afterward, she turned to her mom: "I miss Jacob so bad."

.   None of it had deterred her from going, though, nor did a final hurdle after she'd climbed down out of the truck, delighted with her beige dance tights and the black figure-skating costume. "It's a long drive here, but it's worth it," she said, to no one in particular. "I look so professional." As Ava rounded a corner outside the building and headed toward the entrance, she pulled a sleep mask over her eyes. Walking alongside, Mary placed a hand on the top of Ava's blue backpack to guide her.

"Are we almost there?" Ava asked.

"Almost there," her mom said, referring to the image of a pistol with a red slash through it on the automatic sliding glass door in front of them. NO CONCEALABLE WEAPONS ALLOWED, the sign read, because in South Carolina, someone with a license could carry a gun almost anywhere, and Ava didn't want to think about guns here, her favorite place in the world. Inside the lobby, she took the mask off and said hello to one of her friends, another home-schooler. Mary helped lace up her pink-and-white skates, and Ava put on a pair of black gloves. She stretched and hopped around, warming up until her coach arrived and leaned down to give her a hug.

"Hey, Ava!" said Breigh-Anna, a tall, slender brunette with the cheerful energy of a teenager and the poise of a woman twice her age. "How are you?"

"I'm okay," she said.

"I love your dress," Breigh-Anna told her.

"Thank you," Ava said. "This used to be my mom's. It's velvet."

"Are you ready to start level two today?"

"Uh-huh." Ava nodded.

"Yeah?" Breigh-Anna said, excited. The coach sat next to Ava on a bench and touched her index finger to the girl's hand. "Look at your gloves," she marveled.

"Thank you," Ava said. "I love this skating dress. It's so cozy."

"It looks really cozy."

"I like your skate colors," Ava told her, referring to the blades. "They're very glittery."

"My dad got 'em for me for Christmas one year, but they're kind of falling apart now."

"Mm. It's what happens," Ava said, as if talking to an old friend, and soon, the two of them were holding hands out on the ice, where Ava wore her purple headphones to muffle the country music blaring through the speakers.

"So, we have a lot of fun things to do today," Breigh-Anna said, speaking up so Ava could hear her.

"Ohhh," Ava cooed.

"We're starting basic two, but it's going to be a little trickier," her coach said.

"That's okay," Ava told her, because out here, even without Mikey and Bowers, who remained in the blue backpack, she had somehow found the confidence that evaded her nearly everywhere else, and what made that most remarkable was how unpredictable this environment could be. The music was never not loud. Strangers, sometimes teenage boys, zipped all around her. Ava, still a novice, knew she could fall at any time, and regardless of what happened, she couldn't quickly reach her mother, who watched from the bleachers.

"All right. Let's do our warm-up and we'll go up and down the blue line, and then we'll take our lap before we start," Breigh-Anna said. "Do you want to do it with me first or by yourself?"

"With you—get used to it," Ava said, and as Breigh-Anna helped her toddle along the line, toward the center of the rink, she asked a question: "Is it safe out here?"

"Yes," her coach said, and Ava believed her, so on she went, until they reached the far side. "All right, I'm going to let you go down the line by yourself this time, okay?" Breigh-Anna asked. Ava nodded, then she did it, by herself, every step nourished with encouragement.

"Good," Breigh-Anna said. "There you go," she said. "That's it," she said.

She knew about Ava's history before they met—the shooting, the PTSD, the innumerable triggers that could lead to spontaneous violence—but the teenager didn't hesitate to take her on. Like Ava, Breigh-Anna had been home-schooled, a sometimes isolating experience for kids, but ice-skating had provided her with a cherished outlet and an up-close look at the influence someone who genuinely cared could have on a child. Breigh-Anna's coach, who cut the price so her parents could afford lessons, was more than her teacher. They discussed schoolwork, friends, siblings, hobbies, and hard times, and by her early teens, Breigh-Anna knew she wanted to be that person, too.

At Ava's first lesson, the girl barely spoke in the beginning, but as she began to feel secure—"I got you," Breigh-Anna told her dozens of times—she opened up, and the two of them discovered how much they had in common. They talked about *Junie B. Jones* and *Magic Tree House* books and the ways that brothers annoyed them, about their shared interest in science classes and boredom with history, about Frosted Flakes' best flavors and how much they liked South Carolina in the fall. In Ava, she saw a brilliant, thoughtful little girl capable of no less than any other student, so that's how Breigh-Anna treated her, and it worked. Ava kept a notebook of her skating goals and carefully tracked her progress. In time, she didn't always need to hold her coach's hand, to hear "I got you" after every breath of uncertainty. Now, at her latest practice, Ava had come to the end of the blue line, and Breigh-Anna was asking her another question.

"All right. Do you want to do your lap first or do you want to jump into new things?"

"New things," Ava answered, her tone devoid of fear, and in the minutes that followed, she learned scooter pushes, backward swizzles, and one-foot glides. Afterward, they came off the ice and said their good-byes before Breigh-Anna started with her next student.

Ava swigged from a water bottle and took off her headphones, then decided to head back out onto the ice, this time on her own.

"Very proud," her mother said, giving Ava a hug before letting her go, and that, too, was significant, because Mary had gradually begun to realize that her obsession with protecting Ava could, at times, make things worse. "She really responds to your emotions" is how French, the therapist, eventually put it, and I'd seen that firsthand. At their home, often when Ava exhibited even the slightest sign of a coming tantrum, Mary, brimming with anxiety, would spring to her feet and stare at her daughter. Ava would look back at her, and as if she'd just seen the wave of a green flag, the implosion would begin. Once, during lunch at an Applebee's, Mary noticed Ava nervously picking at a cut on her thumb, and her mother suddenly became preoccupied with taking her to the doctor if the wound worsened. Ava started to panic, begging not to go and verging on hysterics until David intervened, assuring his daughter that they wouldn't take her to the doctor and that this wasn't the time to discuss it. "I think I lost myself at some point in all of this," Mary told me later, after she'd started taking a mild sedative each day to calm her nerves. But in the same way that skating was preparing Ava, her family hoped, for a more normal future, these hours in the rink also stretched Mary.

From the bleachers, she watched Ava ease back out on her skates, arms extended to maintain her balance. As a song by Little Big Town played overhead, a pair of teenagers glided by before an older man did the same, but on Ava went, solo, toward the other side of the rink, skates clacking against the ice. She extended her arms in front of her and formed a circle, briefly dipping her legs. She pressed her right blade down and slowly jerked her body around 360 degrees, the nascent makings of an elegant spin. She wobbled out to the center and raised her hands over her head in the shape of a V, just like the skaters she'd seen in the Winter Olympics. Then, as Ava tried another twirl, she lost her balance and fell backward, landing on her butt. She put her hands down, stood, then gave a thumbs-up to her mother. Mary, who'd forced herself to remain seated, gave one back.

Those bits of progress encouraged Mary, but she couldn't help but worry about what would happen if something triggered Ava while she was out there on the ice. Would she disassociate? Would she scream and curse at Breigh-Anna? Would she hurt herself or someone else? And if she did, would she be allowed to come back? Would she lose skating, one more thing she loved, and how much harder would the loss make her path to recovery? To Mary, an episode seemed inevitable, and she was right. A few months later, Ava arrived at the rink to discover a loud, unexpected noise. She looked over to see maintenance men with drills working on the sound system.

"I'm sure they'll be done soon," Breigh-Anna said, trying to reassure her.

"I might hold on to your hands a little bit more today," Ava said, and her coach told her that was fine. Ava, who didn't have her purple headphones that afternoon, tried to ignore the sound at first, discussing a book she'd read about a cricket and a pair of novels from the *Warriors* series Cameron had picked up from the library. With each pull of the drill's trigger, though, Ava glanced back over. She had just finished a series of backward swizzles when another screech startled her.

"It's too loud," she said, and as the angst took hold, Breigh-Anna quickly led her off the ice.

"It's okay," her coach said, but she could see in Ava that it wasn't. Her eyes welling, they rushed with Mary into the lobby. The girl's gaze darted around the room as her mother took her through breathing exercises she'd learned.

Willing herself to stay in control, Ava sipped a cup of hot chocolate while Breigh-Anna knelt down and untied her skates. On other days, in other places, this is when she came undone—screaming, running, spitting, kicking, crying. None of that happened. Fear had come for her again, but in this moment, the girl endured, and though that didn't mean she always would, it proved to her, at least this once, that she could.

Ava put on her shoes. She stood up. She hugged her coach.

"I'll see you next week," Ava said.

CHAPTER 9

"TELL ME WHEN IT'S GOING TO BE NORMAL"

A Return to Townville Elementary

Meghan Hollingsworth's students spread out across the rug, each standing in their own brightly colored square as they faced a digital screen on the classroom's front wall. The kids seemed especially groggy that morning, so she scrolled on her computer through a collection of silly videos meant to wake them up.

Kidz Bop, one child suggested.

"Every time I put *Kidz Bop* on, you guys laugh. You don't sing and dance along," Meghan said, highlighting one of the challenges she'd discovered teaching third-graders. By this age, her students had started wanting to look cool, or at least to avoid looking *uncool*, and with each new activity, it was hard to predict on which side of that fuzzy line they'd find themselves. She knew what Jacob would have done, had he been there. It was hard not to imagine him singing and dancing to any video she picked, and when he did, everyone else would have, too. But Jacob wasn't there, and neither was Ava, and neither were others, both students and staff, who had been at Townville Elementary on the day of the shooting in 2016, but who had left the school in its aftermath. Among those who had remained, though, were two people whom no one could have blamed for never coming back: Meghan, the teacher who'd been shot in the shoulder before she watched Jacob bleed out on the floor of the school, and Collin Edwards, who'd been shot in the foot before he watched the same thing alongside her.

Remarkably, Meghan had returned after Jacob's death to finish that first-grade year, but she'd switched to third grade the year after. That meant she would teach on the top floor rather than the bottom, an arrangement that would spare her from having to walk by the places where everything had happened. It also meant that, in 2018, she was once again going to teach at least some of the students who had survived that harrowing day on the playground, including Collin, the kind, easygoing kid who liked to play on the swings with Jacob and call him "Little J" because that made his dear friend throw his head back and laugh. Now here, on a winter morning in Room 229 at Townville Elementary, was a remarkable sight, though one far from unheard-of in modern American schools: a teacher and her nine-year-old student doing their best to heal, together, from the horror they'd witnessed and the bullet wounds they still bore.

"I'm gonna see if they've got anything new," said Meghan, who kept scrolling through the silly videos as Collin, still on his red square, waited to find out what she would pick.

"'No Crust'!" somebody said, motioning to one option.

"All right. 'No Crust,'" Meghan said, hitting Play on a video in which adults dressed in black wave their arms around and sing about wanting a peanut butter and jelly sandwich with, well, no crust. Only three of Meghan's thirteen students followed along. Collin, standing in the back row, kept his hands in the pockets of his red hoodie, lightly tapping his left foot until the song ended.

"All right. We'll do another one later. Go ahead and have a seat," Meghan said, prompting a collective groan. "You guys weren't singing or anything. You were just kind of standing there."

They begged for one more. She relented.

"*Kidz Bop?*" someone asked.

"No. We'll do the roller coaster one," she said.

"Yaaaaaaay," they responded in unison, springing back to their feet. She pressed Play.

"*I* love this roller coaster—*you* love this roller coaster," sang two men on the screen while pretending to ride on a digital track. This time, the kids sang along. Meghan walked over and stood next to Collin.

"Hands up!" the men ordered, and Meghan's hands flew up in the air, as did Collin's. "To the side"—and they leaned to one side. "To the side"—and they leaned to the other. "Go craaaaaazy," and the teacher and the student each wiggled their arms. By the time they stopped, both of them were smiling.

In the eyes of many Townville parents and teachers, Collin seemed more vulnerable to psychological damage than any other child. Before learning to tie his shoes, he'd been shot and seen adults he trusted try and fail to save his friend's life. The scary dreams never came, though, and even after returning to Townville Elementary, he felt safe as long as one of his stuffed animals was within reach. His father, a two-hundred-pound construction worker, broke down about what had happened more often than Collin did. It wasn't that the boy didn't care, because he did, especially for Jacob's sister, Zoey, whom he'd often hug when he saw her at school. But even when I first met him, at age seven, he could discuss the experience with striking clarity and composure.

"Everyone was going straight, but I couldn't fit through, so I went around the table near the cubbies, and that's where one of the bullets went, and that's where I got shot, near the cubbies," he said of what led to his wound. "It was moving through the air superfast," he said of the bullet. "I didn't even feel the exit hole. It was just the enter hole that had the most pain in it," he said of how much it hurt.

"There was a huge puddle of blood out in the hallway, from Jacob, when he got shot. I kept looking back at Jacob," Collin said of his friend. "He wasn't even moving."

Collin was a chunky kid with short blond hair, light blue eyes, and a round face that, most of the time, wore a serious expression. At his home one day, I watched him head behind a bunk bed covered in *PAW Patrol* sheets and, in the corner of his room, rummage through a blue plastic toy bin. He had already shown me his wound that day, pulling off his sock to reveal the dark nickel-size splotch on his ankle. Collin had explained that he could run again, though he had to take breaks sometimes because of the pain. A question about the shooting had sparked the idea that led him to his toys. He picked past a *T. rex* figurine, a Burger King crown, a black Franklin baseball glove, the Captain America mask he wore to Jacob's funeral. Then Collin found what he was searching for and held up a plastic pistol with an orange cap on the barrel.

"His gun looked like that," he said, his tone matter-of-fact as he explained to me how the Dollar General toy from China resembled the weapon that had nearly killed him.

Collin didn't think much about Jesse unless someone brought him up, as his friend Siena had once done on the playground, when she pointed out a hole in a ladder, likely the result of rust, that she was certain had come from a bullet. She, too, had stayed at Townville Elementary, and on that morning when Collin and Meghan shimmied to the video, Siena and her classmates were just down the hall, with the school's other third-grade teacher. Siena was the girl who had beaten on the school door and begged to be let back inside. For a long time after that, she thought about Jesse every day.

"What if he gets out?" she asked her parents over and over, and even when they explained that Jesse was in jail, that she was safe, Siena couldn't stop obsessing over the fear of his coming for her again. A lanky girl with straight brown hair, she was a voracious reader whose mind, and imagination, seldom paused. Like Collin,

Siena began carrying stuffed animals as a form of protection. In those first days back at school, she would slip a tiny pink teddy bear named Lovie into her pocket and squeeze it when she walked onto the playground. At home, next to a sign beside her top bunk that read NIGHT, NIGHT, SWEET PEA—SWEET DREAMS, she relived the shooting in her nightmares. On the mornings after many of those nights, she repeated the same negotiation with her parents. "I don't want to go to school today. I don't feel good," she would say, and at drop-off, she would search the parking lot for the cruiser of the police officer assigned to Townville Elementary after the attack. She needed to know that he was there. One day, Siena announced to her mother, Marylea, that she couldn't go to summer camp anymore: "They don't have a police officer."

Even at home, she'd lost her sense of security. Siena, whose mom was earning a master's degree at Clemson and whose dad ran a business, lived on a peaceful cul-de-sac in a two-story house overlooking a lake. She would dead bolt the front door when no one was looking, and at the sight of unfamiliar cars, she'd scurry inside. Once, outside a Publix supermarket, a car backfired, and Siena dove to the ground before darting into the building.

Many of Siena's schoolmates shared this intense fear of loud, unexpected sounds, which posed a complex problem for the principal, Denise Fredericks, and her staff. At the school's Valentine's Day dance, a balloon popped, and the room went silent. Some kids cried. Others dropped to the floor. Denise rushed to turn the lights on. "Noises are different now," she told me. The principal later banned balloons at the spring festival.

Preparing for any sort of emergency became an ordeal. Before the first fire drill, teachers showed their students how to evacuate, but Denise refused to pull the alarm while the kids were still in the building. She had also arranged for firefighters to gather in the parking lot, where they let the kids play on their trucks. For a tornado drill, protocol dictated that many students should shelter in the same tiny bathrooms where they had hidden during the shooting. Instead, Denise allowed teachers to take their kids across the hallway and into other rooms. When the children emerged, volunteers from Oakdale Baptist gave out hugs and high-fives.

For months, some children couldn't go to the bathroom with the door closed, and others dealt with so much stress that a rash of headaches and stomachaches broke out. "Why did he want to hurt us?" ailing students in the nurse's office would ask Angie Langdale, who had given Jacob CPR. "I don't know," she would tell them, because that was the truth. Along with the superintendent, Joanne Avery, Denise had worked every day to make the school feel safe again, revamping security and bringing in the resource officer, comfort dogs, and counselors for children and adults. But as hard as they tried, no one could have been prepared for how much wreckage five pulls of a trigger would cause in the minds of Townville's children, parents, and teachers, including the one at whom the barrel was first pointed.

SMILE, READ THE word atop a mirror near a back corner of Meghan's classroom, just above a sheet explaining the differences among triangles, parallelograms, rhombuses, and squares. On the same wall, surrounded by her students' photos, was another message, delivered in their teacher's impeccable handwriting—THE BEST PART OF OUR CLASSROOM IS WHO WE SHARE IT WITH!—except the exclamation point was punctuated with a heart instead of a period. Similar themes appeared on every wall, in every corner, in every possible direction a child's eyes could wander. Before the school year began, Meghan pasted stickers in the back of all their cubbies, so they'd see the messages each morning. STAY POSITIVE, read one. BELIEVE IN YOURSELF, read another. On their route to them, she placed a small, square wooden sign on a ledge: YOU ARE LOVED. Nearby, she hung a placard on her whiteboard that read FEEL GOOD FRIDAY, and beneath that, she included a directive to take a sticky note. WRITE SOMETHING NICE ABOUT THE PERSON ON THE STICKY, it continued. Meghan had at first let her students write about whomever they wanted, but when she realized that some kids didn't get anything written about them, she changed the system and instead had everybody direct their kindnesses to one child a week. On her door, she taped a large white sheet titled SOCIAL CONTRACT. How would they treat each other? it asked, and they jotted down their answers below: "nicely," "Godly," "Joyful," "happly." Finally, at the end of each day, if somehow the affirmations had escaped them, another laminated sign at the door asked whether they'd had their *H* yet. On the way out, the kids got a hug, a handshake, or a high-five, though most of them chose the hug, even on days when they'd gotten into trouble.

During twelve years at Townville Elementary, she had always designed her rooms to encourage her students, though for this group, she had offered a bit more than usual. In truth, her classroom probably resembled thousands of others in schools across the country, but that didn't make hers any less remarkable, at least to me, because by the time I saw it, I knew what Meghan had gone through.

Aspects of what happened after the shooting have faded from her memory—what exactly she said to Jacob in the room where he was being treated, what she told her husband, Trevor, when they first saw each other at the hospital, what she felt in the sleepless days that followed. The details of those seconds just before and during the gunfire, though, remain cruelly clear, because Meghan has replayed them in her mind hundreds of times, both when she's awake and asleep. What if she had taken the class out a minute later? What if she had moved in a different direction? What if she could have been standing in this place or that one or the one over there? What if she hadn't let Jacob help her at the door? What if he had stayed inside?

"What if I was the one who got hurt worse," she asked, "and he was okay?"

It wasn't the first significant trauma she had faced. At age seven, Meghan's mother died of illness, and the loss forced Meghan and her sister to grow up fast. She drove a used Chevrolet Astro van in her late teens and twenties, because she couldn't afford anything nicer, and she worked at an Irish pub throughout college before taking out loans to cover graduate school. "She has been running her life for a while," said Trevor, who met her at the pub while they both attended the College of Charleston. Meghan had known since childhood that she wanted to be a teacher. She was a natural with kids and especially enjoyed playing "school" with her brothers, who were eleven and thirteen years younger than she. That desire only grew when she got to college, leading to a job soon after graduation. In 2007, she and Trevor, also an educator, moved to Anderson County, near where his family lived. There, at Townville Elementary, Meghan was popular with her students and colleagues, earning a reputation as a teacher who was both compassionate and unwilling to tolerate nonsense. Her rooms were fastidiously organized, her lesson plans arranged well in advance. She was warm but demanding, occasionally whimsical but always in control.

So much of that last trait—control—had been stripped away because of the attack, and Meghan knew it. She couldn't manage the feeling of guilt over what she'd been unable to do for Jacob, just as she could do nothing to stem the added heartache that her students had to return to school at first without her, because she just wasn't ready yet. She couldn't squelch her fear, caused by the PTSD, of being alone or hearing a door slam or other trivial things that once wouldn't have fazed her. She couldn't prevent her five-year-old daughter, who hid in a kindergarten bathroom during the attack, from screaming in the middle of the night, demanding to see her mother's face. She couldn't shake the urge to have the piece of shrapnel removed from her lip or the despair when she learned, after an operation, that her surgeon had failed to excise it. She couldn't ward off the crushing pressure on her chest that would arrive without warning, which meant she couldn't stop taking her antidepressant.

Complicating her recovery was the fact that just weeks after Meghan returned to school, a suicide bombing in Afghanistan killed her father, a government contractor. When the news came, Trevor called Denise to let her know that his wife needed more time off. The principal assumed, at first, that Meghan had just come back too early and was feeling overwhelmed. Then he told her.

Oh my God, Denise thought. *How is she ever going to be okay?*

Meghan sometimes wondered that, too, but she never seriously considered quitting, because that felt like one thing she could control. She was determined to go back, even after burying her father, because her students needed her and she needed them, and she refused to let a teenager with a gun also deprive her of the work she felt called to do. The job she returned to, however, was far different than the one she'd left.

"When I came back, some of their faces were so sad, like, they didn't care that I was trying to teach them to add," she said. "I just wanted them to *want* to be there. A lot of them didn't want to be there, like it was constant: 'I don't feel good.' So, I just wanted them to—whether or not they were learning everything—I wanted them to—I just wanted them to . . . want to be back and be happy to be at school."

So, on many days, they abandoned reading picture books and working on fractions to raid what Meghan called her "indoor recess cabinet," where her students had their choice of LEGOs, Candy Land, dominoes, and Lincoln Logs. Making the kids feel at ease also meant projecting an ease that, deep down, Meghan often struggled to find. By the time she started back, someone had placed a teddy bear in Jacob's desk, and though the stuffed animal served as a constant and at times tormenting reminder to her that he wasn't there, Meghan wouldn't have considered taking away something she knew gave the children comfort. She began to obsessively count the number of students in her class, down from fifteen to fourteen, to make sure no one was ever missing. She hated it when people told her everything was going to be okay, because it could never be okay, not really, but when the torrent of hurting heads and stomachs swept through her class, she forced herself to say those words—*everything will be okay*—because that's what they needed to hear from her. To her surprise, at the end of that year, Meghan's first-grade class did better on their test scores than any other she'd had before. The results didn't mean her students weren't still contending with serious emotional challenges, because some of them were, but it reinforced her decision to finish the year and helped motivate her to teach again the year after that.

Not everyone on Townville Elementary's staff could handle returning to the building day after day, and some ultimately left, but many others, including Meghan, found a haven in the same place where they had faced the worst moments of their lives. For her, she found that support in Denise and the other teachers and also, many times, from her classes. In that first year teaching third grade, a boy who was new to the school poked his head into her classroom one day and yelled, "Hey, were you the teacher who got shot?" Before she could answer, her students swarmed him, making clear he should never repeat that question. In a way, she felt an even deeper comfort the year after that, when she once again took on the kids who had gone through the shooting with her. At the back-to-school night before classes began, one child's mom gave her a kiss on the cheek and told her how thankful she was that her child would be in Meghan's class a second time.

By that winter day in her room, when she and Collin wiggled their arms side by side, the ease that she had once forced herself to project looked entirely organic. By then, Meghan had learned new ways to cope with loud noises. She removed from her supply list metal pencil boxes, which tended to plummet to the floor with a disturbing clamor, and when construction workers had to do maintenance on the building, she joked to her kids that they were tap dancers. "I mean, Collin laughed. Collin doesn't laugh unless it's funny," Meghan recalled, so that was the story she stuck with, and the noise never bothered her or them again. Not long after, she went to court and put her eyes on Jesse Osborne for the first time since he shot her, and the next time Meghan went, she heard the teen admit to a judge that he was guilty of the charges against him. To claw back some of the control he'd stolen, she and Trevor got matching turtle tattoos for their tenth wedding anniversary, a nod to the couple's memories of Charleston from their college years. Meghan got hers on her left shoulder, erasing any trace of the scar the bullet had left. She had also begun to let go of the guilt, telling herself what her therapist had repeatedly insisted: "That I did what I was supposed to do. . . . I did what was best, and that was not a situation that I was in control of. I did not *do* it. It happened *to* us."

She didn't believe those words every time she said or thought them, but she had also accepted that not every moment, or even most of them, was going to be easy, no matter how much time passed. She still needed to take her antidepressant, and she still snapped at Trevor now and then in ways and for reasons she wouldn't have before, and she still had nightmares of the gunfire, of Jacob on the floor. Those dark days, though, gave Meghan all the more reason to envelop her students in light, because she understood that their days were sometimes even darker. "This is your class family," she would tell them, and they believed Meghan, who was, in their view, the family's most treasured member. Amid the many words of encouragement on her walls was one space, behind her desk, dedicated to the words the kids had offered her in return.

"How I feel with you," one child had scribbled above a smiley face with a rainbow mouth. "I Love You!!!" another wrote inside a red heart. Several just drew things they thought she'd like: a tree dotted with pink and yellow flowers, a "carmal frapicoo" from "Starbucks," a hand turkey along with the message "Im thackfull for you." Collin, who aspired to be an artist when he grew up, sketched a neatly symmetrical heart and colored it in with pink. "To: Mrs. H," he wrote. "You are the best teacher ever!" The messages all meant a great deal to her, of course, but she also displayed the drawings to honor the kids who had created them, because she knew even the quietest recognition mattered. She had, in a way, done the same thing for Jacob. After his death, someone found an image that he had drawn and showed it to Meghan, and right then, she knew what to do with it. Now, just on the inside of her left ankle, is a tattoo with the boy's initials, *JLH*, beneath an exact duplicate of a cross he sketched, its edges uneven, its blue color spilling over the lines.

SITTING ATOP A stool inscribed in cursive with her nickname, "Mrs. H," Meghan slid on a pair of dark-rimmed glasses and pulled up a book on her computer that the class had started earlier that week. The story, now displayed on the screen at the front of the classroom, was about a girl in China who wanted to get an education rather than a husband. The kids, parked on the rug beneath her, all followed along, except for one of them.

"Karson, take your hood off, please. And sit up," Meghan said to a boy sitting cross-legged, hunched forward with his hood pulled low. He rubbed his head and looked up, then did what she asked.

"Thank you," she said, continuing on with the book for another two minutes, until she noticed that, again, Karson's head had slumped back into his lap.

"Karson, can you sit up for me?" she said gently, and once more, he did as she asked. The boy propped his chin on his hands, struggling to keep his eyes open as Meghan resumed reading, before she paused again four minutes later.

"Boys and girls, if you're not sitting up, I want you to sit up," she said. "Karson, do you need to sit in a chair?"

He shook his head no.

"Are you sure?"

He nodded.

"Okay," she said. "I'm almost finished."

Deciding what to do with him was never simple for Meghan. Karson, who'd already missed nearly two dozen school days in third grade, had arrived late that morning looking much the same way he did on many other mornings: shoulders hunched and sorrowful brown eyes rimmed with dark circles. He was the boy who had jumped the fence at the sound of the first gunshot, and he was also the boy who turned seven and celebrated at a Chuck E. Cheese on the same day Jacob died. Karson had never been the same.

The shooting had played a significant role in his somber moods—he was diagnosed with PTSD because of that experience—but the growing rift between his parents had affected him, too. He often didn't see his dad, who had split with his mom, for long spells, and that made Karson resent her. His home life had long been difficult anyway. In the year after the shooting, he and his three younger siblings lived with their mother, Kayla, in a dilapidated home that, from the outside, looked abandoned. Littered with trash, it was spare of almost of any furniture, and holes pocked the interior walls, doors, and window screens. By third grade, they had moved, and at the new place, he slept on a futon, alongside a teddy bear, in a cramped living room where his siblings regularly gathered to watch movies on a box TV. At school, Meghan tried to balance holding him to the same standards she did everyone else, because he was a bright student, with also letting him rest, because she suspected he wasn't getting much of it at home. She tended to push him to keep up in the morning but found time to let him take naps in the afternoon.

"He worries too much for a kid," Meghan told me once, and she could relate to that feeling, just as she could to the other one that had dominated his mind for two years before that day in her class: guilt. Like Ava, Karson had felt responsible for Jacob, who'd stood a half foot shorter. In Karson's mind, he was big and Jacob was little, and the big kids were supposed to look out for the little ones.

"Maybe I should have waited," he told his mother. "He could have jumped over the fence with me."

It was an irrational thought, because Karson couldn't have done anything to save Jacob, but it spoke to the challenge of treating children who have suffered trauma and loss. Their life experience is limited, as is their understanding of time and space, all of which makes it harder to persuade them that, logically, they shouldn't think what they think. But if intelligent, educated adults, including Meghan, struggle to accept the reality that they had no power to stop something from happening, consider how much harder it could be for a child to accept the same. It's what trauma experts call a "false assignment of causality," and to change young minds takes considerable effort. Karson's family tried, insisting that it wasn't his fault, but nothing could convince him.

The shooting had also left the boy with intense separation anxiety—he'd follow his mother, who worked at Subway, when she stepped out for a smoke—and led to bouts of anger his family had never before seen in him. He used to be the child his mother bragged was the "perfect kid," the one she wished all her others would act like, and now that same kid often refused to talk, to listen, to do anything but sit in silence. A doctor offered to give Karson medication to deal with his depression, but his mother feared what the pills would do. For a while, he made progress with the counselor Townville Elementary had brought in full time to help the students. Karson trusted her, and she taught him ways to cope with his anger, but when the woman moved away and someone else replaced her, he regressed. Eventually, he stopped talking about what had happened or how he could have prevented it. He seldom mentioned Jacob's name, and he hated it when other people did. But the boy remained on his mind. One Valentine's Day, Karson wrote a card in his memory: "I loved him but he diyd but he is stil a life in my hart."

JUST SHY OF two years after Jacob's funeral, a new kind of pain settled over Townville Elementary's campus, and it lingered there, even months later, on the cool, gray day when I visited. The initial aftermath of school shootings in this country play out with extraordinary consistency: the memorials and prayer services, the fund-raisers, the outbreak of #WHEREVERSTRONG signs, the public declarations of unity, almost always sincere. Then time passes, life resumes, and much of what's left behind are parents desperate to fix their broken children. In Townville, as in many communities before and since, that desperation led to lawsuits, and lawsuits require someone to blame. When the attorneys decided that would be, among others, the school and its staff, the hurt that inflicted on them was immense. Most parents agreed with Karson's mom, Kayla, who, despite her son's profound problems, said she never could have gone after Townville Elementary because, in her view, the people there had done all they could to save Jacob's life and protect their children.

Like Ava's parents, though, a few families couldn't help feeling they were owed something. If their children still needed mental health care years or decades later, who would pay for it? If their children were too debilitated to one day go to college or find good jobs or live on their own, who would support them? Even if what had happened wasn't the fault of anyone at Townville Elementary, as so many people believed, the families knew it wasn't theirs, either.

Those questions had become increasingly real for LB's family, who were among those who filed litigation. LB lived with his great-grandparents, whom he called Nanny and Papa. (I'm referring to the student and his family by their initials and nicknames because they agreed to speak with me on the condition of anonymity). They had no idea how close he had been to the gunfire before he brought it up days later. LB had at first thought it was all a drill, until he'd heard Meghan scream for the children to run—and then he noticed something on her face. "I seen my teacher's mouth bleed," he told them. Before that, LB had been a typical kid, earning decent grades, making friends, playing baseball and football. He liked to ride the lawn mower and work on cars with Papa and spend hours bouncing on the trampoline at his cousin's house. Now the sound of firecrackers sent him sprinting back inside, and he refused to spend the night at relatives' houses, insisting that his great-grandparents pick him up before bedtime. Each evening, he fell asleep next to Papa. LB, who thought often about Jesse, came to believe that he was never safe in public unless someone with him had a gun. At recreation league baseball games, he would demand that his uncle show him the pistol in his pocket before he went out onto the field. His family told him that teachers at school secretly carried guns, even though they didn't, and when LB went out with his great-grandparents, they told him they did as well, even though neither did. "Well, let me see it," he asked Nanny once, and she explained that she couldn't pull the weapon out or a criminal might see it. He began to obsess over getting his own gun when he got older. Maybe an AK-47. LB decided he wanted to become a policeman or go to war, because in those jobs, he could shoot bad people. Once, Nanny overheard him talking to his cousin about killing Jesse when he got out of prison.

Much of that anger stemmed from the overwhelming shame he'd begun to feel because of his worst and most inexplicable symptom: an inability to control his bowels, sometimes several times a day. Nanny and Papa, who by then had been raising children for more than three decades, were baffled. They didn't know what to do.

"You want to know the bad part, that I feel guilty about?" Nanny told me, voice trembling and eyes welling. "When he was first doing that, I would get on to him and I told him, 'I'm going to tear you up if you do that again.' So, you know what he did? He started hiding it. He started taking his clothes, and we would find them all over the house."

They took him to a psychotherapist, and a doctor prescribed the boy antidepressants that Nanny refused to give him because he was seven years old at the time, and she couldn't imagine that was the best way to treat a seven-year-old for anything. He was also given laxatives, in the hope that he could go at night instead of on himself at school, but they didn't help. Nanny would sometimes sit next to LB in the bathroom, watching him cry until she did the same. "I can't do it," he'd say. Eventually, they couldn't have guests at their house because it smelled like a convalescent home. Their teenage granddaughter, who also lived there, was so affected by LB's suffering that she, too, got therapy. Nanny and Papa had to discard their mattress, dozens of towels, and one set of LB's clothes after another. For a time, LB, who dropped 20 pounds, stopped attending school, so a teacher taught him privately. His symptoms would occasionally recede, sometimes for weeks, but they returned again and again, even after he finally left Townville Elementary for another school.

"Is he gonna be like this forever?" Nanny asked his therapist during one meeting, and the words he said in response have never left her: "Probably not . . ." "It's a long road ahead . . ." "I believe that one day . . ."

"What does that mean, you know?" Nanny said to me. "Tell me when it's going to be normal. Tell me something that I can feel better about it, too. I mean, this is freaking real, and then I get pissed off at my own self because I think, 'Well, you really got it made when you compare it to Renae'"—because Renae's boy, Jacob, was dead, and her boy, LB, was still alive.

But he wasn't the same boy she had sent to school that September morning. Not at all. And no one knew that better than LB. One day, he called himself a baby, and when Nanny scolded him for that, he said he knew how different from other kids he'd become. He was about to turn nine, LB told her, and he was so scared all the time that he still had to sleep every night with his Papa.

IT WAS LUNCHTIME at Townville Elementary, and as I trailed Meghan's class into the cafeteria, a pair of photographs on a wall stopped me. I stared at them, briefly unsure of what I was seeing. Denise approached. "I saw Spencer's . . ." I said, my voice trailing off, because she knew right away what that meant. Spencer was Jacob's brother, then a kindergartner in Kerry Burriss's class. For a school project, the kids had dressed up like their grandparents and had their photos taken. For his grandmother, Spencer put on a sunhat and a floral scarf, and for his grandfather, a black top hat and an oversize blue coat. In both photos, he wore glasses, just as Jacob had, and in both, he shared his brother's round cheeks, toothy smile, button nose. I told Denise that, for a moment, I thought the photos were of Jacob. She shook her head.

"There are times that we've seen pictures and it will just almost jar you, you know?" she said. I did know. Chill bumps dappled my arms.

The radius from the blast that was the playground shooting had rippled across Townville and beyond, reaching hundreds of families, but no two survivors had lost more than Spencer, who was four on that day at school, and his sister, Zoey, then six. Their big brother was gone, but it didn't end with that. Even after receiving the $125,000 in donations, the kids' parents, Renae and Rodger Hall, fell apart. Seven months later, Renae was charged with drug possession, one of three arrests before an extended stint in a rehab program for her meth addiction. Over time, the kids saw their parents less and less, leaving them to be raised by Renae's parents, Stephen and Sandra McAdams. At Jesse's arraignment in September 2018, Rodger had appeared to be in agony, clenching a necklace, rocking forward and back, wiping his eyes with tissues—all within view of a half-dozen local TV cameras. On the same day, in the very same building, a hearing was held to discuss what to do with two of his living children, Zoey and Spencer. Rodger didn't show up.

Soon after, Renae's parents were granted permanent custody, and as devoted as the couple felt toward their grandkids, caring for them full time wasn't easy. Stephen, a sixty-four-year-old former welder on disability, was legally blind and afflicted with arthritis. A heavyset woman, Sandra, fifty-six, had worked as a cashier until she quit to care for her husband and deal with her chronic obstructive pulmonary disease. And now, in an aging mobile home that smelled of cigarette smoke, they took on two children whose young lives had been ravaged by chaos and loss. The kids were sweet but also stubborn, so much so that each of them still sucked on pacifiers and refused to give them up. Spencer couldn't remember much about Jacob, but Zoey did, and what she didn't recall about him and his death, the girl obsessively filled in, spending hours on her Android tablet looking up news videos and photos. Not long before my visit to Meghan's class, Zoey showed me how much she knew. Seated on the blue carpet in her bedroom, she had intense dark eyes and a shock of brown hair that dangled below her shoulders. When she smiled, revealing two missing front teeth, her cleft palate all but disappeared. At three foot two, Zoey could have passed for a child half her age, which only made what the girl told me next that much more jarring.

"This is the name of the one who shot Jacob, Jesse Osborne," she said, pointing to a photo she'd found online with her tablet. Sandra, listening in silence, sat atop the *PAW Patrol* comforter on the bottom mattress of the bunk bed Zoey shared with her brother. "First, he shot his father. Then he came to the school with his . . . keys and put them in his father's truck and drove to Townville and Miss Fredericks, our, umm, what's"—she paused, looking at her grandmother for help, until the word came to her—"Principal. She came on the announcement saying to get in the bathroom, and we got in the bathroom. It was when I was in Four-K.

"And our teachers told us to be quiet," the first-grader continued, putting an index finger over her mouth. "And they was both holding the door shut, but they had it locked so nobody could break in. And when it was over, we unlocked the bathroom and we went out the back door . . . I saw Nanny, and she picked me up and said, 'Where's Jacob? Where's Jacob?' And then they said he had been flew into Greenville Memorial Hospital, and they did all they could to keep him alive. He lost so much blood. And they shot him right there," Zoey said, pointing to her right leg. "And it didn't go sideways. It went straight. And it hit his thigh, and he lost very much blood. And when they show it on TV, I freak out."

The six-year-old returned to her tablet because she had more to share. She couldn't read yet, but she'd figured out how to use voice commands to search Google.

"I want to talk to Jesse Osborne," Zoey said into her tablet.

"You know you can't talk to him," said her grandmother, who was intimidated by the technology that her grandchildren had already mastered.

"I know, but it's just a good way to get the video on," Zoey replied, turning back to me with an image of Jesse smiling beside his mother. "This is the picture that he's really creepy in, that I do not like."

Zoey didn't stop there, either. The first-grader knew that Jesse had come to court once in a wheelchair because he had hurt his leg playing basketball while in juvenile detention. She knew that he had once posed with an Airsoft rifle: "You can see him with the gun *in his hand*. I don't like it. I don't like it when *he* killed my brother." She knew what the teacher's aide Pamela Sanchez had testified to in court, quoting her precisely: "Jacob, when he was laying there like this," Zoey told me, slumping on her back, "he said, 'Miss Sanchez, my leg hurts. There's something wrong with my leg.'"

She had thought about what all of it meant, too, for her and her family, for Jesse and for people all over. And Zoey told me what she had decided. About what the teenager who killed her brother deserves: "I think he should go in hell, where all the bad people go." About guns: "I think all the guns should be in the trash can where nobody could buy them guns, where they won't shoot people. Because guns are not good for people." About what she hoped to be when she grew up: "I want be a teacher where I can teach all the kids in school how to do safety things. Be safe and they should tell the teacher when they see something, and I want to be there when they see something where I can make sure that's fine. Where I can get all the kids in the room to lock the room where we can hurry up and get in the bathroom."

She showed me a TV news segment about Renae's arrest on drug charges. "This is my mama," she said. "Listen." She showed me another video, of Rodger talking about the pain of losing Jacob. "This is my daddy," she said. "He broke up with my mama."

Then Zoey noticed that Sandra, still on the bed, had begun to sob.

"Oh gosh. I probably should sit with my Nanny," she said, walking over and wrapping her tiny arms around her grandmother. Spencer did the same.

"I know you're upset," Zoey told her, because the little girl had heard those words said dozens of times, too. "It's okay to cry."

"WHEN I SEE that your group has cleaned up, we will line up for recess," Meghan announced to her class, and suddenly, their pace quickened. It was nearing the end of the day, and her students had just finished making Wanted posters for South Carolinian heroes of the American Revolution, Meghan's latest attempt to generate some interest in an era of U.S. history that they had found, up to that point, pretty boring. Now, however, they'd come to what was still their favorite time of the day, and everyone hustled to put away their markers and pull on their coats. Dressed in a red hoodie, Collin, whose official classroom job was "line leader," stood next to the door, in his appointed position. Karson waited just behind him.

"All right, where's my red bag?" Meghan asked herself.

"Right there on the floor," one girl answered, pointing to her teacher's "EVAC PAC," adorned with a red cross above "#townville-strong." Packed with medical kits, flashlights, and alert whistles, they had been assigned to every teacher after the shooting, and the kids, at least in Meghan's class, understood why. To the students, the bag served as just one reminder among several, in this room devoted to optimism, that on any day at any time, the next Jesse Osborne might show up at their school with a gun. Next to the sign asking whether they'd gotten their hug, handshake, or high-five that day, a sheet of paper in a clear plastic sleeve hung from the wall, detailing how to react in various emergencies: WHEN YOU HEAR IT. DO IT. On the door, just above the Social Contract that asked students how they would treat each other, a shade was attached to the top of the window, allowing Meghan to black out the glass if an intruder entered the building. Such pairings appeared all over the school, including on the bottom floor's double doors that her third-graders would soon reach on their way outside for recess. YOU WILL NEVER REGRET BEING KIND, read one sign. IGNORE THE DOOR! KEEP YOUR SCHOOL SAFE! read another.

Those sobering juxtapositions illuminated a larger truth at Townville Elementary. As much as the staff and students wanted to heal, to move on, the trauma of their past often felt inescapable, and no one wrestled with that more than Denise Fredericks did. "We're not raising children, we're raising adults," the principal would say, because she knew that, one day, her kids would join a world that didn't care about what they'd gone through, and they needed to be ready for it. A woman of both great faith and grace, she constantly tried to balance how to preserve Jacob's memory without lingering on his death, how to offer kids the space for weak moments without giving them excuses to fail, how to keep students safe without focusing on unseen dangers.

After the shooting, Townville Elementary had been inundated with letters, ornaments, photos, posters, and plush toys, many of which the school had put on display in the months that followed. Over time, Denise knew that most of it had to come down. Some things went into storage, and others were discarded. The most unique item—a framed dreamcatcher embellished with blue beads, brown feathers, and a Native American phrase, LET US SEE EACH OTHER AGAIN—hung on a gray wall inside the school's front lobby for more than a year. Before arriving, it had already traveled to four other schools shattered by gun violence, and the name of each was listed on the back: Columbine High in Colorado, Red Lake High in

Minnesota, Sandy Hook Elementary in Connecticut, Marysville Pilchuck High in Washington State. It, too, needed to go, so a month after the Parkland shooting, Denise and her superintendent, Joanne Avery, traveled seven hundred miles south to Florida. There, they attended a ceremony where Stoneman Douglas students held the dreamcatcher and counted off seventeen seconds, in honor of every person killed there. Afterward, it was officially retired.

Then, of course, there was the playground, the most obvious, and haunting, reminder of Jacob's death. It took nearly two years to pay for and build a new one, but the end result looked nothing like its predecessor, and that was the point. The upgraded playground had a pair of adjustable basketball hoops looming above a tidy blue-and-gray court, sprawling jungle gyms atop a springy lawn of artificial grass, a half-dozen sets of monkey bars, swings, corkscrew slides, modern merry-go-rounds, and a circular pit surrounded by a three-foot-high black plastic fence—and that's where most of Meghan's class now headed as they rushed through the double doors and into the chilly afternoon air.

"The champ is here!" shouted Patrick Henry, the school resource officer, who wore a pistol on his hip, as he joined Collin, Karson, and eight other students in the circle for a game of "gaga ball," a variation on dodgeball.

"No, you're not!" one of the kids yelled back.

Meghan, radio in hand and emergency bag strapped across her body, watched from nearby. "It's *highly* competitive, and it's the same ones who win again and again. I can't play without hurting myself," she said, laughing, just before Collin was tagged out unexpectedly early and headed for one of the merry-go-rounds. About then, the other third-grade class emerged from the building, and Siena and a few of her friends rushed toward a climbing net. A game of basketball broke out. Collin pulled himself up a ladder to get a better view. Two girls played tag, and another, on a swing, rocked to and fro, reaching higher, her orange sneakers kicking up toward the sheet of white clouds overhead.

To a passerby, someone who didn't know what had happened at this school, at this spot, to these people, it would have been impossible to tell in that moment. No one would have suspected, for example, that Collin had begun to write Jacob's initials in the dirt because the memories of the boy he once called his "best, best friend" were slipping away. Or that, at home, Karson had suddenly started to explode in anger, throwing his books, breaking his toys. Or that Siena assumed another shooting would probably happen one day and, because of her fear, she'd already picked out a hiding spot in a closet in the second-floor music room, where she just knew the gunman wouldn't think to look. Or that two children who should have been there at recess, Ava and LB, were in places far away, each of them hoping to reach the end of the day without another humiliation. Or that Meghan wondered whether she'd have the will to attend Jesse's eventual sentencing hearing and look him in the eye and tell him how much devastation he had caused in her life. Or that the principal of this school, the steadfast woman whom so many leaned on now, felt a sense of dread when her husband left town and, on those solitary nights, slept with a loaded gun under her pillow. Or that, inside the redbrick building, a first-grader named Zoey worried so much about the brother who was still alive that, at lunch, she would sit where she could see him in case something bad happened again.

It was because of all those things that the scene on the playground might have been a mirage, a blip of momentary joy rather than a tangible sign of progress, but it didn't feel that way, most of all when the third-graders gathered around their favorite contraption, a rotating, horizontal pink wheel they held on to as long as their grip allowed. Collin fetched the school resource officer, who walked over as the kids clung to the metal rim.

"All right, are we ready?" Henry asked.

"Oh goodness," Meghan said, smirking. "C'mon, Officer Henry."

He spun the wheel, and off the children flew, thumping against the turf. They screamed and screeched, in the way kids are meant to on playgrounds. They giggled. They stood back up. They shed their jackets, wiped the sweat from their foreheads. They smiled and asked to go again.

CHAPTER 10

"THERE'S NO GUARANTEE I'M GOING TO LIVE"

When the Help that Children Need Never Comes

Tyshaun didn't want to feel angry, but he did, almost every day. The rage that took hold in the weeks and months after his dad's body had been lowered into the ground in DC was like nothing he'd displayed before. The smallest difficulty—a tough math problem at school, a lost toy at home—could set him off. Once, after losing a game of *Fortnite*, he kicked a hole in his bedroom wall. At school, when he got frustrated with a classmate or his second-grade teacher, Nikki Lee, he no longer just put his head down or walked out of the room. Instead, the boy flipped chairs and tore signs off walls. "I don't care," he would say when confronted. He had never done any of that before, Nikki said, and knowing how to deal with it posed a challenge. "What are we going to do with Tyshaun now?" a security guard at Eagle Academy, Isaiah "Ike" Minder, heard staff members ask one another, because they didn't know whether it was best to punish him after he acted out or give him a pass. Nikki believed in holding every child accountable, regardless of their circumstances, but she also knew that many of her colleagues couldn't force themselves to reprimand Tyshaun anymore.

His mother, Donna, wrestled with the same dilemma. Even when Andrew was alive, she'd served as the disciplinarian, and after he wasn't, Donna continued to take away Tyshaun's electronics or confine him to his room when he misbehaved. None of it seemed to tame her son's fury, though, so Donna did whatever she could to keep his mind off what he'd lost. She took him to Cub Scout meetings, where he was bored with the coloring sessions but enthralled by the s'more making. On Tyshaun's birthday, his ninth and the first since Andrew's death, Donna took him to dinner and bought him a massive sundae topped with whipped cream and a chocolate chip cookie. Two days after what would have been Andrew's birthday, she splurged on a weekend trip to Las Vegas, where Tyshaun shot aliens at an arcade, bounced on an indoor trampoline, gorged on candy at Hershey's Chocolate World, posed in front of a red Ferrari on the Strip, giggled next to a massive sculpture of a nude woman. The distractions were fleeting, because he could never escape the reminders of his father. A family friend had given Tyshaun a pillow printed with the image of Andrew holding him when he was a toddler. He slept beside it every night. He also couldn't avoid the reality of his father's violent end, because he had to pass the spot where Andrew was shot every time he walked from school to his grandmother's house. "I don't like this," he told his mom one of the first times they took that route, but she insisted that he try. "You've got to face your fears," she said. Far less obvious sights could trigger him, too. "I'll never forget that laundromat," he told her once, as they passed it in the car. "Me and my father used to go there."

Then there were the unavoidable milestones: the youth football game when he didn't hear his dad yelling to him from the sidelines to stay low; the Christmas when Tyshaun went to Andrew's house but didn't get to fall asleep beside his dad or wake him up a few hours later, just past sunrise, too excited to wait any longer for his presents; the Father's Day when, instead of making Andrew a card

with a painted handprint and going to a cookout and tugging on
his dad's dreadlocks, Tyshaun visited his grave and released balloons
into the sky. Nothing was the same, and in time, Tyshaun stopped
returning to the cemetery, a place he had come to hate. He'd gone
once with some of Andrew's friends, and next to a polished black
stone that read BELOVED SON AND DEVOTED FATHER, one of them
had taken a photo of Tyshaun, his arms around each of his brothers.
"I was fake smiling," he told me later.

Feeding his bitterness was the idea of his dad's shooter, an object
of obsession for Tyshaun. Donna didn't tell him what the guy's name
was, but Tyshaun still asked, constantly, whether the man would
ever be released from jail. The boy fantasized about arranging for
snipers to shoot him the moment he walked free. To Tyshaun, he
deserved to die. "'Cause he killed somebody that I love," the boy told
me. "I hope that they bring back the death penalty just for that man,
and then they take it back out."

Donna encouraged him to express himself in ways other than
through anger, but she understood his reluctance, especially at school.
Growing up in Southeast DC, surrounded by children whose lives
had also been shaped by violence and trauma, he never wanted to
show weakness, and he seldom did. "Tyshaun doesn't talk about his
feelings at all," Nikki said, and his social worker at Eagle, Ashley
Watkins, knew why, because she'd seen the same thing in so many
other children. "It's not okay to be emotional," she explained, describing how simplistically many students viewed conflict: "If I'm
upset, I'm going to hit you." In fact, when students had disputes and
the staff called their parents, they often acknowledged that they'd
told their kids to fight rather than make peace.

Tyshaun talked to no one about his father's killing, in large part
because he felt such a deep sense of humiliation over it. He saw other
kids' dads pick them up every afternoon, something his was no longer around to do. In a community where gun violence permeated

so much of everyday life, dying, in some children's eyes, also meant losing. "They look at it like somebody dogged my father," said Ike, the security guard.

"If I tell somebody, and they were my friend at first, then now we're not friends, I don't want them to know about my dad 'cause then they might start making fun of me," Tyshaun explained to me once. "People like to use stuff against you."

He and dozens of his schoolmates had developed what Ashley called a "survivor's mentality"—and why shouldn't they? Before Tyshaun reached his tenth birthday, he knew six people, personally, who had been shot to death. That's what most frightened Donna about her son's struggle to harness his emotion, and it was why she at first didn't tell him that Andrew had a gun on him when he was killed. "I don't want him to think he has to grab a gun, you know, to solve his problems," Donna said. "And his father was his best friend, like his role model, so I don't want him to think like, 'Oh, my daddy had a gun, so I can go get a gun, too.'"

She did all that she could to make him understand the cost of bad choices. When a family friend who used to buy him ice cream was shot to death right outside Andrew's old front door, Donna showed her son news stories about it. When the fifteen-year-old honor student Maurice Scott was gunned down at the market around the corner, Donna made Tyshaun watch a video of the shooting. "When you get older and you out in the world on your own, there's going to be people who can't take you talking to them and saying something mean . . . So, you may be mad and y'all have a little argument. You can't control what you're saying, and they can't control how they feel, and the next thing you know, he's pulling out a gun," she told him. "I'm just trying to get him to realize that it can take your life. It can hurt your life, so learn now how to control your anger."

Donna felt certain that her son could change, too, because she and the staff at Eagle had seen flashes of what was possible. Ashley once noticed a classmate of Tyshaun's with some developmental delays stop to tie his shoes while the rest of the class walked ahead. Tyshaun stayed behind with him until he finished. Before a school trip to Kings Dominion, an amusement park in Virginia, Tyshaun told his mom he could skip it if it cost too much, because he didn't want to put a burden on her. He had remarkable patience with his chattering younger cousin, Noah, who was so devoted to him that the family called Tyshaun his "father." Amid his hatred toward the person who had killed his dad, he once told me, unprompted, that he often thought about the man's family. "I feel bad for the mother that actually had to raise him," he said. "I don't want to see a mother have to deal with somebody killing somebody."

At no time did his care and compassion come through more clearly than during his video calls with Ava, whom he could talk to for hours. "We went through the same thing, losing somebody that we care about, and we like to chat a lot, and we both know how each other feel when we get emotional and stuff," said Tyshaun, who so cherished Ava that he tried never to talk to her when he was angry. "I don't want to say something on accident and it messes up our friendship." Once, Ava confessed to him that, during an especially bad episode, she'd smashed a picture frame into her parents' bedroom wall, punching a hole in it. In response, he showed her on camera the divot he'd kicked into his bedroom wall, because Tyshaun figured that seeing it might make her feel better.

With Ava, Donna said, her son became a "whole different person," and she wished he could stay that person, not just because of the anger that so often consumed him. Now and then, she'd get a glimpse of the sorrow buried beneath it all. During a drive home one day months after the shooting, he was quiet, deep in thought.

"I wish I could die so I could see my dad," he finally told her. "So I could be with my father."

SINCE THE MOMENT she'd told Tyshaun that his dad was dead and he'd crumpled to the floor, Donna knew that her son needed therapy. DC Police had offered to pay for the family to get counseling through a center that provides treatment at a pair of local offices, but when Donna called one, she said they told her nobody could see Tyshaun for months, and when she called the other, they told her they had room for him but only with students still in training. Wary of letting someone so inexperienced see him, Donna declined. Later, she tried to get him into a camp that provided group counseling to kids who had lost a loved one, but before he was admitted, a therapist interviewed him. Afterward, the woman told Donna he wasn't ready. He needed individual help first. "He's mad," the woman explained. She feared that he would either refuse to share or blow up when asked to.

At Eagle, Tyshaun saw Ashley, his social worker, twice a week for thirty to forty minutes per session. She would sometimes sit with him on the floor and play a board game meant to help children express their emotions, but Ashley's primary job was to help Tyshaun succeed at school, not work through his grief. She tried to make sure he always felt safe with her and, on his bad days, reiterated the difference between right and wrong, encouraging him to make good choices. She talked about his father's killing only when he brought it up, which was rare. For a time, when he seemed to struggle to accept the permanence of death, she gently explained to him, as Donna also had, that his dad could never come back.

Because Donna couldn't afford to send him to a private therapist, she hoped Tyshaun could see Dr. Oron Gan, a psychologist assigned to the school but who worked for the city's Department of Behavioral Health. When Donna tried to arrange it, she said, school staff asked for her insurance, assuming that she, like many of Eagle's parents, was on Medicaid. Donna had private insurance that, as she far as she knew, didn't cover any mental health care. Fearing that the treatment with Gan would cost more than she could pay, Donna dropped it.

As she and Ava's mother, Mary, got to know each other better, they talked about how hard it was to get their children treatment. Both mothers wondered what would become of their kids if they never found someone to talk to. How different would Ava's and Tyshaun's experiences with the mental health care system have gone if they'd actually been struck by bullets? They questioned whether that's what it took, in the planet's richest country, for kids wrecked by gun violence to get help. For Tyshaun, what it took was an eruption the next school year, in third grade, when he blurted out that he wanted to kill himself. Gan arranged to meet with the boy for at least an hour a week and told Donna there would be no charge.

"He really needs it," Gan told her.

SHE HADN'T MET Tyshaun, but the teenager knew what happened to kids like him when they never got the help they needed, because she'd grown up alongside them all her life. Now Kaitlyn Towles, seventeen, was in a meeting with someone she hoped could make a difference. "Change is something that everybody is just sitting around praying for. I was always taught 'when you want something, you have to go out and get it. No one is going to get it for you,'" Kaitlyn read from her speech as she stood at the front of a classroom inside Anacostia High, a school in Southeast Washington less than three miles from Eagle Academy. Trayon White, the DC council member who represented her ward, listened from a table in front of her as Kaitlyn clicked on a PowerPoint slide that detailed precisely what she wanted: "to bring more awareness to something so tragic . . . your babies dying from gun violence."

The person who'd led Kaitlyn to speak up that day was her best friend, fifteen-year-old Gerald Watson. They'd met earlier that year in Deborah Lyons's fifth-period geometry class, where he'd introduced himself the first day, asking her name and age. A skinny kid with a baby face and the early fuzz of a mustache, Gerald appealed to Kaitlyn right away. He was goofy and charming, but polite, one of Lyons's favorites, too. Always looking after his friends, he often stopped by the teacher's classroom to discuss them with her—*she's so smart; if he would stay out of the hall, he'd do better.* In a school where fistfights were a near-daily occurrence, he presented a swagger—"A false bravado," Lyons said—but stayed away from the worst of it. "He was a relationship kid," his teacher said, and that's why she paired him with Kaitlyn in class. Studious and focused, Kaitlyn helped him work through math problems, and Gerald, always ready with a joke, helped her work through the stress of her turbulent home life. It was more upheaval with her family that, in October 2018, forced her to withdraw from Anacostia and return to her mom, who lived in public housing in Virginia. The teen left so abruptly that she didn't get a chance to see Gerald before she went.

"Really Yu left me you a fake best friend," he messaged her on Instagram.

"No im not fake dont do that bff i got all love for you! and imma come and see you," she responded.

"Imyy," she wrote him a week after that—*I miss you.*

"Imy2," he wrote back.

Two months later, to the day, two people in ski masks chased Gerald through the courtyard of a DC apartment complex and into a building. "Are they coming?" he asked a tenant, moments before they caught the boy and, as he screamed for help, shot him seventeen times in a stairwell. Within days, police charged a sixteen-year-old, who stood five feet four inches tall and weighed 130 pounds, with first-degree murder. The killing, investigators said, stemmed from a petty neighborhood dispute.

Gerald's death was just one more blow to Anacostia, where 80 percent of the student body qualified as "at risk," a term used for children who have been held back for more than a year or are homeless, in foster care, or in a family that receives welfare. In a school home to just more than three hundred students, Gerald was one of five shot that year. A sense of fatalism settled over the campus in the aftermath of his death, forcing Anacostia's first-year principal,

William Haith, to sit with students who no longer saw the point of an education and talk them out of quitting. "There's no guarantee I'm going to live," he heard them say, and it was a hard point to argue, because Haith understood that most of his students, if not all, knew more people who'd been killed than ones who'd gone to college and gotten good jobs.

"They believe the odds are better that they're going to die," he said, "than that they're going to make it."

Central to the problem was how seldom any of them felt safe, a necessity for a child's healthy development. Many of his students, Haith said, hid weapons—knives, pipes, pepper spray—in bushes outside the school because they needed to protect themselves walking to and from the building each day. A boy once pulled up Google Maps on a computer to show school psychologist Byron McClure just how treacherous it was for him to commute down streets and through neighborhoods that were feuding with his own. That student later left Anacostia and was either shot or stabbed, McClure recalled, but he couldn't remember which, and it immediately struck him how sad that was. Violence had become so pervasive in the community that when a child survived an attack, most people didn't linger on it. "'This person got shot, but he's okay.' *No*. He's not okay," McClure said. "It's crazy to think of it like that."

Kaitlyn transferred back to Anacostia shortly after her friend's death. She'd returned too late to contribute to the makeshift memorial of photos and notes at his desk in the back of Lyons's room, but the girl was determined to do something. With her teacher's help, she started a group, Voice of the Youth, and taped flyers on walls all around the building. "You Can't Build Peace with a Piece," they read. "Say No to Guns." She also contacted Councilmember White's office, which led to their meeting in the classroom and a promise from him to push for as much money as he could for the school and to promote her cause on social media. She wanted stricter gun laws that made it harder for people to obtain firearms, because she had seen how easy it was for any kid with a grudge to get one, but Kaitlyn also knew that such change from the senators and congressmen across the river, on Capitol Hill, would take time. What she thought her schoolmates needed most, and immediately, was better mental and emotional support. Fear, despair, anger, and years of relentless trauma—all that, she believed, was driving many of the kids around her to kill and be killed. Simply staffing schools with more counselors and social workers wouldn't fix it, she said, because they would never know about most students' problems or have the time to address them all. The care had to start with the teachers, coaches, and administrators who dealt with the teens' everyday travails.

"There's so many kids who actually be having depression or anxiety," she told me. "That really be having problems and just can't find the comfort, I guess, to really go to someone to say, 'Hey, like, I need help.' Some kids just don't."

The consequences for children who go untreated are extraordinarily high because the chronic stress that perpetual community violence exacts can follow them for the rest of their lives. Besides the increased likelihood that they'll develop PTSD, become more aggressive, do worse on tests, and struggle to control their impulses, research also shows that the community violence children face can have such a potentially devastating effect on the health of their hearts that it may actually shorten their natural life spans.

Haith, thirty-eight, could relate to his students' struggles as well as anyone because he, too, was a product of Southeast's streets, first encountering gun violence at age eleven, when a bullet burst through his kitchen window and lodged in the table in front of him. Before his eighteenth birthday, he was robbed four times at gunpoint, and once, when he was in the tenth grade, a man pistol-whipped him. As a teen, he'd considered getting his own gun for protection, but didn't, thanks to how much he respected his mother and feared jeopardizing his chance to play football, which eventually earned him a college scholarship and a way out. He took over at Anacostia with nearly a decade of experience in education, two master's degrees, and a vision to reinvent a troubled campus that some people suspected would inevitably close one day. After his arrival, he and the school psychologist, McClure, also a recent hire, began work on a plan to make Anacostia fully "trauma responsive," part of a burgeoning movement among educators to train *everyone* in their schools, from the security guards to the principal, on how to recognize trauma and address it.

The inability of school staffs to do that very thing has, for years, put affected students at a debilitating disadvantage, said Marleen Wong, a professor at the University of Southern California. She is one of the country's leading experts on trauma-informed education, an approach that takes into account the emotional, physiological, and academic consequences of the adversity a child has experienced. She pointed to the hugely disproportionate number of black children who were being suspended or expelled from schools before the Obama-era Department of Education began to highlight the discrepancy. In Los Angeles, she said, children from high-crime areas were sometimes kicked out of school before they even reached kindergarten. The offending administrators "never asked or did an assessment of what caused the situation. What were the factors that were underlying the kids' behavior, leading to some kind of aggressive or dangerous activity? . . . So they just suspended or expelled without providing any kind of assessment services," she explained. "Every adult in the school needs to understand that it's not about necessarily bad kids . . . It's about kids who come into the school traumatized by exposure to violence."

Teachers recognizing what their children have gone through isn't enough, though, because even at a place like Tyshaun's school, founded with the goal of reaching a marginalized community, teachers—not just mental health specialists—have to know what to do once they've identified the source of a child's behavior. "We didn't get training on trauma at all," said Nikki Lee, Tyshaun's second-grade teacher, who was twenty-five when her student's father was killed. "I did the best that I could."

Haith and McClure believed that their teachers were doing the best they could, too, but the way things had long been done at Anacostia hadn't worked. The rates of discipline remained high, while attendance, test scores, and graduation rates remained abysmal. As soon as he started at Anacostia, Haith began overturning the punishments his staff would dole out, often to their frustration.

"My team gets mad at me all the time because I take suspensions away. I reduce suspensions, because . . . I talk to the student and the parent and I start hearing, like, what the problem is," he said. Haith tells his staff: "It's easy to come here, push a button, and suspend a kid. But just know, every time we suspend a kid, they're not in this building and we don't know what they're doing out there."

As an alternative, McClure instituted "restorative practices," allowing students who misbehaved to enter mediation. When one girl disrespected a teacher, for example, he brought her and the staff member together, giving each a chance to explain what had happened, how they felt, what factors outside that episode might have led to it. Afterward, all of them agreed that, instead of serving a suspension, the girl would clean up the cafeteria for three days.

"It's a huge win," said McClure, but as Haith noted, it took a lot more work than sending the child home would have, highlighting perhaps the biggest challenge for schools attempting to launch an all-encompassing approach to dealing with traumatized students: the additional demands it places on already strained teachers. In fact, Wong, her colleagues, and other experts still developing best practices have discovered that many teachers struggle to participate because they're too overwhelmed with their own trauma, experienced either directly, because they live in the same communities as their kids, or secondarily, because they're so immersed in the students' suffering. Addressing those complexities requires resources and time. At Anacostia, McClure suspected it would take three to five years, perhaps longer, to train the staff, develop the programs, establish consistency, and, above all, change the school's culture.

Knowing how hard that process would be, he had tried, as a first step, to create a mentor program in partnership with a woman from a local nonprofit supporting the school. Research has made clear that even for children who've gone through years of discord at home and on campus, having the support of a single trusted adult can carry them through it. McClure hoped to pair each staff member with half a dozen students with whom they already had good connections, providing every child with at least one person who would regularly check in on them. "It wasn't anything above and beyond," he said, but months after launch, the nonprofit cut the woman's position, leaving no one to manage the program. It quickly fell apart.

For students like Kaitlyn, who were paying attention, those failures only reinforced how inequitable the system felt—how much less their lives seemed to be valued than those of students from wealthier, whiter neighborhoods. She wondered how the world would have reacted if, say, five students from a private school in affluent Northwest DC, a fifteen-minute drive away, had all been shot in separate incidents over the course of a single school year. Would that have made national news? Would those children's schoolmates have had the opportunity to share their pain with people who could help? What Kaitlyn knew for sure is what would happen to her schoolmates if they didn't get that help, because it had been happening to them for years, well before her best friend was shot seventeen times in a stairwell: More fear, despair, and anger. More trauma and violence. More dead children.

THE INCIDENT BEGAN, as they often did for Tyshaun, with a misunderstanding. It was the spring of his third-grade year at Eagle, and he'd been switched months earlier from one class to another because he couldn't get along with his original teacher, a no-nonsense veteran educator who didn't believe in coddling. Now Tyshaun was with another teacher, Matt Wong, an earnest young man less than two years out of college. On that April Monday, Matt was trying to prepare his students for their standardized exam the following week. Tyshaun had just finished a practice test, after which he was supposed to sit and wait for his classmates to do the same. The boy, already frustrated with how hard the questions had been, didn't know that, so he retrieved his school-issued iPad and began to play a game. When Matt, twenty-three, noticed, he thought Tyshaun was disobeying and threatened to bar him from that afternoon's picnic at a park down the street. Before his dad's death, Tyshaun might have objected, even raised his voice, but he and the teacher likely would have worked out the disagreement and moved on. This time, he lost all control. "What do you want from me?" he screamed, storming out the door and slinging a chair down the hallway. Ike, the security guard, quickly escorted him down the stairs to the first-floor "Pride Room," a place for kids having bad moments to cool off.

Indignant, Tyshaun walked in shouting. He kicked the wall and punted a bin of building blocks, scattering them across the floor. Robert Hagans, one of the behavioral specialists who managed the Pride Room, avoided giving Tyshaun any attention until the boy began throwing the blocks, accidentally hitting a student seated at a nearby table. Robert turned on a machine that dispersed a lavender-scented oil into the air and asked Ike to dim the lights, techniques meant to make the space more peaceful. Unwilling to let Tyshaun hurt someone else or himself, Robert stepped behind the boy and wrapped both arms around his shoulders, lowering him to the floor as he waited for the tantrum to pass. "I hate you," Tyshaun yelled, but Robert ignored that.

The two had known each other since Tyshaun was in first grade, back when Robert had seen his behavior steadily improve. Then came the five shots, the funeral, the months of all that growth unraveling. In early March of his third-grade year, during a week when

Tyshaun acted out every day but told no one why, Robert reminded his colleagues that it was the anniversary of his father's killing.

Before Gan, the psychologist, started meeting with Tyshaun, Robert had included the boy in a monthlong "check-in/check-out" program. At the start of each day, kids who'd been floundering in school would stop by and review with one of the behavior specialists a list of daily goals: "Always Do Your Best: Complete your assignment or activity," "Be Prepared: Stay in assigned seat or area," "Consider Your Character: No arguing or fighting." Tyshaun struggled so much that, at the end of the program, Robert kept him in it for another month.

Now, ten minutes after the outburst in the Pride Room began, Tyshaun stopped screaming, and his shoulders relaxed. Robert let him go, and a few moments later, they sat side by side, their backs to the wall, on a rug covered in encouraging words: PROTECTIVE, THOUGHTFUL, FUNNY, RESPONSIBLE, LISTEN. "I'm not upset at you," Robert said, telling him that he knew where the frustration was coming from, but that it still didn't excuse the way he'd acted. It couldn't. So, before the nine-year-old went upstairs to apologize to Mr. Wong, and before his mother took him shopping at Marshalls for the upcoming school dance and he immediately picked out an orange-and-blue checkered shirt because it looked just like the one his dad wore in the casket, Robert reminded Tyshaun that it was his last year at Eagle Academy, a place where people understood what he had gone through. The world was a tough place, and someday, someone somewhere would not understand. In Robert's mind, just as is in Donna's, Tyshaun *had* to grasp that point regardless of his age, because it could mean, as it had for so many other boys they knew, the difference between graduating and failing, freedom and incarceration, life and death.

"You know what I'm talking about, right?" Robert asked, and Tyshaun nodded.

CHAPTER 11

"IT'S MORE THAN JUST PROTECTING CHILDREN FROM BULLET HOLES"

What Campus Lockdowns Do to Kids

Two miles from where Tyshaun's father had been shot outside the boy's elementary school on that chilly morning in March 2017, a silver sedan rolled to a stop around the corner from another elementary school on another chilly morning in Southeast DC. Three men stepped out of the car and, at 10:42 a.m., they pointed their guns and pulled their triggers, discharging more than forty rounds in less than ten seconds. It was the third shooting in the neighborhood in as many months, and in the immediate aftermath of each one, the nearby school, DC Prep, sealed off its campus and sequestered its students. Remarkably, none of the bullets hit anyone, which meant that police didn't assign a bevy of detectives to find out who was responsible. No reporters sped to the scene, and no press conference was held. The shooting, classified by officers as "destruction of property," didn't appear on the police district's online Listserv because it didn't qualify as a serious crime. And yet, those bullets wreaked enormous damage because of what they did in the minds of children who were never struck by them, never saw them, never even heard them.

One of those kids was MaKenzie Woody, who had huddled with twenty-five other DC Prep first-graders in the darkness behind their green classroom door. The little girl sat on the vinyl tile floor against a far wall, beneath a taped-up list of phrases the kids were encouraged to say to each other: "I like you." "You're a rainbow." "Are you ok?" In that moment, though, MaKenzie didn't say anything at all, because she believed that a man with a gun was stalking the hallways of her school, and she feared what he might do to her.

"The lockdowns," as MaKenzie called them, changed her, because she remembered what it had been like before them, when she always felt safe at her school, and she knew what it was like afterward, when that feeling disappeared. Three weeks after the November 2018 gunfire, dozens of parents, politicians, activists, and school officials gathered in DC Prep's cafeteria to discuss what to do about the unrest in their neighborhood, and as they debated, I met with MaKenzie and her mother in the lobby. The girl boosted herself up into a chair next to me, and her purple-soled sneakers dangled off the edge. She had walnut-brown eyes and long braids, at the end of which hung marble-size clear plastic beads that clacked together below her shoulders. She wore a baby-blue polo, part of her school uniform, and beneath that, a bright yellow long-sleeve shirt speckled with pink flowers, offering a glimpse into her personality.

MaKenzie, who cherished school as much as anything in her life, told me that every class was her favorite, except for language arts, her "favorite favorite." She could read well beyond her grade level and had nearly memorized the chapter book *Monsters Don't Scuba Dive*, said her mother, Gabrielle Woody, who worked in an after-school program at DC Prep. The campus was part of a network of charter schools that, like Tyshaun's, had been intentionally planted in communities struggling with poverty and, in many cases, violence. MaKenzie had excelled, though, earning a spot on the "Principal's Cabinet," which meant her behavior, attendance, and grades ranked among the best in her age group. In the photo marking that honor, later stapled to a bulletin board outside her classroom, she looked elated: pink socks pulled up to her shins, left hand on a hip, right hand flashing the deuces sign, bright beads in her hair, and a grin revealing the baby teeth she'd begun to lose.

MaKenzie didn't stop loving school because of the lockdowns, but she did think about them often. About how upsetting it was that they had interrupted her time to learn new words and different ways to add up numbers. About how scared she'd felt when some of the kids wouldn't stop making noise and how her teacher had offered them Smarties if they could just stay quiet for a little longer.

If, by the time I met MaKenzie, my years of reporting on gun violence had taught me anything, it was that America had grossly miscalculated the epidemic's true scope, and no two children had made that clearer to me than Tyshaun and Ava. We can't talk about the tens of thousands of men and women killed by guns every year without considering the irrevocable harm done to the tens of thousands of children who are left behind, just as we can't talk about the dozens of students who have been massacred at their schools in the past two decades without considering the anguish inflicted on the more than 240,000 who were on those campuses when the blood was shed.

So, how, then, should we talk about students like MaKenzie? MaKenzie, who, at age six, had stopped wanting to spend recess on the playground, where games of tag and climbs across the monkey bars had once been among the highlights of her days. "Until the lockdowns happened," she told me. "I don't want to be outside because what if someone was shooting and we had to leave and we were too late and everybody got hurt?"

MaKenzie's reaction was not unique to her age or race or neighborhood. Two weeks later, just outside Omaha, Nebraska, a young man was spotted with what turned out to be a BB gun at Fremont High, leaving teenagers weeping as they hid for nearly two hours in a girls' locker room with the lights turned off, until police barged in and ordered them to put their hands up. In the Florida Panhandle, a sixth-grader at Bailey Middle messaged his grandmother, certain a shooter was in the building after social media threats triggered a lockdown. "Please check me out before I doe," he wrote, then corrected his misspelling: "die." On Staten Island in New York City, rumors of a firearm on campus at Susan E. Wagner High panicked students, who desperately texted and called their parents, begging for help, telling them, "I love you." In Birmingham, Alabama, after someone threatened to shoot up Jones Valley Middle, a twelve-year-old boy took out a sheet of paper and scribbled down a will, detailing who should get his Xbox and dirt bike after he was gone. "I love you my whole Family," he wrote, "you mean the most to me."

School shootings remain rare, even when accounting for the twenty-five in 2018, a year of historic carnage on K–12 campuses. What's not rare are lockdowns, a hallmark of modern American education and a by-product of living in a developed country that has prioritized giving so many of its citizens unfettered access to lethal weapons over guaranteeing that children are not shot to death in classrooms ten or fifteen or twenty times a year. Lockdowns save lives during real attacks, but even when there is no gunman stalking the hallways, the procedures can take a considerable emotional toll, and the number of children who have experienced these ordeals—the MaKenzies of our nation—is extraordinary.

More than 4.1 million students endured at least one lockdown in the 2017–18 school year alone, according to an analysis I conducted at the *Post* along with my colleague Steven Rich, who reviewed twenty thousand news stories as part of the reporting. The number of students affected eclipsed the populations of Maine, Rhode Island, Delaware, and Vermont combined. But the actual total is likely far higher, because many lockdowns are never reported in the news, and I discovered that a huge number of school districts, including in Chicago and Detroit, don't track them: after contacting nearly ninety of the largest in the country, just thirty-one provided me data. That means, in a single year, there could have been as many eight million kids, more than 10 percent of America's *entire student body*, who, for at least a brief moment, thought they might die at school.

"STAGGERING," SAID STEVEN Schlozman, a child psychiatrist and assistant professor at Harvard Medical School, after I described to him the figures our analysis had turned up. And he was right. They were staggering. The number of lockdowns in that single school year, for example: more than 6,200. The number of school days between Labor Day and Memorial Day when at least one campus locked down because of gun violence or the threat of it: all of them. The number of elementary-age children who were subjected to a lockdown: more than 1 million, including at least 220,000 who were in kindergarten or pre-kindergarten.

To Schlozman, who had written for years about how fraught even lockdown *drills* can be, the numbers were particularly disturbing, because he knew what the science showed: such terrifying experiences will leave some percentage of children with lasting symptoms, such as depression, anxiety, sleeplessness, and substance abuse, all issues that can thwart progress both socially and academically. "Given the potential scope of the problem, we are in dire need of more information," he told me, exasperated. "We have the capacity to study these things. And these are our *children*." He imagined how America would react if millions of students suddenly contracted welts at their schools. "We'd be on this in a heartbeat," he said, and yet he knew of no one who was researching lockdowns' long-term consequences.

Even for Steven Rich, one of the country's best data journalists, identifying reliable patterns in our findings wasn't easy because we knew they didn't include millions of students who had gone through lockdowns no one ever officially noted. Three things, though, did become clear: First, most lockdowns, perhaps even the vast majority, are related to firearms. Second, they happened everywhere, in every type of community, regardless of demographics or affluence, location or security. Third, a leading cause of lockdowns—threats—and a common effect—anxiety—are contagious, and they're each exacerbated by actual gun violence.

In the month after dozens of people were slaughtered at a Las Vegas country music festival on October 1, 2017, the number of lockdowns in Nevada's Clark County School District spiked 42 percent to a total of thirty-seven, the largest count during the entire school year. Similarly, the seven days with the highest number of incidents leading to lockdowns across the country that school year occurred in the two weeks after the bloodshed at Stoneman Douglas.

On the second Friday after Parkland, thirty-three separate incidents led to lockdowns, the most we identified during any single day that school year. A campus in Florida locked down after a fourteen-year-old showed two students what looked like a pair of guns during a FaceTime call, before saying he was going to attack their high school. Campuses in Vermont, North Carolina, Texas, and Michigan locked down because of online threats, the same thing that led a rural district of three schools in Oregon to shutter *twice* that day. The second warning sounded so alarming that the superintendent ran outside seconds later, just as his elementary school let out for the day. The thirty-year veteran educator stood guard, unarmed, as he scanned the crowd for unfamiliar faces, devising a plan to draw fire away from the kids if a gunman approached. In DeKalb County, Illinois, after administrators learned of a Snapchat message stating that "at 2pm no one is safe here," all eleven campuses in the district locked down. School officials quickly confirmed that the message was bogus, and hadn't even been directed at any of their schools, but neither revelation quelled the worry that had already spread from cell phone to cell phone, student to student, many of whom went home early. "Kids are very aware," Superintendent Jamie Craven told me later, "of the things that have gone on around the country."

Lockdowns are such a staple of the modern American childhood that dramatic descriptions of them have become a sort of Gen Z ghost story kids read or watch to frighten themselves. A YouTube video titled "3 Creepy True School Lockdown Stories" has been viewed 22 million times and attracted more than 85,000 comments that are littered with other stories of lockdowns kids said they'd experienced. "So glad that I live in Australia and we dont have FRICKEN GUNS," one person replied.

A recent survey by the Pew Research Center found that nearly 60 percent of American teens, and 63 percent of parents, feared a shooting could happen on their campus. The fact that only a minuscule percentage of the tens of millions of students in America ever go through them does nothing to comfort a group often referred to as both the Columbine and Lockdown Generation.

"There was once a time where we could say schools are the safest place for a child to be, and they would agree," said Steven Berkowitz, a psychiatrist who has worked with kids for twenty-five years. "They wouldn't now, even though it's still true. The perception of safety is no longer there."

A faction of readers, though small, dismissed our analysis of lockdowns with a consistent criticism. Wrote one: "I remember school drills where we were taught how to survive a nuclear attack by the Soviet Union. Of course, back then everyone was stoic and there was no social media to incite mass hysteria." Wrote another: "Just a short reminder of how lockdowns worked in the 50s and 60s during the cold war . . . any trauma there?" And another: "Any grey-hairs out there who were 'traumatized' when we crawled under our school desks regularly to prepare for the Nuclear Holocaust?"

While I acknowledge that I didn't grow up during the Cold War and can't know what those drills felt like, such an analogy is like comparing apples to watermelons, in small part because they were, in fact, *only drills* and in large part because no one had already dropped nukes on kids in Florida and Colorado and Texas, a point made with chilling clarity by another commenter:

Just for the sake of comparison, I grew up in a time and place where we had Civil Defense sirens tested once a month on the same weekday each month, but we didn't do "duck-and-cover" drills for them; they were just a regular expectation to make sure the system still worked. Then, when I was in high school, the movie *The Day After* about nuclear holocaust was aired. The sirens were scheduled to be tested the next day as always, but when they went off everyone else in my English class hit the floor and crawled under their desks crying. I watched in confusion and amazement, then realized that these kids had been traumatized by the movie and were acting on primal instinct unable to distinguish that this was just a test and not the real thing. *This* is what the mind of a child does with such information. Now imagine the minds of the children who have been through endless lockdown drills being told that they might die at school at any given moment.

Ajani Dartiguenave, twelve, became one of those children after he heard on his mom's car radio in the fall of 2018 that a student at Charlotte's Butler High, about twenty miles away from him, had been gunned down in a hallway. Ajani said nothing about it at the time, and his mother, Claudia Charles, didn't discuss it with him. They lived in an upscale neighborhood where crime was rare. Ajani had never seen a gun in person or heard shots from his bedroom, and Claudia, a nurse, wouldn't even let him play with water pistols. Not once did she imagine that what they'd heard about on the radio would make him feel unsafe.

Eleven days later, Ajani was studying English literature at Governors' Village STEM Academy when someone on the intercom announced a campus lockdown. The seventh-grader didn't know that an anonymous threat, never in danger of being carried out, had elicited the response. He knew only that a boy in the community had been shot inside another school a week before, and that made Ajani think he would get shot, too. So, as he and his friends sat on the floor, Ajani reached into his bookbag, adorned with a smiling cartoon anime character. Without making a sound, he pulled out a pencil, writing first on an index card and then on a sheet of notebook paper. At the top, he scribbled his home address and his mom's name.

"I am sorry for anything I have done," he wrote.

"I am scared to death."

"I will miss you."

"I hope that you are going to be ok with me gone."

EVERY DAY, DOZENS of school administrators, most of whom have no expertise as threat assessors, are asked to evaluate threats and to do so in seconds, often based on nothing more than a vague image and a few menacing words posted on Snapchat or a warning from police that a crime has been committed somewhere near campus. In this era, educators should never overlook even minor red flags, because the cost of ignoring them can be, and has been, dead children, but that also doesn't mean the appropriate response to every potential danger is to seal doors, turn off lights, and pack children into darkened corners.

John Czajkowski, a former teacher and naval officer who heads security for a forty-thousand-student district near San Diego, uses a brilliantly simple analogy to help people understand the purpose, and impact, of a lockdown. "It's like an air bag," he told me, because they save drivers' lives in car crashes, but the devices might also break noses and deliver concussions. His point: full-scale lockdowns should be employed only when absolutely necessary.

The system Czajkowski oversees, Sweetwater Union High School District, dealt with seventy-one student threats during a single school year, he said, but only seven times did schools lock down, and five of those were prompted by off-campus danger, such as a burglary or gunfire. In eleven instances, schools went into what they refer to as "secure campus" mode, in which classroom and exterior doors are locked and no one enters or leaves the buildings, but teachers can continue with instruction.

Some school districts still categorize that or similar measures as lockdowns, while others call them "lockouts," "building mode," or "sheltering in place." Though those scenarios can also rattle children, the experiences are usually less jarring than turning the lights off and hiding in the corner. The National Association of School Psychologists has developed a set of commonsense guidelines, emphasizing that nothing is more important than preparation and clearly communicating with staff and students, before, during, and after actual lockdowns. Still, because there are no universally followed best practices, schools take dramatically different, and sometimes haphazard, approaches to preparing students for potential danger.

Ten months after Parkland, on a Florida campus two hundred miles north, Lake Brantley High declared a "code red" emergency over the intercom, indicating that the 2,700-student campus faced immediate danger. "Active Shooter reported at Brantley / Building 1/ Building 2 and other buildings by B Shafer at 10:21:45," read a text sent to teachers. "Initiate a Code Red Lockdown." Students wept, had asthma attacks, messaged parents good-bye—but the threat wasn't real. It had been a drill, kept secret "so people will take it seriously," a spokesman later argued, insisting it was "the only way to get their attention."

That sort of thinking, though not uncommon, is misguided and harmful, says Cathy Kennedy-Paine, head of the National Association of School Psychologists' crisis response team. "To do that to children, I think that's unconscionable," she said. "The impacts can be very large from this kind of a thing." As the furious parent of one sixteen-year-old student put it, "It's more than just protecting children from bullet holes. It's protecting them from the anxiety and trauma they're now experiencing."

It was an inability to do the latter that devastated DC Prep's principal, Neema Desai, in the moments after the shooting around the corner on that late fall morning. As the school's lockdown was lifted, she watched a trio of her preschoolers emerge from a conference room where they'd hunkered for twenty minutes. The kids, who had been on the playground when the shooting started, were still wearing their jackets because the staff had quickly rushed them back in. The looks on their faces so unnerved Desai that she struggled to describe them to me later, before settling on "detached." She had never seen expressions like those before, but Desai supposed they epitomized the looks of children who had been subjected to "significant trauma." She imagined what the kids were thinking as they shuffled by: "I'm three, and I'm trying to process what just happened in the school, in the place where my parents trust my teachers, where I'm supposed to be safe." In the hours that followed, her students came undone:

"Who's going to shoot me?"

"I want to shoot people."

"I want to shoot myself."

That was the price her school paid for gun violence that did not qualify, by any measure, as a school shooting, that left no one bleeding from spiraling lead or hysterical from what they'd witnessed. The injury those kids suffered was exclusively psychological, born of fear from what they knew could happen because it had happened in so many other places. The ripples of those experiences extended well beyond the students. Teachers who had willed themselves to project calm amid their own terror struggled to recalibrate after the last lockdown, and in some cases overcorrected, demanding that their classrooms return to normal right away and disciplining kids who wouldn't or couldn't. "We saw the people who work in that building every day almost reach a breaking point," said Michelle Hess, DC Prep's senior director of student support. She and her staff realized the teachers needed as much space to recover as the kids did.

"We just didn't know what to do," Desai told me, and neither did parents. Monique Moore worked as the school's operation manager, and she had been thrilled with her three-year-old's progress at DC Prep, where he'd learned twenty-four letters and memorized every number up to ten. But the boy had also been outside, on the playground, when the three men fired their guns. "What's more important," Moore asked herself as she began to consider sending him elsewhere, "his safety or his academics?"

Shanta Suggs also wrestled over what to do with her own son, Zayden Saxton, who was seven and had excelled in the school. She sensed his angst and frustration after the lockdowns, and when she talked to him about transferring, he objected, but for a reason that stunned her. "What about my other friends? They're still going to be there," Zayden said, concerned that the kids in his second-grade class might get hurt after he left. "I didn't have an answer for that," Suggs told me.

After the last lockdown, Desai and other administrators changed their security protocols, announcing at a meeting with teachers in early December that the school would initiate full-scale lockdowns only if danger reached campus. Short of that, it would go into "building mode," a far less disruptive response. The next day, on another cold morning in Southeast DC, someone around the corner fired a dozen shots. Desai and her staff hurried to lock the doors to the school, but in a classroom on the second floor, MaKenzie and the other first-graders didn't stop learning new words or ways to add up numbers.

CHAPTER 12

"ARE YOU GOING TO KEEP KIDS SAFE?"

How Ava Found Her Voice

"Dear Mr. President," Ava wrote in pencil on a sheet of notebook paper, just a few hours after her brother left for school one morning. Cameron had been at home, on a break, and it was his first week back. Ava hated that. His move from Townville Elementary to another campus had offered her little comfort, because she knew that school shootings could happen anywhere, and on that day, she had felt more worried than usual. Years earlier, she had written a letter to President Obama, asking about his job, what he liked to read, the advice he'd offer if she wanted to become president. His office responded, so she decided to send a more serious plea to President Trump, hopeful that the most powerful person in the world would want to help. Propped in a white chair at her family's kitchen table, Ava's usual letter-writing spot, the girl explained to him what she had been through on the playground.

"I heard and saw it all happen and I was very scared. My best friend, Jacob, was shot and died," she continued, forcing herself to write the words that so unsettled her. "That made me very sad. I loved him and was going to marry him one day. I hate guns. One ruined my life and took my best friend. I don't want that to ever happen again. Are you going to keep kids safe? How can you keep us safe? Please don't let any more bad people get guns and hurt kids. My brother goes to school and I don't want anything bad like that to happen to him again. Please keep kids safe from guns."

Four months later—a span in which guns had hurt another eleven kids in American schools, leaving three of them dead—a manila envelope arrived at Ava's doorstep. "THE WHITE HOUSE," it read in the top left corner. Her mother opened it first, scanning the message to make sure it didn't include anything that might spark Ava's anxiety. Mary then called her daughter into their living room, where they sat together on the couch. She gave Ava the note, which, at the top, included the presidential seal.

"Dear Ava," it read. "Thank you for your letter. It is very brave of you to share your story with me. Mrs. Trump and I are so sorry to hear of the loss of your friend, Jacob."

"Wow," Ava said, marveling at Trump's massive, jagged signature, scrawled in black marker at the bottom of the page.

"Is that real?" she asked her mom, and it was, though a White House spokeswoman wouldn't tell me whether the president had read Ava's letter or contributed in any way to the response that bore his name.

"Schools are places where children learn and grow with their friends," the letter continued. "Their halls should be free of fear. It is my goal as President to make sure that children in America grow up in safe environments, giving them the best opportunity to realize their full potential. I will continue to focus on protecting Americans and improving the safety of our Nation. Mrs. Trump and I hold you close in our hearts. We hope you always remember that no matter what may happen, there are so many people in your life who love you, support you, and want to see you fulfill all your dreams."

For a few days, the words of reassurance made Ava feel better, until something about them started to bother her. "He didn't say *how* he could keep kids safe," she told her mom. So, Ava sat down to write another letter.

AVA HAD BEEN enamored with the written word since she started reading it, at age four. By the time I met her, she'd finished hundreds of books and could recall her favorite parts of many. Filling her kindergarten and first-grade notebooks were stories of lunches with her brother, riding down a slide on the playground, and the joy of friendship. ("I listen with my heart. I do not argu.") She'd written her first note to Santa Claus, then others to her parents and grandparents, before the one to Jacob in which she asked him to come over for lunch and marriage and which, after the shooting, she realized had gone undelivered. Following his death, letters took on a new and more profound meaning in her life. Fear of what she might hear or see or feel or, most of all, do had shrunk Ava's world, confining her almost every hour of every day within the walls of her home. She lost her teachers and her friends, and she also lost control, and with it, a central piece of the person she had become. But in the pages of her letters, that person remained—a little girl brimming with the creativity, curiosity, and empathy her parents worried all the trauma had stripped away.

Rosey Colautti didn't know what to expect when she wrote to Ava one summer day in 2017. Rosey, who'd worked as a teacher for thirty-two years before retiring, read my *Washington Post* story on the attack at Townville Elementary and immediately felt compelled to do something. She understood how odd it might seem for someone to write a letter to a child she didn't know living nine hundred miles away, but there was something about Ava that Rosey couldn't shake. "I've got to talk to her," she said, so that's what Rosey, sixty-three, tried to do. "I thought I would write to you and tell you that you and your friends are very brave. I'm sorry that you lost a dear friend. I want you to know that your story will stay with me," she wrote. "I think there are lots of people who are wishing you good things, Ava. Especially Rosey in Toronto, Ontario, Canada."

Ava was thrilled, quickly writing back on stationery bordered with cat faces. "I didn't know that anyone in Canada would read about me and my friends. Your card made me smile. Does it get very cold where you live? I like to look at weather stuff. I would like to do the weather on TV someday. That is nice you were a teacher. Did you teach little kids like me? My mom is going be my teacher this year. I hope to learn about Canada. Thank you for reminding me nice people are thinking about me. I hope you have a nice day!" she wrote, and after that, she included a smiley face and a final detail: "PS. My middle name is Rose."

The letters continued, for months and then years, and if not for Ava's youthful handwriting, they could have passed for exchanges between old friends. Rosey sent books about Ontario and the planet and another titled *The 12 Bugs of Christmas*. Ava sent photos of herself and her brother and asked all sorts of questions: "Was it fun teaching? My brother wants to teach one day." "How was your Christmas? Mine was okay." "Have you had much snow?" "Do you enjoy spring time? I love spring here! I love seeing the colors and pretty baby animals!" "Do you have any pets?" "Have you been to an apple orchard?"

Rosey talked about her husband and her three sons, including one, Jesse, whose name Ava had to scratch out because she couldn't bear to look at it. Rosey told Ava that it was sometimes lonely in her house because her kids were all grown, but that she looked forward to one of their upcoming marriage ceremonies. "I asked my son Ben what song we can dance to at his wedding. He asked for 'You Are My Sunshine' and 'High Hopes,' songs I used to sing to him at bedtime. I wonder what the dance will be like. My friend is taking me shopping on Friday . . . a dress for the wedding. I'll tell you about what I find." When she learned that Ava enjoyed ice-skating, she scoured shops for a gift until she spotted a silver-colored skate ornament near the checkout line at a grocery store. "Oh my God," Rosey said when she saw it, and after she explained the reason for her exclamation to someone nearby who overheard it, the woman cried. "I love it so much!" Ava responded. "I've never seen one like it before! I've decided to start collecting them." Rosey kept sending books, too, including one of her favorites, the Dr. Seuss classic *Oh, the Places You'll Go!* "I read the book with my mom every night," Ava wrote back. "It helps me remember that good things are coming."

There was a sincerity to Rosey's messages that put Ava, who resented nothing more than being feared, at ease. Rosey encouraged but never preached, because she understood what it felt like for strangers to claim they knew best how to overcome suffering. A decade earlier, Rosey had been diagnosed with stage-four Hodgkin's lymphoma. "I got a lot of stupid stuff from people, about positive outlook. If I got books, I sent them back," she told me. Rosey wasn't sure if she would survive, because so many of the people receiving chemotherapy along with her didn't. She did, though, and because of that, she started sending thank-you notes to anyone who made an impact, however small, on her life, from a waiter at a restaurant to the head of an art gallery she enjoyed.

"I decided that was my version of being brave," she told me, and that's what led her years later to write Ava, who, in return, gradually opened up. "I am sorry I haven't written sooner. I have had a lot of mad and sad days. I am trying to feel better," she confided once. Ava also told Rosey why she liked to read so much: "I don't have to focus on anything but my book." And why ice-skating had helped: "It is very peaceful for me." In time, it occurred to Rosey that their friendship meant as much to her as it likely did to Ava, and it wasn't just because she felt gratified from doing a good thing. "This was somebody I could talk to," Rosey said, "even though she was little."

Mandy Gaither understood that better than anyone. After I wrote about Ava for the *Post*, Mandy, a local TV reporter who had covered the shooting's aftermath, also interviewed the girl. Ava so appreciated how Mandy, a mother of two boys, handled their discussion that she wrote the woman a thank-you and asked, "Will you be my new BFF?" Of course, Mandy responded, and for a long time, their letters were mostly a series of cheerful questions and answers, punctuated with hand-drawn cats. Ava asked Mandy about her job and her favorite things and how she would describe herself, and Mandy asked Ava just as much—about her favorite game ("Monopoly Junior"), favorite movie ("*Sing!*"), where she would like to travel ("Washington D.C."), what she would do if she had a hundred dollars to help strangers ("give people food"). Then, three months after their correspondence began, one of Mandy's coworkers was killed while on assignment after a tree fell on his car. He was her best friend. "Dear Ava," Mandy wrote many weeks later, "I'm so sorry it's taken me a while to write you back. We've had a sad time at my news station, but I'm trying to be strong, JUST LIKE YOU!" Mary explained to her daughter the basics of what had happened, and soon Ava sent Mandy another message. "I am so sorry that you have felt sad! I hope that things have been happier," she wrote, and now that she knew the two of them had something more in common, she asked a new question: "What do you do when you are mad to feel better?"

By the time Mandy responded, she had left her job at the news station, unable to keep going back to a place that was a constant reminder of her colleague. Still, she answered Ava's question. "You also asked what I do to feel better when I'm mad or sad. I've felt a lot of that lately with the loss of my friend. I know you know the feeling. What I've learned to do is breathe. Take in a deep breath through my nose, hold it for 4 seconds and exhale. I do this over and over. Then, I remind myself of all the blessings I have in this life and I focus on those. I know my friend, Mike, lived a happy life and would not want me to be sad, so I smile for him," Mandy told her, and then she said her favorite pizza toppings were pepperoni and mushrooms and that she'd just gotten a new kitten, named "Pickles" by her five-year-old son.

"I will try what you do when you are sad," Ava responded, and in a letter just after that one, she offered her friend something more. "I am glad you understand feeling sad-mad. I know most people don't understand it," Ava wrote, adding that she had taken Mandy's advice. "I do try to think of good times. One time in kindergarten, Jacob and I ate crayons! That's funny, isn't it!"

Mandy, then forty, knew how significant it was for Ava to offer that detail, or even to utter Jacob's name to her, and she suspected the girl had done it, at least in part, to reciprocate; Mandy had shared about her loss, and now Ava had shared about hers, because that's what friends do. The difference in their ages didn't matter. "We have that common bond, when it comes to loss," Mandy said.

Ava wrote often to other people, too, including Ricky Carioti, the *Post* photographer I worked with on the original story, and to me. Along with one note I found inside my office mailbox was a certificate with an illustrated cat. "You've got a positive cat-titude," it read. Below that, Ava wrote what she called me: "Mr. John." And below that, the reason for the honor: "Helping people tell their story." Her longest-serving pen pal was Chris Justus, a meteorologist at Mandy's news station whom Ava had first contacted for a school project before the shooting. After it, he gave Ava and her brother, Cameron, a tour of the studio, where he and the producers made sure she wouldn't see or hear anything from the broadcast that might bother her. That day, in a rare moment, Ava's mother took a photo of her daughter smiling. Another time, Chris's family met Ava's at a local children's museum. He had worried how she would handle going to such a public place, but when Ava met his two sons, then ages one and two, she was smitten, doting on them the whole day, and not once succumbing to her anxiety. They were too young for Ava to write to, but she did start to send them gifts, Beanie Babies and Matchbox cars, paid for with her own money and always in pairs, so each boy had his own. Chris was struck by her thoughtfulness.

"Deep down," he told me, "she wants to help other people not to be sad, like she is."

For that reason, of course, Ava first wrote to the boy she cared about as much as anyone, Tyshaun. He was the only person her age, other than Cameron, with whom she had regular contact. She wanted to be his friend so badly, in fact, that she ventured beyond her letters and talked to him through video chats, an initially terrifying prospect for Ava, who was convinced Tyshaun wouldn't like her. But Tyshaun was gentle with her in a way that his mother had never seen before, and Ava was comfortable with him in a way that *her* mother had never seen before. The two of them, the girl thought, shared something most adults didn't understand, especially the ones in charge, and it was because Ava believed they needed to understand that she kept writing her letters.

"DEAR MR. PRESIDENT," Ava jotted at the beginning of her reply to Trump, before thanking him for his initial response. "I sometimes still think about that day in my head thinking it will happen again. When you wrote me, you said that you will keep kids and schools safe, and I'm glad to hear that. If you have the time, I have some ideas to help keep kids and schools safe. Sometimes people who have lived through a school shooting have better ideas. I will list my ideas for you. Please let me know if you need any more ideas after this."

Ava told him what they were: Put schools in safer places, build them in circles and put the playgrounds in the middle, give kids a spot to run to if something bad happens. She folded both pages and slid them into an envelope, and as the carrier took it from her mailbox in Townville, she hoped that somehow, everything would get fixed before any more kids got hurt. Then, two weeks later, a teenager in a small Kentucky community that was a lot like her own took a gun from his stepfather's closet, packed it in his bag, and headed to school, where he opened fire just before classes started. Two kids died, and a dozen more were wounded. The shooter, who was fifteen, later told investigators he had done it as an experiment, to see how the world would react.

In Washington, DC, America's leaders reacted the way they had many times before, with denouncements and calls for thoughts and prayers. Thirty hours after the last bullet was fired, just before a tweet about his administration ushering in a "new era of Peace and Prosperity," the president mentioned the shooting. "We are with you!" Trump wrote, in his only public comment about it. "The president believes that all Americans deserve to be safe in their schools," press secretary Sarah Huckabee Sanders told reporters, but she offered no specifics on how the president would try to keep them safe. Then there was another school shooting the next day, in Alabama, and another seven days after that, in California, and another thirteen days after that, in a Florida town named Parkland.

During a visit to his grandparents' house, Cameron heard about the seventeen people killed at Stoneman Douglas High, and when the boy came home, he let it slip to Ava, prompting another outburst. Ava knew she had to get past that, though, because not long after, she was to meet South Carolina's Republican governor, Henry McMaster, who had heard about the girl's story and invited her to the statehouse. Two weeks to the day after the Parkland massacre, Ava dressed in a girl's suit, black with white trim, put a blue bow in her hair, and tucked her feet, in white stockings, into child size-twelve flats whose toes featured silver hearts. She slid Mikey, the stuffed Ninja Turtle that had once belonged to Jacob, inside one of her pockets, and into the capitol building Ava went. After she'd met the governor and taken a seat beside him, she removed from her backpack a black-and-pink notebook. On its cover were some of the words she liked most—PEACE, LOVE, SMILE, LIVE—and inside was the list of all her ideas on how to keep kids safe. She'd already removed the sticky pieces of pink paper that normally covered the words she disliked most, the ones Ava jotted with her eyes closed.

"Somehow help people to understand what happens to kids like me who have seen and heard what happens when a gun hurts someone," she'd written as number five.

"Keep guns away from kids or if they do have them make sure they stay locked up where someone can't grab it who is not supposed to have it, especially kids," she'd written as number seven.

"Get rid of guns," she'd written as number eight.

Ava didn't know what, if anything, would come of their discussion, but she did know that she had gone to an important place and told an important person what she thought, and she felt proud of that, because she figured that's what the women she admired most would have done, too. Without knowing what the word meant, Ava had become something of a feminist. "Girls can be just as good as boys" was how she'd explained it to me, and that's why she'd decided to make her Belle doll, from *Beauty and the Beast*, a firefighter, and her Tiana doll, from *The Princess and the Frog*, a scientist.

After another frustrating session with a therapist in Greenville one day, Ava's parents took her to a Barnes & Noble, a place she adored. She wore her purple headphones and carried Mikey and Bowers, her stuffed polar bear, under her arm as she walked up and down the aisles. At the end of one, she spotted a red sign that read, INSPIRING STORIES FOR UNSTOPPABLE GIRLS. Below that was *She Persisted*, an illustrated book written by Chelsea Clinton. Ava picked it up. "I just think it's pretty cool," she told her mom, who quickly skimmed through it, searching for trigger words, before returning it to Ava. The girl continued perusing the store, but held on to the book. She approached a display of plush cat toys. "Anyone who doesn't like this is crazy," she told me, as she picked one up, then put it back. She gasped at a stack of American Girl dolls, ogled Barbies, Shopkins toys, and *Minecraft* figurines. She saw a book titled, *Ava and*

Taco Cat. Her eyes widened. "That's *so* cool," she said, but she put that back, too, and when they finished shopping and Ava knew she could pick only one item, because her parents couldn't afford more than that, she chose the book about the unstoppable girls. When she got home that afternoon, she sat on the couch and read every page, and in the months after, she found other books about strong women, all of which became her favorites, depending on the week: *Hidden Figures*, about three African American women instrumental in NASA missions to space; *I Dissent*, about Supreme Court justice Ruth Bader Ginsburg; *She Persisted Around the World*, about international heroines, including the author of the Harry Potter series. "I told Cameron that J. K. Rowling's a girl," Ava bragged to me later. "He was like, '*What?*'"

On the afternoon that Ava met with Governor McMaster, he shared a photo on Facebook of himself next to Ava, his finger on her open notebook. "She is a precious, gifted child, and a reminder of both the need to do whatever it takes to keep our children safe and the bright future that our state has in their hands," the governor posted, saying nothing about guns or the meaning of "whatever it takes." Exactly two weeks later, and exactly one month after the killings at Stoneman Douglas, thousands of students across the country walked out of their classrooms, demanding that Congress pass gun control legislation. Reporters asked McMaster to comment.

"It is not about the tragedy. It is not about the schoolchildren. What we should all do, and what these students should do, and I imagine a lot of them intend to do, is pray and to hope for the families of those who were slain," said McMaster, who, with an A rating from the NRA, condemned the student walkout. "It sounds like a protest to me. It's not a memorial. It's certainly not a prayer service. It's a political statement by a left-wing group, and it's shameful."

The governor's office never reached out to the Olsens again, Mary said, but that didn't dissuade Ava, nor did a second letter from the White House that mentioned a school safety bill but, again, included not a word about guns. Immersed in her world of books and letters, Ava thought often about those women she so looked up to: Ginsburg and Rowling, Rosey and Mandy. In the face of hard times, they hadn't given up, so neither did Ava, sending fresh pleas to her state's senator Lindsey Graham and to Alexandria Ocasio-Cortez, the representative from New York, and, one last time, to President Trump. Mary told her daughter that she wasn't alone, that other children were fighting for change, too. Ava's mom talked to her about one of them in particular, a Parkland survivor named Emma Gonzalez, who had led demonstrations and given speeches advocating for gun control. Mary showed Ava photos of Gonzalez online, and when the girl asked if people listened to her, given that she was older, her mom said that yes, some did, but others didn't want to hear her opinion and said unkind things about her.

After Ava heard that, she took a seat early one morning at her kitchen table and opened two notebooks, one small and the other large. Wearing a plastic headband that looked like cat ears, she silently outlined with a yellow pencil the things she wanted to say in the small one, listing twelve ideas in all. "I might need the cat things," she told her mom, referring to the thin sticky notes, which bore illustrations of cat faces, that Ava used to put over scary words.

"Dear Emma," Ava wrote with tidy print letters in the larger notebook, explaining who she was and where she was from. "I am sorry that you had to go through a school shooting," she continued, immediately covering "shooting." "I lived through one too. I think you are very brave. I think that even when people are mean to you, you are still very brave. I know adults don't listen sometimes. I think nobody should have to worry about getting hurt."

"Okay, I think I'm done," Ava said at the end, before adding a final line: "Have a nice day!" At the bottom, she drew a picture of a smiling cat, and when Mary picked up her daughter's notebook to tear the pages out so they could mail them, Ava covered both ears with her hands.

CHAPTER 13

"THAT'S TWENTY-NINE
THOUSAND DOLLARS A KID"

The Business of School Security

Long before Emma Gonzalez and millions of other people demanded that America's political leaders do more to protect schools from gun violence, the superintendent of a rural district in South Carolina had become fixated on the idea. Joanne Avery oversaw six campuses, including Townville Elementary's, at the time of the shooting there. A slender, polished woman with a refined Tennessee accent and a PhD, Avery never shied away from the fight that Gonzalez and her classmates took on many months later, writing an op-ed (for an overwhelmingly conservative readership) that called for laws preventing people who pose a threat from having access to firearms, ridiculed state politicians who had debated solutions without ever asking her or Townville's staff what they thought, and condemned a proposal to arm teachers. "Putting more guns in close proximity to children is not the answer," Avery wrote. She understood, though, that the country, and especially South Carolina, wouldn't fix its gun problems any time soon, and that meant, in the meantime, Avery had to do whatever she could to guarantee that her students were safe from another attack. Making sure she did kept her up at night.

Avery toured each of her schools with members of the sheriff's office, asking them to point out vulnerabilities. On each campus, she had boxes installed that contained campus maps and radios the police could access in case of an emergency. She updated surveillance systems and connected them to her cell phone so she could see what the cameras saw, at any time, day or night. She added resource officers, increased the number of active-shooter drills, installed trauma kits, and provided receptionists with panic buttons.

Then along came 2018, and suddenly, ensuring that students were safe from another attack was keeping thousands of superintendents up at night. By every significant measure, that year of school shootings stands as the worst in at least the past two decades, but almost certainly in modern history. In total, twenty-five K–12 campuses suffered incidents of gun violence immediately before, during, or just after classes ended, considerably more than the previous high of sixteen four years earlier. Among the ninety-four people shot, thirty-three were killed, each breaking the prior records. The number of students who experienced gun violence on their campuses in 2018 could have filled all twenty thousand seats inside Madison Square Garden and another five thousand outside it. Of course, the deadliest incident, at Stoneman Douglas, led a new wave of congressional leaders, state legislators, school boards, administrators, teachers, and parents to raise the same question that Avery, and Ava, had been asking for months: how do we keep kids in schools safe from guns?

Eager to provide solutions—just as they had been after Columbine in 1999 and Red Lake in 2005 and Sandy Hook in 2012—were capitalists, who understood that the carnage represented a significant financial opportunity. Though campus shootings remain rare, school security has grown into a nearly $3 billion market, an estimate that does not account for the billions more spent on armed campus police officers. In a time of such extraordinary desperation that districts are investing in shooter insurance and parents are buying $150 bulletproof backpacks from Walmart, superintendents continue to face intense pressure to do *something* to make kids safer. That climate often leads to rushed, uninformed choices, driven less by logic than by fear.

It was the nation's renewed anxiety, five months after the deaths of seventeen people in South Florida, that drew so many administrators in July 2018 to the National School Safety Conference at an Orlando hotel two hundred miles north of Parkland. Waiting for them there, and intent on capturing a piece of the money they would soon spend, were the entrepreneurs, corporations, and charlatans who had rushed into the void left by politicians who couldn't or wouldn't answer Avery and Ava's question.

ON A SULTRY Florida afternoon, hundreds of superintendents and principals filed down the hotel's hallways as they neared a sign advertising another conference later in the year. ACTIVE SCHOOL SHOOTERS, it read, above a photo of an armed man approaching a half-dozen children at their lockers. Most of the passing educators didn't seem to notice. It was the expo's opening night, and just beyond the sign, inside a sprawling chandeliered ballroom, a band played Jimmy Buffett covers to the rhythm of a steel drum.

Waiters in white button-downs poured glasses of chardonnay and served meatballs wrapped in bacon as a bespectacled man in a navy-blue suit asked passersby to try on a wearable black body shield that he said could stop bullets fired from a nine-millimeter handgun. They were available for $158, a sign at his table read, just below IDEAL FOR STUDENTS, TEACHERS, AND TRAVELERS. In one corner of the room, feet from where guests posed with colorful boas and silly hats at a photo booth, a security company's digital sign displayed hypothetical warnings in bright red letters: ARMED THREAT RUN HIDE FIGHT RUN HIDE FIGHT RUN HIDE FIGHT.

Ten miles from Walt Disney World, the scene, at once festive and ghoulish, perfectly mirrored my conversations with vendors, who could pivot in a breath from uninhibited giddiness over the chance for coverage from a journalist to dour seriousness when asked about the awful things that *had to keep happening* for their businesses to survive. What made the enthusiasm appropriate, even necessary, they suggested, was the country's urgent need for what they had to offer. At one booth, two gray-haired men from Wisconsin were selling a mobile three-hundred-pound ballistic whiteboard, adorned with adorable animal illustrations and pocked with five bullet holes, that cost more than $2,900, or about ten times the price of whiteboards that couldn't stop rounds designed for warfare.

"A teacher can sit there and use it for daily use," Jim Weiss, who was in charge of marketing, said as he sipped on a bottle of Michelob Light. "And then the kids can just run behind it."

"What we want to do is just give the kids, the teachers, a chance," explained the company's general manager, Jim Muth.

"So they can buy a few minutes," Weiss added.

Muth had been in the whiteboard business for nearly two decades when a company that developed ballistic material for airport seating, office partitions, and fencing recognized a prime new possibility. "They said, 'How do we begin to deal with schools?'" Muth recalled. "So, they contacted us."

Elsewhere at the conference, vendors peddled "bleeding control bags" and pepper ball guns, window shades meant to prevent shooters from seeing inside classrooms, and a security proposal that would turn former special operations officers into undercover teachers. Threaded into every pitch was the implication that their product or service would make students safer—that, if purchased, it might save a life.

What few of the salespeople could offer, however, was proof. Despite the billions spent every year, little research had been done on which safety measures actually protect students from gun violence, leaving schools to rely on self-appointed experts and consultants, who almost always base their recommendations on anecdotal information or experience in other industries.

"Many of the activities that schools undertake to promote safety and prevent problems, including use of technology, have not been evaluated," according to a 2016 federally funded study by Johns Hopkins University. "There is limited and conflicting evidence in the literature on the short- and long-term effectiveness of school safety technology."

The vacuum of reliable evidence had not deterred a mass of vendors from venturing into the market and inundating schools with product spiels that make grand promises. A superintendent in an Illinois district that experienced a shooting two months before the conference told me that within hours of the incident, her in-box was "flooded from vendors with some pretty disrespectful and tacky statements: 'had you had this . . .'; 'if you had this . . .'" That attitude was prevalent at the expo, which, at times, brought to my mind stories of eighteenth-century pharmaceutical salesmen who, because they worked in an unregulated industry, made phony guarantees about ineffective products to a nation desperate for relief. In the lead-up to the event in Orlando, so many companies requested space that its organizers ran out, stopping at 105 vendors, an all-time high for the conference and a 75 percent increase over the previous year.

"This is our first show," said Paul Noe, who had come to sell a high-tech, armored classroom door that he claimed could stop bullets, identify the weapon, photograph the shooter, and notify police. The bright yellow one his company had put on display had been shot fifty-seven times. "At four thousand bucks a door, they'd have the Rolls-Royce of school doors. It would do everything," added its inventor, Dale Ryan, then seventy-two, who also insisted that he viewed his product as a "legacy item," not a "profit item."

"We just released it in the past couple of months to be available to schools, and we've been obviously overwhelmed with interest," said Monte Scott, who sells guns that fire spheres similar to paint balls but packed instead with a potent pepper mixture intended to disable a shooter. Scott had just come back from training U.S. troops in Afghanistan on how to use the weapons in a combat zone.

"This is our first school conference that we've ever done," said SAM Medical sales director Denise Ehlert, who, at one point during the expo's first evening, met a girl named Athena who had come with her father, a resource officer at a school in Pennsylvania. "What is this?" the girl asked about a tourniquet, and her dad tried to explain that if a bad person hurt someone at her school, this could help save them. Ehlert saw an opening. "It's not something to be afraid of," the woman said as she knelt down and put the tourniquet on her own arm, then encouraged Athena, who was six, to tighten it. "You gotta keep going," Ehlert urged, until Athena cinched it all the way down, a perfect demonstration that anyone could use their product. "Proved my point," the saleswoman told me later.

Also among the first-time vendors was Jordan Goudreau, whose business concept came to him in Puerto Rico, where he had traveled to work in private security after Hurricane Maria. Goudreau, a former Green Beret, was getting rich on the island, he said, but the new idea was too enticing not to pursue.

"I saw Parkland and I was like, 'Well, nobody's really tackling this, so *I* want to fix this,'" Goudreau explained as he stood in front of a glossy, wide-screen TV playing his tutorials on a loop. Central to his company's plan, which sounded broadly similar to the plot of Arnold Schwarzenegger's *Kindergarten Cop*, was to embed former special operations agents, posing as teachers, inside schools. The benefits over resource officers, Goudreau said, were obvious. First, because the children wouldn't know who his guys really were (or that they were armed and adept at counterterrorism tactics), students would be more likely to open up, giving agents a chance to glean information that could prevent a shooting. "He's just a—he's a cool shop teacher: 'Hey, what's up, fellas,'" said Goudreau, then forty-two, mimicking a potential conversation between an armed special ops man and a child. "Clandestine. I talk to them. I talk to kids. I go sit down with a kid who's alone, playing Dungeons and Dragons, and I just try to see whether there's any problems. I try to develop relationships." Second, Goudreau explained, his staffers are all much more skilled at killing—"They've been in gunfights"—than the police officers whom schools typically hire. "It's the definitive solution. You can either have a guy that you pay $18,000 to $30,000 a year— you get what you pay for. I'm sure you've seen guys walking around, 'I'm a resource officer,'" he told me, motioning to his stomach to imply that they're overweight. "Or you can have a guy who is tactically proficient, in tremendous shape, who makes his shots 95 to 99 percent of the time. That's the difference."

There was a lot Goudreau hadn't worked out yet. I had, by then, spent many days in classrooms, jotting down notes as the kids raised hell and the adults tried to corral them. The job of a teacher, a good one, was among the hardest in existence, in my view, and it was with this in mind that I pressed Goudreau to explain how his band of combat veterans was qualified to do that job. He couldn't, because he had barely considered it, but what Goudreau had considered was his revenue model.

"The beauty of it is it's all for the price of a Netflix subscription, so it's really hard to argue with me about 'Well, it costs too much.' You can't tell me that," said Goudreau, who, in the hope of making a small fortune, would later attempt, and fail, to organize a coup against the Venezuelan government.

His agents weren't in any schools at the time of the expo, but Goudreau, hair buzzed and shirt unbuttoned to the center of his chest, was certain that he wanted to bill the parents of each student directly (for $8.99 a month), so his staff could remain outside any district's "chain of command." Just then, the media relations liaison standing beside Goudreau at their booth interceded, suggesting that, if necessary, they could go through school boards and accept government money. Goudreau stopped him.

"But we don't *want* to. We don't *want* that," he said. "We want private money, because it's faster."

Included with every pitch was an insistence that it really wasn't about the money at all, that the true reason they had come was altruistic, that what had drawn them to the industry was a sincere hope to make a difference.

Among the most popular booths was the one that belonged to Justin Kuhn, whose Ohio company produced an elaborate door security and weapons detection system. As he stood next to his 2,500-pound aluminum-framed vestibule, I asked him what he would say to people who argued that he, and others in attendance, were indirectly trying to profit from kids' murders.

"I don't know. I never thought of that. I don't know what to say about that," he said, and as he struggled to find an answer, one of the consultants Kuhn had brought with him stepped over.

"It's a really good question," Barry Schrock interjected. "Did he tell you his story? His story is that he didn't start this because he was looking to make a bunch of money. He already did that."

Kuhn, then thirty-eight, told me he had previously invented a scraper blade (the Spyder Scraper) and a car wax (Widow Wax), enterprises that had left him with so much wealth that it was offensive to suggest he had started the school safety company to make money.

"It's really about his kids," Schrock said, in front of and about Kuhn, the father of three young children. "Ultimately, when it comes down to it, if people think about it from a financial gain, then they've got it all wrong."

In truth, thinking that would not have been *all* wrong, because by Kuhn's own account, his mind was very much on the business of making financial gains. Although he acknowledged that he didn't know if his new product would have stopped the attack at Stoneman Douglas, this hadn't dissuaded him from trying to leverage the bloodshed. He recalled a meeting in Indiana with one district's head of school safety who had suggested that the price tag for Kuhn's entire system seemed exorbitant.

"If you think five hundred thousand dollars is expensive, go down to Parkland, Florida, and tell seventeen people five hundred thousand is expensive. That's twenty-nine thousand dollars a kid," Kuhn remembered saying. "Every person would pay twenty-nine thousand dollars a kid to have their kid alive."

CONVERSATIONS LIKE THE one with Kuhn, repeated in some form more than a dozen times during the trip to Orlando, made me wonder: what did the educators that had actually experienced shootings learn from those incidents, and what could they teach districts around the country trying to decide what to invest in or whom to trust? To answer that question, I sent surveys to every school that had gone through a shooting since the 2012 killings in Newtown, Connecticut, which prompted a surge of security spending by districts nationwide. Of the seventy-nine schools I contacted, thirty-four provided answers, and the most striking responses were to a question about what, if anything, could have prevented the shootings on their campuses. Nearly half said there was nothing they could have done, and just a single school suggested that any kind of safety technology might have made a difference. Several, however, suggested that other specific steps would make a difference.

"Sensible gun control . . . We are largely powerless from determined shooters with high-capacity, high-velocity semiautomatic assault rifles," responded Richard Fitzpatrick, superintendent of a district in California where a man attacked a school in the fall of 2017 with an AR-15-style rifle he had built with parts, many of which are readily available online.

"Better Mental Health Services (for shooter)," suggested representatives from Sandy Hook Elementary's district, in reference to Adam Lanza.

"We could have armed SROs at the entrance of the school checking student IDs for every car coming onto campus. But that's not realistic, and even that is no guarantee the shooting would have been prevented," wrote Kevin Christian, a district spokesman in Florida, of a teenager who wounded a student with a shotgun inside Forest High in the spring of 2018. "Had this former student been supported at home, perhaps he wouldn't have felt the need to reach out for the attention he received . . ."

Christian's answer echoed many others that suggested no amount of investment in security, regardless of a school's location or demographics, could ensure immunity from gun violence. Take, for example, Huffman High in Birmingham, Alabama, and Freeman High in Rockford, Washington. The schools, located 2,300 miles apart, have almost nothing in common. Huffman, which was 95 percent black and in a city of more than two hundred thousand people, routinely ranked among the state's worst schools, with abysmal test scores and high rates of poverty among its students. Freeman, which was 85 percent white and in a rural town of fewer than five hundred people, routinely ranked among the state's best schools, with excellent test scores and a largely middle-class student body. But both their campuses had, in security parlance, been "hardened," a term that has migrated from antiterrorism circles to school board meetings—and yet, both still failed to prevent shootings. At Huffman, cameras mounted inside and out, periodic checks with both handheld and walk-through metal detectors, and a trio of resource officers couldn't stop a seventeen-year-old boy from unintentionally firing a handgun in the school, killing a senior two months before her graduation. At Freeman, a surveillance system, door locks, extensive active-shooter training, and an armed resource officer couldn't stop a fifteen-year-old boy with a handgun and an AR-15 rifle from taking the life of one student and wounding three others in a hallway.

"You want to rationalize in your mind that you could have stopped it or something could have been done," said Randy Russell, the superintendent in Freeman's district. "There's just nothing, outside of a crystal ball, that would have allowed us to know this was going to happen. . . . We don't control as much as we think we do."

What every school should strive to control, said a number of them, is the development of deep, trusting relationships with students, who often hear about threats before teachers do. "Communicating with kids is the number one thing we can do to stop to these things," safety consultant Curtis Lavarello, who organized the conference and expo in Orlando, told me just before noting that his vendors wouldn't appreciate his saying that.

In cases in which shootings cannot be stopped before they begin, administrators consistently pointed to simple, well-established safety measures as most effective at minimizing harm: carefully planned drills that teach rapid lockdown and evacuation strategies, doors that can be secured in seconds, and resource officers, or other staff, who act quickly. At Forest High, for instance, teachers and students who had undergone safety training locked classroom doors and piled chairs and desks in front of them immediately after realizing that the nineteen-year-old man with a shotgun was in the hallway. He fired into one classroom and injured a student but surrendered when he failed to get inside. A month later, at Dixon High in Illinois, resource officer Mark Dallas rushed toward the sound of shots near the school gym and, in a firefight, hit the shooter, who was quickly arrested.

Of the twenty-three surveyed schools that had officers at the time of their shootings, seven indicated that those officers played a part in limiting the harm done, but contrary to the role many people assume resource officers play in shootings, what Dallas did is extraordinarily rare. Before that day, just one other officer during the prior nineteen years had gunned down an active shooter. (Meanwhile, at least seven shootings over the same period were stymied by malfunctioning weapons or the gunmen's inability to handle them.) Though the officers' mere presence may deter some gun violence, in dozens of cases, it didn't: among the more than 225 incidents on campuses since 1999, at least 40 percent of the affected schools employed one.

Beyond armed security or any sort of high-priced piece of safety technology, schools consistently emphasized that what saved the most lives in their moments of crisis was being prepared for them. No school better exhibited this than Rancho Tehama Elementary. Early on the morning of November 14, 2017, staff at the rural school in Northern California heard what sounded like gunshots in the distance and hurried the children who were outside into the building. All students and staff had locked down, something they frequently practiced, forty-eight seconds after a secretary called for it—and just ten seconds before the man with the homemade AR-15-style rifle reached the quad. The gunman, who had already killed five people during his rampage, fired more than one hundred rounds, shattering glass and ripping holes in walls. He tried to come in through exterior classroom doors and the main office, but all were secured. Six minutes after arriving, he gave up and left, killing himself a short time later. One student, age six, was wounded but survived.

Rancho Tehama's security procedure worked "flawlessly," said Fitzpatrick, the superintendent, highlighting that well-planned lockdowns, executed only when a threat is both real and imminent, can prevent harm. But even as the school's conventional response drew praise and headlines, more and more districts were turning to a different type of active-shooter training, one that suggested the responsibility of keeping kids safe from being shot to death in their schools was, in part, on the kids themselves.

THE YOUTUBE VIDEO opens with a little girl who appears to be about thirteen and is wearing an ivy-print dress and a bow in her hair. Along with her partner, a sock puppet meant to look like a rabbit, she explains to the students of Lange Middle School in Columbia, Missouri, what they should do in case a gunman ever comes to their campus. The training, she says, is known as ALICE, which stands for Alert, Lockdown, Inform, Counter, and Evacuate. Much of what she explains next are widely accepted strategies for how to respond, focusing on clear and quick communication, the importance of securing doors, knowing when to flee rather than hide—all protocols that schools, including several I surveyed, credited with saving lives. It's not until the 10:42 mark that the letter *C*, in a cartoonish yellow font, appears on the screen, introducing a strategy developed by an Ohio-based company, also named ALICE, that has become one of the leading active-shooter training providers in America.

"*C* is for 'counter.' Think of it like 'counterattack,'" the girl says. "You keep moving, and you throw things as you go along."

"Wait, did you say *throw things*?" the rabbit interjects.

"Yes," she tells him.

"That's awesome!" the puppet shouts, before the video, which has been viewed more than 73,000 times, cuts to a scene of a shooter in their school's hallway. A man in an orange ski mask and a black trench coat walks alone, carrying what looks like a long green-and-orange Nerf gun. Dramatic music, as if from a Hollywood thriller, plays in the background. "Attention, students and staff. This is a not a drill," says a voice over the intercom, before describing a strange man with a weapon headed toward the main hall. He walks in, and a student yells as a group of four hides under a table. The shooter walks up, cocks his weapon, and fires, simulating the execution of each child. One of them screams, another moans. Eventually, they all stop squirming, and as the kids pretend to die, the puppet and the girl pop back into the frame. "Wait a minute, that's not how it was supposed to go. You said they should keep moving and throw things," the puppet says to the girl, and she agrees—because, sure, the students didn't do what they were supposed to do when facing a two-hundred-plus-pound man armed with a shotgun who has come to their school to kill them. So, they try again.

This time, when the intruder walks in, one of the kid's shouts,

"Holy crap, he has a gun." Without hesitation, the children bombard the intruder with books, folders, and toy balls. Like hardened Marines, five of them charge straight at the gunman, who drops his weapon and crumples to the floor.

Back up comes the rabbit.

"Those kids just attacked a guy with a gun," he observes.

"Yep," the girl says cheerfully.

"You never said anything about attacking a gunman," he tells her.

"Yes, I did," she says, holding up her hand in a C shape. "Counterattack."

Thousands of superintendents and principals have adopted the ALICE approach in recent years, and many have taught their classes—even in elementary schools—the counter tactics. Yet, much like the extravagant safety technologies districts have embraced, there is no proof that students are made safer by confronting armed attackers, regardless of the circumstances.

"What if the person is ex-military or the person has police training, and you're teaching the student to throw a can of green beans or attack?" asked Joe E. Carter, vice president of business development and marketing at United Educators, an insurance company that covers more than eight hundred K–12 schools around the country. "I haven't seen any data out there—real data—that this is something that makes it safer." In fact, the federal instructions on school emergency preparedness published in the aftermath of the Newtown massacre specifically state that only adults should consider attacking a shooter when cornered.

Numerous ALICE training videos online—typically produced by educators after they've paid for the company to instruct their staff—depict the same scene that played out at the middle school in Missouri, with students instantly reacting, launching objects, and rushing the shooter, who surrenders without a fight. But it's absurd to believe that children would behave with such decisiveness and precision when facing a real gunman intent on doing them harm.

"It presumes an ability to transform psychologically from a frightened kid to an attacker in the moment of crisis, the ability to successfully execute the attack on the shooter (e.g., hit the shooter with the book or rock, knock them down, etc.), again in a crisis situation, the ability to not accidentally hurt a classmate, the reality that unsuccessfully going on the attack might make that student a more likely target of the shooter," Katherine C. Cowan, spokeswoman for the National Association of School Psychologists, told me. Her organization teamed up with the National Association of School Resource Officers to produce a guide for active-shooter training, and it emphasized that "lockdown drills implemented according to best practices have been suggested to increase knowledge and skills of how to respond appropriately without elevating anxiety or perceived safety risk," but that there was "no empirical research regarding school-based armed assailant drills."

Stephen Brock, a school psychologist since the early 1980s and one of the guide's authors, recalled ALICE's founder, Greg Crane, a former police officer, first pushing his theories after Columbine, but not until years later did the concepts catch on. "I think a shift took place following Sandy Hook. That's when it got traction. And I think it was more or less out of a sense of hopelessness," Brock said, theorizing that parents and schools so longed for change that when the major gun reforms many of them counted on didn't happen, they turned to extreme alternatives, including teaching kids to fight their attackers. "It gave us something to do, in other words," he said. "The problem with that something is it costs money, it takes time, and maybe, to a certain extent, it's diverting our attention from other tried-and-true safety measures."

Representatives from ALICE, a for-profit company, maintain that the counter strategies should be used as a last resort and that their job is only to train law enforcement and school staff, who must then decide what's best for their students. But educators aren't security experts; they're educators, with limited expertise. In one case, the open-ended guidance from ALICE led a superintendent in Pennsylvania to equip students with five-gallon buckets of river stones. "If an armed intruder attempts to gain entrance into any of our classrooms," he told reporters at the time, "they will face a classroom full of students armed with rocks, and they will be stoned."

Colleen Lerch, a marketing specialist at ALICE, also insisted that their instructors recommend "SWARM" techniques, in which kids may gang-tackle shooters, only to students who are at least thirteen or fourteen years old. "At this age, it is statistically very high that the shooter will be the same age as potential victims. A room full of 14 year old's can easily control another 14 year old," Lerch asserted in an email, though she provided me no evidence to support either claim.

Lerch wouldn't say what she considered to be a "very high" percentage, but the truth is that a third of shooters who attack middle schools and high schools are older than their victims. Also, teachers, coaches, and other staff have taken down more than a dozen armed intruders since Columbine—including on at least three campuses that underwent ALICE training—but the company could not provide me a single case in which students used its counter techniques to subdue a gunman.

What we do know is that kids have been killed after confronting intruders, whether accidentally or on purpose. In late 2017, a seventeen-year-old was fatally wounded when he came upon a former student in the bathroom who was readying an attack at Aztec High in New Mexico, and a seventeen-year-old girl was struck when she did the same thing at Alpine High in Texas a year earlier. At Freeman High, the school in rural Washington State, Sam Strahan decided not to flee on that morning when a classmate started firing in the hallway. Instead, he approached the gunman, trying to intervene, and the boy shot him. Sam, who was fifteen, didn't survive.

NICOLE HOCKLEY DECIDED that America's approach to school safety was broken almost immediately after the murder of her son,

Dylan, who died at Sandy Hook three months before his seventh birthday. She watched as the nation, in response to the slaughter of twenty first-graders, didn't address the proliferation of guns or the ease with which they're bought and sold or even the shortcomings in our mental health system. Instead, Hockley watched our country turn to the schools—the victims of the crisis—and say, in essence, *You fix this.*

"They're looking at this in the whole wrong way," she said. "It's so much focus on imminent danger and what you do in the moment, as opposed to what you do to stop it from happening in the first place."

Hockley understood the cost of failing to stop it from happening as well as anyone. She had switched from a career in marketing to one in gun violence prevention, and not just to honor her dead son's memory. She also had another son at Sandy Hook that day, but Jake, then in third grade, came home. She didn't send him back to any school for a long time, but eventually, even in the face of her breakdowns and panic attacks, Hockley's surviving child had to go. Determined to keep him safe, she cofounded Sandy Hook Promise, which in its earliest days fought for the sweeping policy changes (including increased background checks and an assault weapons ban) that the U.S. Senate struck down in April 2013. In defeat, Hockley didn't stop working at it, because Jake and millions of other kids didn't get to stop going to school. Sandy Hook Promise changed course. "We decided we'll be that organization that teaches people about gun violence, teaches people about the causes," she once wrote, "and gives them the tools to actually prevent it where they live."

In early 2018, Hockley and her colleagues unveiled a free service intended to do just that. The Say Something Anonymous Reporting System allows users to privately submit safety concerns to a crisis center through a computer, phone, or app, addressing the one thing that a number of the surveyed schools told me could have stopped the shootings on their campuses: a tip from someone who knew it might happen. Most shooters are children, and most children commit their acts of gun violence at the schools they attend, and in most cases, someone knows or suspects something before a shot is ever fired. Hockley had long understood that, but as she implored students around the country to speak up if they were aware of a threat, many kids told her that they were afraid to, often because of potential retaliation. The anonymity the system offers is meant to alleviate that concern, and over its first two years, the app received more than forty-eight thousand tips. The results were significant.

In one instance, a student informed the crisis center that an eighth-grade friend was cutting herself and considering suicide. The girl was soon placed in treatment. In another case, the organization said, a tipster reported that a student who might have access to guns had talked about shooting gay classmates. Staff immediately contacted local law enforcement and school district leaders, who intervened.

On the spectrum of America's gun violence epidemic, the problem of school shootings often feels as if it's among the most intransigent, but the solutions are not unknowable or unattainable, as Hockley's reporting system illustrates. It's also likely that some percentage of the products and services for sale at the Orlando expo actually would save lives, but without good research (the same kind that, more than a decade ago, showed the effectiveness of lockdown drills that strictly followed best practices), schools will continue to invest blindly in what they guess will work best.

And then there are the answers that don't require any financial investment at all. Joanne Avery, the South Carolina superintendent, had never stopped wondering what might have been had the middle school Jesse Osborne attended not lost contact with him after he was expelled, effectively severing his ties to the outside world beyond family and the internet. It was then, in his isolation as a home-schooler, that he became immersed in first-person shooter games, deranged online chats, and an obsession with mass murderers.

Jesse, who would eventually be sentenced to life in prison, remained in her mind two years later, when she learned that a student at one of her other schools had talked on social media about bludgeoning classmates. The principal there wanted to kick him out immediately, something that Avery, the superintendent, might have agreed to years earlier, but this time, she said no. "I'm not just going to expel him and be done with him," she recalled telling the principal. "You're going to increase your chances of that person coming back to your school and doing harm."

Instead, Avery met with the sheriff's office, a prosecutor, and the area's executive director for mental health, which led to criminal charges against the boy. Avery attended his first court appearance, and although the student's mother argued that he should be released, Avery had asked the prosecutor to make sure he got help. The judge honored her request, sending the boy to juvenile detention and ordering that he undergo a mental health evaluation. At another hearing months later, the child's mother argued once more that he be released. Avery didn't oppose that, but she insisted that he continue to receive support. And again, the judge listened, sending the boy to an alternative school and ordering that he and his mom receive additional counseling. A probation officer was also assigned to check on him every week. Avery didn't know whether he ever would have carried out his threats, but she had witnessed the damage Jesse Osborne caused in just twelve seconds—Jacob in a miniature casket, his classmates stricken with trauma, adults tortured by guilt, a community splintered—and she did know what her time and effort cost: nothing.

CHAPTER 14

"REMEMBER, YOU CAN'T SEE DADDY ANYMORE"

Father's Day and the One Who Wasn't There

Tyshaun had just finished a bowl of Cheerios in his third-grade class-room when a friend approached him with a question. "You going to the cookout today?" the boy asked, referring to the party Eagle Academy was hosting just before Father's Day on that Friday after-noon in June 2018. "Yeah, my grandfather coming," Tyshaun said, referring to Carl Potts, his grandmother's boyfriend. Most of the time, the boy referred to him simply as Carl, but on this day, he was his grandfather.

"Mr. John, when does the Father's Day start?" he asked the teach-er's aide a few minutes later.

"One p.m."

"So, what time is it now?"

"Nine fourteen."

Tyshaun shrugged. That sounded like a long time to wait. He had begun the morning more subdued than usual, acutely aware of what the day represented, but he looked forward to going to the cookout, comforted that at least he wouldn't get left out. It helped, too, that he and the rest of the class didn't have much to do that day, exactly one week before the third-grade graduation marking the end of their time at Eagle. So, instead of laboring through the math work sheets a substitute teacher had handed out, he and a few of his classmates had some fun. When one of them played Migos' "Walk It Talk It" on a cell phone, Tyshaun danced "the Floss," grinning, swinging his hands back and forth, shifting left and right. Then he tried a chicken dance he'd seen in the video game *Fortnite*, along with his own, custom version of Michael Jackson's "Thriller."

He had originally planned to perform at the day's event, just as he had for the Mother's Day brunch a month earlier. Curtis Murray, one of Tyshaun's favorite teachers, had selected a group of kids who seldom got picked for things, bribing them to practice with a pizza party. For the moms, the boys sang and danced to "My Girl," by the Temptations. They'd dressed in jeans, white button-down shirts, and red bow ties, and Tyshaun, whose grandmother attended while Donna worked, had beamed onstage. Curtis asked the same group to perform for the dads, and Tyshaun at first agreed, before changing his mind. In years past, Andrew attended the cookout with his son, posing for photos, munching on burgers and hot dogs. But now he was gone.

"I'm not dancing for no fathers," Tyshaun had said to Curtis, who told the boy he understood.

Now, as the performance approached, his classmates were about to go to the cafeteria to change into their outfits and rehearse. Tyshaun, who didn't want to be around for that, headed to the first-floor Pride Room to see Charnita Newburn, one of the behavioral specialists. It was her birthday. Just as he arrived, the sound of screaming drew near, and in came a boy with one of the teachers' aides. The kid, who'd erupted in another third-grade class after the man took a toy from him, walked straight to a desk and picked up a pencil, holding it in his tiny hand like a knife. Charnita, wearing a hat that resembled a baby-blue cake, walked the child over to her desk and wrapped both arms around him.

"Breathe, breathe, breathe," she repeated, until the screaming faded.

Tyshaun stood by the wall, staying out of the way. Unaffected by the outburst, the sort he saw nearly every day at Eagle, he glanced at a girl eating at a nearby table. "What is that? Pizza?" he whispered. When the crying boy had calmed down, Tyshaun walked back over to Charnita, who let both of them scroll through her phone so they could each pick out a Beyblade, a spinning top toy she'd agreed to buy them as graduation presents.

"They leaving me. They better come back and visit," she said, but Tyshaun's mind was on his gift.

"What days do y'all get paid?" he asked.

"None of your business," Charnita said, laughing.

Tyshaun gave her a hug and soon headed upstairs. "That's my third-best friend," he told me, speaking about the boy he'd just watched implode. I asked if that kid got upset a lot, and Tyshaun said that he did. "Me, too," he added. "I get mad."

Back up on his third-floor classroom, with his friends still at the practice, he began to wonder what time Potts would arrive. He and Potts, a subdued man who'd lived with the boy's grandmother for years, weren't especially close, but they still considered each other family. He walked Tyshaun home from school when no one else could, and in years prior, he came along for the Grandparents' Day event at Eagle. Potts, forty-eight, could never fill the void Andrew had left behind, but on days like this, he was asked to play a more significant role in Tyshaun's life than he'd ever expected to. Now the boy went to the back of the room, taking out his cell phone, the one with a lock-screen image of himself in his father's arms. He called his mother.

"Ma—Mom. Is Grandfather coming?" he asked, pausing to listen.

"What time?"

"Oh."

Soon, 1 p.m. arrived, and the show began, but still, Potts wasn't there. Tyshaun phoned his mom again. She didn't know what to tell him, so he called his grandmother, who didn't pick up. He returned to a table where the kids left in the room were still playing with their Beyblades.

"My grandfather, I don't know where he is. I don't think he came," Tyshaun said, now after 1:30, but nobody paid attention to him. The boys, all in their white shirts, burst through the door, smiling, short of breath.

"Y'all already danced?" he asked.

"Tyshaun, you should have come," one of them said. He didn't respond. They talked about the dance battle they'd had with the girls, the hot dogs they were going to eat when they went back down to see their dads.

"My grandfather down there," Tyshaun said, but he knew that wasn't true. He went to the back of the room, pulling out his phone again. He tried his grandmother another time. Nothing. He called once more.

"She's not answering. Pick up, pick up," he said, but she didn't.

"Ugh," he groaned, at 1:55. "I want to go with my grandfather."

He sat back down, and a boy he knew from another class walked in, bumping him at his desk. Tyshaun, whose patience had disappeared, realized the kid had done it on purpose. His neck stiffened, fists clenched.

"Boy, what is you doing?" he asked, and when the child darted back into the hallway, Tyshaun chased after him.

"Hey!" he shouted, catching the kid and shoving him into a wall.

Isaiah "Ike" Minder, the security guard, quickly pulled them apart, placing his massive arms on Tyshaun's shoulders as the other kid took off down the hallway. "Calm down. Calm down," Ike pleaded, and when Tyshaun pulled away, trying to go back into his classroom, the guard stopped him, telling him to walk to the opposite end of the hall. "Calm down a little before you go in there, all right?"

"C'mere, Zaire. C'mere," Ike shouted at the other kid, assuring him that it was safe to return. "You good. You good. You all right."

At his end of the hallway, Tyshaun kicked a trash can. "It's a misunderstanding," Ike said, motioning for him to come back. "Man, come here. Come here, Ty!" he repeated, raising his voice, so Tyshaun came. "It's a misunderstanding."

Ike told them they needed to make up, but Tyshaun pulled away. "Shake hands, man. Come on, Ty. Ty. *Ty*. Come on." Tyshaun finally extended a fist, and he and the other child bumped knuckles. "All right, that's good. There you go. Good job. Baby steps. Baby steps," Ike said, allowing Tyshaun, still furious, to return to his classroom. Inside, a boy stepped in front of him, and Tyshaun extended an arm into his chest, pushing him against a wall. The boy looked confused, unsure whether Tyshaun was being serious.

"What is you doing?" the boy asked. He let him go.

"Kill you," Tyshaun muttered as he walked away.

At 2:10, his grandmother, Jessica Jackson, called. The family matriarch worked long hours as a caretaker for the elderly to support her family, but nothing mattered more to Jessica than her grandkids. Sensing Tyshaun's rising frustration, she promised that Potts would be there soon. After he hung up, the substitute announced it was time for recess, and all the children not attending the Father's Day cookout began to get ready.

"I'm not going outside. My grandfather's coming," Tyshaun said, asking if he could go downstairs to look for him. The substitute agreed, and when he reached the second floor, Tyshaun called his grandmother again.

"Do you know where Carl at?" he asked, and she told him that Potts was there, somewhere, and that he'd find Tyshaun soon.

"But we about to go outside," he said, at 2:29, voice quavering, eyes glistening. She assured him again, and Tyshaun hung up. He sighed, then headed back to his classroom, where everyone had lined up to go. Tyshaun joined them and marched down the stairs. At the door that led outside, he lingered, staring back to look down the busy hallway, where children and their fathers were walking, talking, laughing, holding hands. He turned around and stepped outside, heading to the playground with the rest of the class.

A few minutes later, Potts appeared at the top of the hill, calling down to him. Tyshaun trudged up, and Potts, a thin, bespectacled man with a shaved head and graying goatee, extended his hand. Tyshaun slapped it but didn't say anything. When they reached the cafeteria, Potts asked how he'd been. Tyshaun said he was fine.

"You want to get a picture?" Potts asked. Tyshaun shrugged. They stood in front of a black sign with a red-and-yellow *Superman S* above the word DAD. A woman from the school pointed a camera. Potts put his arm around Tyshaun and smiled. Tyshaun kept both hands by his sides. He stared ahead. He didn't smile.

Potts headed for the back of the line while Tyshaun took a seat at a table covered in gingham paper plates and black-and-white flyers. "A sturdy, steady hand to hold to in times of strife and stress. A true friend we can turn to when times are good or bad. One of our greatest gifts and blessings," they read. "The man that we call Dad." Tyshaun looked around the cafeteria, its walls lined with signs decorated for the occasion. A DAD IS, read one, surrounded by adjectives: AWESOME. HARDWORKING. SUPER. STRONG. LOVING. Near the entrance, Tyshaun noticed a little girl adjusting the collar on her denim jacket before she and her father posed for a photo. Each of them flashed "I love you" hand signs and grinned. Tyshaun looked down at his phone, pulling up on the screen a YouTube video of a first-person shooter game. Behind him, near the stage, a man picked up a microphone.

"It's good to see a bunch of fathers here today supporting their kids," he said, explaining that his own son had started at Eagle in pre-kindergarten and was now in third grade, about to graduate.

"Right now we in a crisis, and all of the violence . . . is up because we have a lack of fathers, but to come in this space and see all the fathers does a lot for me. So, it's encouraging, in today's time. To say anything to encourage you all, I'll say that, you know, keep motivating other brothers, because a lot of us have friends and family who's not stepping up like we step up. So, if we encourage them and hold them accountable, we can help control some of this violence that's going on in the community, because it stems from not having fathers with their kids," he said, and Tyshaun stopped listening. The boy had heard this speech many times before, so, instead, he returned to the violent video game playing on his cell phone.

ON ONE EVENING each summer, dozens of children and teens, most of them black, gather before sunset on the banks of a lake in Maryland just outside Washington, all holding tiny wooden boats. Some are painted with bright colors or elaborate designs. A few carry drawings and dates, and many include names. Each one represents a life cut short. The exercise, part of a grief camp for local kids hosted by the Wendt Center for Loss and Healing, is meant to provide catharsis, a way to memorialize loved ones who have died, often from gun violence. In groups of five or six, the kids step forward and raise the boats above their heads. As they approach the water to release their creations, a drummer pauses and Stephanie Handel, who runs the camp, reads off the child's name and the person they lost.

"I can't tell you how many fathers we remember and honor. In an entire group, I can say, 'John remembers his father, Sean remembers his father, Destiny remembers her father,'" said Handel, a grief and trauma psychotherapist. "Father, father, father, father."

The children those fathers leave behind are, like Tyshaun, among the unseen victims of gun violence in Washington, DC, and in other cities all over the country. That's especially true in Southeast, a thirteen-square-mile triangle where, in 2017 and 2018, bullets took the lives of no fewer than 109 people—stripping at least 119 children of a parent.

"Clinically, I wonder about levels of early anxiety and depression, attachment disruption issues and feelings of hopelessness, particularly in boys, who are experiencing the death of a generation of men," said Handel, who has treated traumatized children in the city for more than two decades. "How can they believe that there will be a place for them within their own community when so many men have died?"

Complicating the grieving process for kids and young adults in violent neighborhoods is the potential that they, too, may be in danger, a reality detailed by a University of Maryland researcher during interviews with forty male teens and young adults in Baltimore, home to one of the country's highest homicide rates. "Young men's residential location within unsafe neighborhoods might constrain their abilities to process traumatic loss and contribute to unresolved grief," the study reported, noting that "existing research has failed to capture the frequency at which the lives of Blacks are buffeted by the traumatic loss of homicide. The lived experiences of Black males as homicide survivors have been almost entirely overlooked."

Researchers have just begun to understand the full effects of losing a parent to violence at a young age, but studies have already shown that such episodes place children at an increased risk of physical illness as well as homelessness, PTSD, depression, anxiety, and instability in their adult relationships. A study at the University of Texas found that black Americans are considerably more likely to experience the death of a parent or sibling at a young age, creating a "unique source of adversity . . . that contributes to lifelong racial inequality."

Tyshaun and his brother Zah'Kyi were both eight at the time of their father's death, and each child's mom expected from the start that they would struggle to deal with the loss, but even the boys' younger sibling, two-year-old AJ, dealt with profound anguish after Andrew's killing. At preschool, the boy lashed out at classmates when they crossed him, screaming, pushing, throwing. "He's hurting," a school counselor told his mother, Benica McManus, who, in time, saw his behavior change at home, too. Small things—being told to go to bed or denied a honey bun—would set him off in ways she'd never seen before. Her mother died of cancer the same year Andrew was shot, and afterward, Benica attended one of her son's therapy sessions. She watched AJ, then three, play with action figures in the sand, until he started to bury them in it. "They died," he announced. "This is their funeral."

Even as the months passed, the memories of his father remained clear to him. AJ always asked for tilapia, because that was Andrew's favorite. When he and his mom walked outside and heard music boom from a passing car, he'd stare, telling her that's what his dad used to do. For months, he couldn't accept the immutability of the loss, asking his mother during a birthday party whether his daddy was going to come. "Remember, you can't see daddy anymore," Benica said, but she assured her son that his father would watch over him. That wasn't enough for AJ, who saw classmates with two parents, who saw kids on the fields tossing a ball with their fathers. "Can you get me a new daddy?" AJ asked her, because he, too, wanted someone to toss a ball with him.

Benica missed Andrew's presence during so many moments, from small ones, like when she was trying to guide her son through the complexities of potty training, to big ones, like when she started imagining what she would tell AJ about how to deal with the police as he got older. She could show him how to work hard in school and in life, which is why Benica brought him to the graduation ceremony for her master's program—so he could see one of his parents achieve something great—but she couldn't show him how to stay safe on the streets of DC, how to fight if he needed to stand up for himself.

When AJ asked for the first time how his dad had died, Benica was so caught off guard that she lied, saying that Andrew had been sick. She couldn't stomach telling her son the truth, not yet, but she knew she would have to eventually, and when she did, Benica wanted him to process it the right way. She'd already discarded AJ's water pistols and allowed him to play only with Nerf toys that fired discs instead of the darts or pellets that resembled bullets. "I don't want him to be around here thinking that guns should be glorified," Benica said. She had known for years what that sort of thinking led to. Three weeks after his birth, in the summer of 2014, her cousin was shot to death because of another inconsequential neighborhood quarrel. At the vigil, Benica, who was holding her infant, listened to the cousin's mother say that she had regrets, that she wished she'd been firmer with her son. "This is not your future," Benica whispered to AJ. "You're not going to be a statistic." That scene, and those words, haunted her in the months after Andrew's killing. "He's still a statistic," she told me, because, like hundreds of other black children in their community, AJ was one more whose father's life had been lost to the epidemic of gun violence.

STANDING BENEATH A basketball hoop inside Eagle's gymnasium, Tyshaun zipped up the front of his white gown and squeezed his head into the matching graduate's cap. He draped a blue sash behind his neck and over both shoulders, noticing the gold letters inscribed on each side. "'Moving Up,'" he read, prompting a wiggle and an abbreviated version of the *Jeffersons* theme song. "Moving on up," he sang.

It was graduation day for the third-graders at Eagle, and about seventy-five of them were spread out across the teal-colored floor, quickly growing bored. Tyshaun and a classmate found a pair of foam pool noodles in the corner of the room and started whacking each other with them before their teacher, Matt Wong, told the boys to stop. Just then, Andrew's former girlfriend, Aisha, arrived at the gym door, holding a half-dozen balloons. She and Donna had become close after the funeral, and because Aisha suspected this might be a tough day for the family, she'd come to support Tyshaun and his mother. He walked over to say hello and see the balloons before noticing that Aisha had brought a shirt featuring a photo of the boy with his dad. CONGRATULATIONS, TYSHAUN, it read. ILY AND I'M PROUD OF YOU!

Reminders of Tyshaun's father, and his absence, were always around, and the boy both embraced and resented that—sometimes, it seemed, all at once. In class, his friends would notice the images of his father on his phone and school iPad, but when they asked who the man was, he wouldn't discuss it. During Spirit Week, when Matt's students were assigned the color black, Tyshaun wore the shirt with REST IN PEACE DADDY on the back, despite his mother's prodding to try something else. Even on those days when he refused to say a word about his dad, he daydreamed about him, sometimes googling random images in class and staring at them before quickly closing the pages so no one sitting nearby would notice. One morning, not long before graduation, Matt used superheroes' qualities to explain to his students how a Venn diagram worked. When he asked about the characters' weaknesses, Tyshaun suggested that one of Batman's was that he didn't miss his father, who, in the comic book story, had died in a shooting.

By the end of third grade, Tyshaun had begun to learn more about his dad, including those unflattering details his mom had tried to keep from him. None of them could sway his devotion. About the allegation that Andrew was in a gang: "My dad wasn't involved in gangs. He just hang with his friends. Because that's the only friends he, like, had. But he wasn't in the gang. He was just hanging around them a lot." And about the gun Andrew had in his car when he was shot: "It was only for self-defense."

Now, in the gym, with all the third-graders organized, the time came for them to head toward the cafeteria, where dozens of their family members awaited. Lining the hallways on the way there were teachers and staff who had known Tyshaun since before he could read. When they saw him, their faces betrayed some blend of pride and anxiety. They knew that, for Tyshaun, Eagle Academy would always be synonymous with his father's death, but because of it, the school had also provided a haven, a place where people under-stood what drove his worst impulses. They wondered, and worried, whether he would find that in the next school.

"What's up, baby boy?" asked Ike, the security guard who had dealt with more of Tyshaun's crises than anyone. "Heyyyy, my man made it," said another staffer, who gave him a hug. "Tyshaun, make sure you do a good job in there. No playing around," said Charnita, the woman from the Pride Room, and she fixed his cap and cupped his cheek in her hand. "Tyshaun, I'm proud of you, baby," another woman told him. And just before he walked into the cafeteria, Matt gave him a final once-over, adjusting the boy's blue sash so it hung evenly off each shoulder.

"Ready, big guy?" his teacher asked him.

"Uh-huh," Tyshaun answered.

That week, Matt had decided to award Tyshaun with a certificate naming him the class's "Most Improved Student." Matt had given it to him, to some degree, as encouragement, but the teacher also be-lieved the boy had earned it. Matt, who'd grown up in middle-class Maryland and worked as a full-time teacher for just two years, at times felt overwhelmed at Eagle, where the depth of students' chal-lenges could frazzle even the most seasoned educator. With Tyshaun, though, he had developed a sincere bond and seen the boy make real progress, with both his grades and his attitude. The latter was due in part to his sessions with Oron Gan, the psychologist assigned to the school. Gan, Tyshaun said, let him play with toys or relax on a bean-bag or, once, frame a picture of his dad with a set of red-and-yellow Popsicle sticks, whatever the boy needed to decompress. When Gan asked how he was feeling, Tyshaun did his best to articulate it, at least some of the time. The doctor gave him tips on how to manage his frustration, telling him to count to ten or to take deep breaths through his nose and release them from his mouth.

Once, in Matt's class, Tyshaun and a classmate were working together to build a block tower when someone else walked by and accidentally knocked it over. Feeling his anger build, Tyshaun approached his teacher. "Mr. Wong, I need to walk," he said, and the man told him to do whatever he needed to do to calm down. Tyshaun stepped outside for a few minutes and when he returned, the boy asked if he could wear headphones and listen to soothing Chinese meditation music that Matt had introduced to the kids. Of course, Matt told him. The teacher would later describe the episode as "profound."

Now, with his cap on straight and his sash aligned, Tyshaun marched with his classmates into the cafeteria, nearly as packed that day as it had been more than two years earlier, when, after his dad and five others were all shot near the school, hundreds of people showed up for a community meeting to demand change that never happened. Following applause for the graduates, Tyshaun took a seat on the last of three rows all facing the crowd. He watched other students win accolades for their achievements and listened to hopeful speeches about all that he and the other kids could accomplish. He yawned. He closed his eyes. When it was over, he met his family in the bustling hallway, shedding his cap and gown. He flipped through his graduation cards and counted up the cash, $90, then fanned it out and flashed it for a photo. He put his arms up so his mom could slide on the shirt with the photo of his dad. He opened his class folder again and lingered on the certificate honoring his improvement. The next year, he was scheduled to attend fourth grade at another charter school just a few blocks away, but everyone, including Tyshaun, knew it wouldn't be the same as Eagle. Just before he left for the last time, he spotted his teacher passing by.

"Mr. Wong, let's take a picture," Tyshaun said, and when the man didn't come over right away, the boy raised his voice. "Mr. Wong!"

"I'm coming," Matt responded. He put his arm around Tyshaun, now holding the balloons, as the boy leaned into his teacher and the two of them smiled for the camera. Afterward, they shook hands, and Tyshaun headed to the lobby and out the front door, turning toward the road. He paused on the sidewalk and released his grip, sending the balloons up toward a pristine summer sky. He hoped they would reach his dad. "They made it, Ty," Aisha assured him, and as his time at Eagle ended, he once more passed the spot where his father had been shot five times, where he'd looked out from the school lobby and seen the red and blue lights flash.

CHAPTER 15

"I CANNOT PROMISE YOU THAT IT WILL BE EASY"

Why Some Kids Make It When Others Don't

The attorney first read about Tyshaun McPhatter while sitting at her desk inside the world's most famous courthouse. An avid reader with a passion for social justice, Tiffany Wright, then serving as a clerk for Supreme Court justice Sonia Sotomayor, had heard lots of stories about kids in difficult situations, but something about the piece I'd written on Tyshaun resonated with her. Soon after she finished it, Tiffany sent me an email.

"I write in regard to your article regarding Tyshaun McPhatter and to inquire whether you would be willing to pass along a letter on my behalf," her note explained. "Your article moved me to write to Tyshaun because of similarities in our childhood experiences."

Even to the people who had never heard about those childhood experiences—who didn't know she was living proof that any kid, regardless of the hardship they'd experienced, could overcome it—what she had achieved sounded remarkable. Tiffany, who is black, had grown up in Southeast DC amid the crack epidemic of the 1990s, attending public schools before going to the University of Maryland. Years later, as she neared age thirty, Tiffany gained admittance to

Georgetown Law but still kept her job as a paralegal in Baltimore, awaking each weekday at dawn, going to work, rushing home to eat lunch with her young son, leaving the office at 5 p.m., attending classes, returning home to study past midnight. A lifetime of insomnia suddenly became an asset, allowing Tiffany to function as a wife, a mother, a paralegal, and a law student all at once. And at Georgetown, she excelled, earning all As her first semester.

"One of the most brilliant people I know," said Edward Williams, a fellow graduate.

In her second year, she participated on the school's moot court team and served as an editor on its prestigious *Law Journal*, the only African American, male or female, to do both at the same time those semesters. She graduated in the top 5 percent of her class and, a year later, began a clerkship for David S. Tatel, a renowned judge on the U.S. Court of Appeals for the DC Circuit.

"She was magical," Tatel told me. "Just extraordinary."

So extraordinary, in fact, that he insisted she apply to become a clerk on the Supreme Court, something she'd hesitated even to consider before he brought it up. More than thirty thousand law school students graduate annually, and the Supreme Court's nine members offer just thirty-six clerkships a year. Being selected, as Tiffany's husband described it, would equate to getting drafted into the NBA. Those chosen enter one of the most exclusive fraternities in the legal world, routinely receiving signing bonuses in excess of $300,000 from their first post-court law firms.

Tiffany had plenty of reasons to doubt she belonged. She was thirty-three then, far older than most of her competitors, and she hadn't gone to an Ivy League school like the vast majority of the lawyers whom the justices tended to choose. She was also a black woman from one of DC's poorest neighborhoods who had never traveled outside the country, and she was trying to join a group that, in decades past, had been dominated by affluent, worldly white men. In a sense, though, Tiffany also believed she'd spent her entire life preparing for that stage. So much terror and upheaval, misery and loss—maybe it all had led to this.

On a spring morning in 2015, before meeting Justice Sotomayor for the most important interview of her career, Tiffany took a detour, returning to the place where her journey had begun. Driving into the city from her home in Maryland, she turned up Trinidad Avenue and slowed as a brown brick row house came into view. She glanced out her passenger-side window and thought back to the night that had shaped every aspect of the person she'd become. *I hope I made you proud*, she silently told her dad, because it was there—beyond the chain-link fence, up the gray steps—that, when Tiffany was seven, her father had answered the front door and been shot to death.

"HE'S GONE TO heaven," Tiffany's mother told her in 1989, and when the little girl on the bed understood that meant her dad was dead, she curled into a ball and sobbed. Tiffany had come to the nation's capital as a toddler, after her parents' divorce, and lived with family in an aging home across the street from a housing project in Southeast, immersing her in a community plagued by gun violence. She heard the pops of discharged rounds nearly every day in her neighborhood, and on several occasions, she saw men inside her home brandishing pistols, demanding unpaid drug debts from her mother or aunts, all of whom had at some point struggled with addiction. Two of her uncles had also stayed there before one, who sold drugs, went to prison for sexual assault and the other served time for armed robbery.

Amid that turmoil, her father, Thomas W. Moore, a stout Army veteran who worked as a corrections officer, had always given her an unwavering sense of security, even when they'd been apart. In her clearest memory of him, she wore a baby-blue shirt that matched the bows in her braided hair, and before her stood a white pony she was too scared to ride. Moore snatched up his daughter and plopped her atop the saddle. Suddenly unafraid, she grinned for a photo until her plump cheeks could stretch no farther. Months later, at the funeral, she stared into his open casket and, at first, thought her dad had just fallen asleep. Then she touched him and felt the chill across his skin. The girl had never faced dread like she did on that winter day: *If I stay here, I'm going to die.*

Tiffany struggled to sleep after that, often lying awake in bed until the sun came up, because it was at night when her father had been shot. At school, she joined a poetry club just to avoid going out on a playground that she worried would leave her too exposed. She never saw a therapist as a kid, and her family seldom spoke of her father, which infuriated Tiffany. To her, it was as if no one cared, a feeling exacerbated by the police's inability to catch the person who shot him. Tiffany's mother didn't even initially tell her daughter's teachers what had happened, further isolating the girl in her sorrow. Normally timid and well behaved, Tiffany felt so much anger, and desperation for someone to acknowledge that anger, that she began to explode at school, screaming at staff and throwing chairs in class. "I didn't get what I wanted," Tiffany said, because she made such good grades that her teachers overlooked the outbursts.

Soon after Moore's death, her mom and stepfather had a baby, and for the first few months of her sibling's life, Tiffany was sent to live with relatives, including an aunt still hooked on crack. Tiffany's grandmother, the family matriarch, felt so unsafe in the home that she smoked her Newports and drank her Miller Lites in her bedroom, behind a closed door secured with a padlock. The girl, who didn't have her own room, saw used hypodermic needles and blackened spoons in the house and, outside it, men trying to exchange money for sex. Neighborhood kids teased her because, they said, her aunt was a prostitute. Once, the woman brought Tiffany with her to a drug house when she needed a fix. Another time, Tiffany awoke on the sofa bed to find that someone had stolen her clothing. "Everything had been sold except my underwear," said Tiffany, who realized that even her most beloved possession in the world, a video-tape of *The Little Mermaid*, was gone. Another aunt, a heroin addict who would die of AIDS years later, insisted one day that Tiffany look at the sores and track marks on her arms. "You don't have to do this," she told the girl.

A group of DC police officers later gave a presentation at her school showing graphic images of dead bodies in an effort to scare the kids from dealing drugs or joining gangs. Afterward, the students were marched by an open casket, the first Tiffany had seen in person since her father's funeral. Inside, it held a mirror.

That incident only reinforced the notion that had gripped her from the day she saw her father's body—that her lone chance at survival was escape. After his death, she learned that the pension and life insurance money he'd left her was being overseen by someone called an attorney. Tiffany expected that person, Leonard McCants, to be white, but when she met him in a fancy Silver Spring, Maryland, law office, he was black, like her, and in a crisp suit and tie. "What do I have to do to be like you?" she asked him. Read a lot, McCants told her, and become a good writer.

That single bit of encouragement forever changed the way she thought about her future. If he could make it, Tiffany thought, so could she. When the girl confided in a teacher that she wanted to be an attorney, the woman told her to forget that idea, suggesting she consider cosmetology school instead. Tiffany didn't listen. The little girl found a library and asked for all the "hard books," and she came back with *Pride and Prejudice*, *The Great Gatsby*, *For Whom the Bell Tolls*, and dozens of others. Over and over, she copied the sentences onto sheets of paper, and at night, during all those hours when her mind wouldn't let her sleep, Tiffany read.

Before ninth grade, she heard about the city's School Without Walls, a public magnet that offered one of the best educations in the region. When her mother and new stepfather neglected to write an essay required for the application, Tiffany did it herself and put their names on it. She got in. That led her in 1999 to the University of Maryland, where she met a fellow freshman named Michael who had wide shoulders and an affinity for smart women. During one of their first conversations, he recalled years later, Tiffany told him she wanted to become an attorney, run her own law firm, and make $90,000 a year.

BY THE END of her sophomore year, none of that looked attainable. She had arrived at college with no idea how to use a computer or the internet, and her grades suffered because of it. She made Bs and Cs, then an F in a statistics class. "It was just devastating," she said. The money her dad left had run out, leaving her with nothing to pay for school. By then, her mother and stepfather had moved to Richmond, Virginia, where he pastored a church. She lived with them that summer and took a job at a cell phone store, and when she got her first paycheck, for $557, Tiffany stared at it. That seemed like a lot to her, and for a moment, she considered quitting college. Then she recalled, again, what her aunt, the heroin addict, had said to her. She thought about her dad.

"All my life I've said I wanted to do this," Tiffany told herself, so she took out a $20,000 loan and headed back to school, making almost all As during her last two years and earning a dual degree in criminology and psychology. She'd finished, but not in the way she'd once expected to. With her middling GPA, law school seemed beyond reach. She looked for a job, but couldn't find one for months, growing so desperate that she ordered a Mavis Beacon Teaches Typing computer program, convinced she would become a secretary who needed to produce eighty words a minute. In her first job, she worked at a law firm, stuffing envelopes and organizing files. In her second, she worked at the U.S. Parole Commission, reluctantly acknowledging during the interview process that her two uncles were on parole. She took a position making recommendations about what to do with convicts who violated the terms of their release.

She'd accepted that this would be her life, until the day after Thanksgiving in 2006, when, seven months pregnant, Tiffany began to suffer severe back pain. As she lay in a hospital bed talking on the phone with her mom, the right side of her body went numb. She dropped the phone. A CT scan showed that four blood clots had traveled from her leg to her lung, triggering a heart attack. "We don't know how you're still alive," a doctor told her. A month after that, she underwent a C-section only to learn that her son was ill. His pancreas had wrapped around his intestines, leaving him hospitalized for weeks.

Much like with her father's death, the agony surrounding her son's birth forced Tiffany to rethink her future. Trying to have another child would likely prove too risky, she thought, but maybe she could do something more with her career. She joined the U.S. Attorney's Office in Baltimore as a paralegal, and the experience immediately renewed her passion. Tiffany helped on major drug and gang cases, showing such a knack for the work that prosecutors pushed her to reconsider pursuing a law degree.

She had never quelled the trauma of her youth, even after her mother remarried a good man, even after she found Michael and they spent years together in therapy. The fear still lingered. As a little girl, Tiffany so hated where her family lived that she collected real estate listings and gave them to her mom, with homes in nicer neighborhoods circled in pen. As an adult, she still slept with a serrated knife under her mattress.

Tiffany couldn't undo the damage from her past, but she also knew that she didn't have to let it dictate her future. Withstanding those experiences infused her with a certainty that whatever she faced next wouldn't compare to what she had already conquered.

"Early in my childhood, I realized that education would be the key to my escape," she wrote in the personal statement that helped her get into Georgetown Law. In the summer before she started, as Tiffany prepared to take on a quarter of a million dollars in debt to pay for her classes, she posted a collage on Facebook called her "2009 Visions & Inspiration": a smiling photo with her husband and son, who was two; a Bible verse from Philippians that encouraged confidence; a picture of Jane Bolin, the first black woman in America to become a judge; an image inside the Supreme Court, with its sixteen columns and nine leather chairs.

Years later, Tatel, the esteemed judge, sensed from the beginning of Tiffany's time on his staff that she could make it to the nation's highest court. "The first piece of work I saw from Tiffany Wright was as good as the best work I get from the best law clerks," Tatel told me. Her life experience provided Tiffany, who stands at just five feet tall, with a rare gift to argue with both ferocity and grace, said clerks who worked with her. Tatel recognized it, too, once assigning her to review a police case that, at first, he thought had no merit. She delivered her analysis with a delicate touch a few days later.

"Judge," he recalled her saying, "I think I have a different view of this case than you do."

"She was right," he said.

On April 8, 2015, twenty-six years after her father's killing, she awoke at 4:30 in the morning to a phone alarm labeled in bright white letters: *SCOTUS DAY!* She put on makeup and fixed her hair, filled a thermos with cold-brew coffee, and prepped her navy-blue suit. Tiffany prayed, too, but for what God wanted instead of what she wanted, because the latter still felt beyond possibility. It had been three months since she'd applied to serve as a clerk for Justice Sotomayor and two weeks since Tiffany had gotten the call: "The justice would like to have you come in and interview."

"Seriously?" Tiffany said, succumbing to tears she almost never shed.

She barely slept in those two weeks after the call, reading seventy court opinions, reviewing at least twenty of Sotomayor's written decisions, and scouring YouTube for interviews that the court's first Latina had given. Tiffany outlined cases that were especially meaningful to her (about the Sixth Amendment, equal protection, voting rights) and filled forty-one pages of notes. "It doesn't matter where you come from, what you look like, or what challenges life throws your way," she watched President Barack Obama say in a video from the day he announced Sotomayor's nomination. Her palms were slick with sweat when she arrived at court. She could feel her pulse beating in her fingertips.

"The justice is here," someone told her. Tiffany stood and walked down a hallway, where a door in front of her opened. There was Sotomayor, smiling, her hand extended.

"Oh, Tiffany," the justice said, "it's so great to meet you."

Eighteen months later, on October 4, 2016, in a room with red velvet drapes and a forty-four-foot-high coffered ceiling, Tiffany took a seat in a wooden chair as a Supreme Court clerk. Bound by confidentiality, she could never speak of the work she'd do for Sotomayor during a year in which the justices would take up cases involving trademarks and free speech, racial gerrymandering, and President Trump's travel ban. But on her first day in the nation's most important courtroom, this is what Tiffany could say: she was the only clerk who was a mother, the only one who was black, the only one who had grown up in Southeast, the only one who had lost a father to gun violence.

"CHILDREN ARE RESILIENT," people say because they've heard other people say it, most often when kids face hard times. After years of reporting on those hard times, it's a saying I came to despise. It ignores the pain individual children carry, even if they seem okay, and it assumes that kids are monolithic, all of them sharing some innate quality that allows them to weather adversity. It's dismissive and based not in fact, but on a wishful belief among many adults that a child who doesn't explicitly express suffering must not be suffering. A less tidy but more accurate way to put it: children *can* be remarkably resilient in the face of difficulty, as Tiffany was, but in almost every case, including hers, they can't develop that resilience without help.

In 2019, the *Clinical Child and Family Psychology Review* published the most comprehensive analysis of resilience in kids exposed to violence ever undertaken. After scrutinizing 118 studies that involved more than 100,000 participants, the authors found conclusive evidence showing that specific influences played essential roles in children's ability to overcome hardship.

"Much of the research on resilience has focused on identifying protective factors within individuals, and although there are qualities (like self-regulation) that are important, this review makes it clear that supportive relationships with caregivers, teachers and peers are the most consistent predictors of resilience in children exposed to violence," the authors told me. "If we want to protect children from the traumatic effects of violence, we need to support their families and schools."

The most important internal quality they noted in children—self-regulation, or the ability "to adaptively manage their emotions and behavior to achieve a desired goal"—also seldom develops without external influences. Some kids learn to control their feelings through parents, mentors, and therapists, while others find direction through ambitions that they desperately want to achieve.

The factors that the authors found made the biggest difference were consistent regardless of the type of violence children encountered, which means that what a kid needs while facing the constant threat of gunfire in a big city may be the same as what one needs after surviving a school shooting in a rural town. William Haith, who was robbed at gunpoint four times while growing up in Southeast, found resilience through respect for his mother, whom he worked hard not to disappoint, and through the love of football, a skill nurtured by devoted coaches that gave him self-worth. Those might seem like simple motivations, but they were what stood between Haith and the temptation to get a gun for self-defense, a choice that might have led him to a jail cell or a grave rather than two master's degrees and the position of principal at Anacostia High, in his hometown. Missy Jenkins Smith, left paralyzed from the waist down at age fifteen after a teenage gunman opened fire in 1997 at her Kentucky high school, also found the strength to recover—from the people who loved her and, eventually, through a clear vision of what she was meant to do with her life. During her five months at a hospital going through rehab, hundreds of letters and gifts from people across the country buoyed her. When Jenkins Smith was released, she returned to a home that had been redesigned to suit her wheelchair, thanks to money the community raised. Her friends continued to include her, too; if the girl's chair couldn't go somewhere, they carried her. She never saw a counselor one-on-one, but at age seventeen, she shared her story with a middle school, and she's kept sharing it for more than two decades.

"My therapy was speaking," she said. "I realized how healing it was."

For children who don't discover such productive outlets, actual therapy can prove critical. Frank DeAngelis, the principal at Columbine High during the 1999 massacre, saw the influence it had on the lives of his students. He began seeing a counselor right away and talked openly about the help he needed, hoping to destigmatize it for the teens. Some of them still refused, insisting they were fine, but for many of them, DeAngelis said, the horror didn't relent. In time, a number of survivors turned to drugs and alcohol, and at least two of them took their own lives. The effects of trauma often lay dormant for years, which, to DeAngelis, underlines the need for parents to be persistent and never to assume that their children are okay just because they say so. Samantha Haviland's mother and father supported her in every way they could after one of her best friends at Columbine was killed, but for years, survivor's guilt prevented her from meeting with a counselor. When she finally sought therapy, it helped tremendously, as did turning her experience into something positive. She earned a doctorate, became the director of counseling for Denver's public school system, and traveled with Crime Stoppers, promoting anti-violence campaigns at schools nationwide.

Finding purpose, along with support from caring adults, has helped sustain thousands of children who've endured violence, including survivors of war and genocide. Two decades ago, Roberta R. Greene, then a professor at the Indiana University School of Social Work, interviewed thirteen Holocaust survivors and reviewed more than three dozen studies that explored their lives. A psychologist who had written extensively about child survivors, Greene found, had "concluded that practitioners needed to rethink the idea that adversity inevitably leads to negative outcomes. She argued that, contrary to popular notions, we learn powerfully from these lives that lifelong emotional disability does not automatically follow early trauma . . . [Rather,] what happens later matters enormously."

What mattered most to children who'd lived through the Holocaust, Greene learned, was not so different from what mattered to kids who'd experienced mass shootings on their campuses or the gunning down of a parent. Faith and family, supportive peers and teachers, all had an impact, as did, time and again, what the children made of their experiences.

Eva, one of the girls Greene interviewed, escaped Germany as part of the Kindertransport program, a rescue effort that brought thousands of Jewish children to Great Britain in the late 1930s and early 1940s. To cope, Greene wrote, Eva found purpose in helping others. "Each girl was given a room and food to eat," Eva told Greene. "The English brought us over, and the rest was up to us. We had to work to support ourselves. I wanted to work at the Bristol Aircraft Factory because they were making arms to fight Germany. I kept going back to the foreman of the company until he gave me the job. All the other girls with me in the rooming house worked and grew up to be productive."

Eva later gave talks to children, telling Greene that kids in urban communities were "living their own personal Holocaust. It is a shame because all children need nurturing. When I speak to children at inner-city schools, I tell them about the Holocaust. I tell them they must give up being a victim. They must find out what they want to do and be, and do it."

TIFFANY WRIGHT, IT must be said, is an extraordinary person: courageous, tenacious, brilliant. In truth, most people, regardless of their circumstances, couldn't replicate the path she forged, but that doesn't mean her story isn't instructive, because, as she told me, her success was not inevitable. No moment after her father's death proved more significant than the one with Leonard McCants, the black attorney who told her that, to be like him, she needed to read a lot and learn to write well. Even the drive to his office through Northwest DC and the Maryland suburbs changed her worldview because, as a second-grader, she had come to believe that all people with her skin color lived in poverty. McCants didn't serve as a mentor in her life, or even a consistent figure, but those few words of inspiration transformed what she considered possible. It mattered, too, that unlike so many other children in her community, then and now, she had access to the resources she needed most: in her case, books from a library.

Other episodes beyond Tiffany's control also altered her trajectory in substantive ways. A different sort of reassurance, from the drug-addicted aunt who told Tiffany that she wouldn't have to live that life, stuck with her, and she didn't underestimate her mother's decision to get clean and remarry a man who viewed Tiffany as his own daughter. She never received the direction from her mom and stepdad that she craved, but they did provide her with a stable home life as a teenager, and she knew that they loved her.

Tiffany doubted that she could have made it to Georgetown had she not attended the School Without Walls, a place where she met kids of different races, who spoke other languages, who shared new ideas. It was in a classroom there that she first analyzed Toni Morrison's revelatory novel *Beloved*, about one woman's torturous experience as a slave. *The pain was so much greater than mine*, she recalled thinking, and that helped the girl keep fighting. The therapy Tiffany finally received as an adult also transformed her. She might have become a clerk on the Supreme Court anyway, Tiffany thought, but marriage and motherhood and happiness of any kind would have been unimaginable without it.

"I was just walking around with all of this grief and anger and everything and had never even spoken about it. . . . It also just showed me how dysfunctional I was as a result of everything. I felt like I was an adult, but I was just not a functioning human being," she said. "I couldn't have productive conversations. I couldn't deal with disappointment, anger, or any negativity in a way that was helpful or useful."

More than a decade of sessions with a counselor made her realize how much of a difference the experience could have had on her life if she'd met with one as a child. Maybe that person would have acknowledged her pain, sparing her from the outbursts that came when she felt that no one cared. Maybe she would have shaken the fear that followed her into adulthood and compelled her to sleep with that knife beneath her mattress each night. But Tiffany had learned, too, not to wallow in the anguish of her past, or what might have made it easier to withstand, because she understood that the sum of her life experience had formed the person she became.

That was why, when she read Tyshaun's story, she didn't see a child who couldn't make it, whose future was devoid of hope. Instead, she saw a kid just like she once was, and sometimes, she knew, all a kid needed to hear were the right words from the right person. So, one day, Tiffany sat down at her desk inside the U.S. Supreme Court Building and began to type, and when she was done, she went home and transcribed what she'd written onto a card.

"Dear Tyshaun," she began, before telling him who she was and what had happened to her father.

I can imagine how you must be feeling—hurt, afraid, sad and sometimes, really angry. After my dad died, I tried to think of what he would want me to do. I knew he would want me to be brave. He would want me to be happy and to be good to my mom. And he would want me to do my best in school. So I did all of these things—even when it was very hard because I missed him so much. I think your dad would want you to do these same things. I cannot promise you that it will be easy. But I promise you that being brave, happy, good to others, and smart in school pays off. I promise you that you can achieve *anything* you set your heart and mind on.

CHAPTER 16

"Y'ALL UNDERSTAND EACH OTHER"

Ava, Tyshaun, and the Anguish that Persists

Ava had waited all weekend to talk to Tyshaun, and at last the time came, so she sat atop her Hello Kitty bedsheets and held her mom's iPhone in both hands, staring at the screen as she waited. The phone pinged, and midway through a conversation with her mother, she stopped and answered.

"Hey, Ava," said Tyshaun, his face appearing on the screen.

"Hi," she replied.

"Happy birthday," Tyshaun said.

"Thank you," said Ava, flanked by piles of stuffed animals. Just before the call, she'd put on a special black dress dotted with miniature stars and Marvel superheroes. "I'm out here if you need me," whispered her mother, Mary, before stepping into the hallway.

"What you doing for your birthday?" asked Tyshaun, who was calling from his mother's bedroom because, in his own, he'd been playing a violent video game with his brother and he didn't want the sound of gunfire to frighten Ava.

"Not really doing anything," she told him.

"Did you want to do anything?" he asked.

"No," said Ava, who had just turned nine. Neither of them spoke for several seconds after, scrolling through dozens of silly virtual masks on their respective Facebook Messenger apps before they each settled on banana-shaped sunglasses.

"What you been doing for the last two days?" Tyshaun asked.

"Eh," Ava said, considering what to reveal to him. "Not much."

"Did you go anywhere?"

"No, not today or the past two days, but tomorrow I'm going ice-skating, for my lesson."

"You want to see my new hair?" he said.

"Yeah."

He cocked his head forward and put it up to the camera lens, revealing a fade with twists on top, the start of dreadlocks that he hoped would someday look just like his dad's.

"Whoooooa. Neat," she told him.

"What was your favorite thing to do for the last four days?" Tyshaun asked, pressing to hear about the fun she'd had over her birthday weekend, because, to him, that's what birthdays were meant to be.

"I think I liked—" she began, then paused.

"Huh?" he said.

"I don't know," Ava told him, withholding the truth that she hadn't done many favorite things that weekend. Tyshaun had called on her actual birthday, but neither she nor her family were recognizing it that afternoon, a holiday Monday in early September 2018. Ava had grown to hate her real birth date because it fell on the same month as the shooting, so she and her family celebrated it, as much as that was possible for her, on the last day of August. Her despair grew more acute as the anniversary of Jacob's death approached, and to Ava, it felt as though her birthday marked the beginning of that unwelcome time of year. Just as she had before turning eight, twelve months earlier, Ava had begun to fixate, again, on the idea that she should have done something to save Jacob's life. Her parents did their best to assure her that wasn't true, but it seldom helped. That weekend, she had exploded again and again, slapping herself, screaming obscenities, writing expletives on her bedroom window with a banana-flavored lip gloss, banging her face into a wall, and snapping the word *MEOW* off the top of a gold-colored head band. "I miss Jacob," she'd said during one of the quiet moments between eruptions. "I don't like today," she'd said during another, at the start of her real birthday, and that feeling only deepened as the hours passed and the call that she'd expected to get from Tyshaun didn't come. Ava lived in perpetual fear that she was going to lose those closest to her, that she would inevitably do something to drive them away. She'd wondered at first, despite her parents' insistence, if that's why Tyshaun hadn't called. Then he did, and now she was as happy as she'd been all weekend, perched on her bed, cycling through more goofy faces on the Messenger app.

"That's weird. My lips are flapping," she said, opening her mouth wide so, in the video chat, she looked like a cartoon character in a wind tunnel. Tyshaun quickly switched to the same one.

"Did you eat any cake?" he asked.

"Yes, my mom made a homemade Funfetti cake."

"Did you like it?"

"Yes, it was really good," Ava said, though she didn't mention that the cake, shaped to look like the head of a pink cat, included no candles or mention of a birthday, that no one sang her a song, that she made no wishes.

"So, is your mom, like, a baker?" Tyshaun asked.

"No, she just—" Ava broke off as Mary walked in to check on her. "But she made a really good cake."

"Have you asked him how he's been doing?" prompted her mother, who, at Ava's insistence, was wearing the necklace with the metal vial of Jacob's ashes.

"How have you been doing?" Ava asked.

"Good," Tyshaun said.

"This is one of my presents I got," she told him, holding up a tiny green foam dragon. He switched to another mask, this one donning him in a bandana and circular sunglasses.

"You look like a biker," Ava said, pulling over the rainbow-colored bear that Tyshaun had picked up for her in Las Vegas. She switched to a mask that turned her cheeks into pineapples.

"Did you ask him how his weekend was?" Mary asked, during another stretch of silence between the two kids.

"How has your weekend been?" Ava said.

"Good," he told her, and they both kept scrolling.

Before her mother stepped out again, she told Ava just to keep asking questions. "You got this," Mary said, giving a thumbs-up, because she knew how much these conversations meant to her daughter. "You got it."

"What do you think you're going to do at school this week?" Ava asked.

"Nothing," he answered, the levity suddenly drained from his voice. "I just don't like school that much."

"I know," Ava said.

What she didn't know—because Tyshaun didn't want her to—was that he'd already begun to struggle in fourth grade at his new school, the other charter just up the street from Eagle Academy in Southeast. The staff there had less tolerance for his fits of anger, especially, during one episode, when he threw a chair and said under his breath that he wanted to hurt a teacher. Furious, his mother, Donna, took away his electronics for a month, but she knew that would only treat the symptoms of his issues, not the cause. The friends of his father who had promised to be there for him, to set an example and give him guidance, had long ago stopped checking in. Desperate for help, she went to his youth football coach, Rick Dupree, who had dealt with the boy's temper on the practice field for weeks. Rick called Tyshaun, explaining that those sorts of outbursts at school could one day lead him to a jail cell. Rick understood, too, that such anger could put Tyshaun's life in jeopardy—at least five players he'd coached during his decade-long career were later shot. "It's okay to cry," he told Tyshaun, convinced that's what the boy needed as much as anything.

Tyshaun missed Eagle, where, in those final weeks of therapy, he felt sure he'd made real progress, almost all of which evaporated when he left. He wished he could talk to the psychologist again. "He knew how I felt," Tyshaun told me once. After the counseling ended, he tried new ways to control his impulses. When he felt his temper about to flare, Tyshaun would tell himself not to act out, repeatedly asking the same question in his mind: "Would your dad want you to do this?" He also began carrying the tiny polyurethane animals Ava had sent him, squeezing them until they popped, as she often did, anytime he felt upset. When Tyshaun ran out of them, he sent her a letter. "Can you please send me some more of those squishy thing's please please they helped me so much," he wrote her, and the morning after his letter arrived, Ava woke her mom up at six to insist that they order him a new batch as soon as possible.

For at least a moment on Ava's birthday, neither of them was thinking about their episodes, those torrents of rage that had come to define their young lives, because that's not what defined her to him or him to her.

Now, on the video chat with Tyshaun, she had someone to introduce her friend to. "Here's my kitty," she said, hopping off the bed to retrieve her cat and bring it back. "This is Ty," she told the cat. "This is Autumn," she told Tyshaun, holding her up to the camera.

"What is your favorite book to read?" asked Tyshaun, who didn't care much about cats but did appreciate how much Ava loved to read, which always made books a good subject for their talks.

"I like the *She Persisted* series, two of them," Ava said, cheerfully, and now her mind was on her birthday gifts and a few of those favorite things from the weekend that had escaped her mind earlier. Her parents had given her a Barbie in a cat dress, and her brother had given her peach ring gummies, which she thought tasted better than any candy in the world. She had tried a few of her dad's old MREs, the instant meals he still had from his military days, and found the flavor of the jalapeño cashews especially entertaining. And, of course, she'd gotten her book about strong women, reading it all the way through that night. Even those flashes of happiness in Ava's life were often tainted, though—when the girl had reached the story of Malala Yousafzai, the Pakistani activist shot as a teenager, she couldn't bear to read it. Afterward, she asked her mom to tape those pages shut.

Her parents sometimes wondered how, when their daughter got older, she would navigate a world so filled with sights and sounds and stories that might trigger her. Would she have to live at home, with them, into adulthood? Would she always need such heavy medication? David still hoped Ava wouldn't always have to take the pills, but Mary believed their daughter would, and that was due in large part, she said, to what the girl's psychiatrist had told them to expect. Ava's ninth birthday arrived a month before she met Holly French, her seventh therapist but the first to make a meaningful connection with the girl. French wouldn't be able to say whether the medication helped or hurt, because she couldn't know firsthand what had changed after the treatment started, but the counselor had hope that Ava would eventually lead a normal life. French had seen other kids with debilitating PTSD make it, so why couldn't Ava?

Donna held out the same hope for her son, but she and the Olsens knew that for their children to heal, they needed to develop trusted friendships, and no better version of Ava or Tyshaun existed than the ones that emerged during their conversations with each other. "I don't have to be hard at all" is how Tyshaun once explained it to me, saying that he wanted the chance to be that person all the time: "Like, myself." That was why, after the kids got into trouble and had to be punished, their parents didn't deprive them of their calls. It was also why, when Donna and Mary caught lulls in the chats, they recommended questions for the children to ask. But the kids, who, like old friends, could often enjoy each other's company without exchanging a word, didn't really need any guidance.

Tyshaun had never heard of the *She Persisted* books, but they did discuss his favorite, *The Tale of Peter Rabbit*, and the new places they'd built in the video game *Minecraft*. They talked about his Xbox and her Kindle, and they cycled through more kooky masks. Then Tyshaun, who could be silly with Ava in a way he would never be with most of his friends, decided to try to make her laugh. He lay on his mom's bed and wrapped his right arm around the back of his head until his hand reached the other side of his face. "Help meeeeeeee," he said, covering his mouth and slapping his cheek. Ava looked closer at the screen, trying to figure out what he was doing. Then she attempted to do the same thing but couldn't quite get her hand around. "I can't do it that much," she said, straining to reach behind her head. Lying on his back, Tyshaun positioned the camera so she couldn't see the right side of his body.

"Where is my arm?" he asked.

"*Whaaaaa?*" she said, briefly baffled. "It's back there! I see it."

He smiled, and she did, too. After that, they talked more about her cats and about his grandmother's dogs, a shih tzu and some other kind he couldn't think of. Ava told him she ate tacos for dinner, and he asked about her favorite foods. "Kale bites," she said. He told her he liked kale a lot, too. They both said they liked pizza, and Ava told him everyone liked pizza, but Tyshaun told her he knew a boy who didn't. "What!?" Ava responded, shocked. "That is *weird.*" They chatted about her ice-skating lessons and how he also enjoyed skating, because he used to play hockey.

"That's pretty neat," Ava said. Then Tyshaun told her he had to go.

"I have to help my mother with the groceries," he said. "But happy birthday. Have a great time."

"Thank you. Bye," Ava said, waving at him as the screen went black. The girl looked up at her mom. "That was fun."

"Yay," Mary replied, because she almost never heard her daughter say those words anymore. "Y'all understand each other."

Charlie, the fat cat, lumbered into the room, and Ava's dad, dressed in his police uniform, popped his head inside. "Gotta go," he said. Ava walked over and gave him a kiss and a hug as her brother, Cameron, came down the hallway.

"Is Ty still on there?" he asked, and Ava told him no, he had to help his mom.

"What'd y'all talk about?" Mary asked.

"He said he used to take ice-skating lessons," she said, adding that he asked about her favorite foods and what she was doing that week.

"What did you tell him?" Cameron asked.

"I just told him I'm going skating tomorrow and next Tuesday," she said, and that reminded Cameron he had to go to school the next day. He discussed his math and reading homework, neither of which he enjoyed. At least, Mary told him, she'd already picked out his snack and selected his clothes. That made him feel better.

As they talked, Ava went quiet. Abruptly, and inexplicably, her mood had darkened. She headed back to the bed, sinking down into her pile of stuffed animals. She sat with her shoulders against the wall and stared off into nothing, retreating once more into an abyss of anxiety and regret. The snippets of joyful relief, even from her calls with Tyshaun, never lasted long, nor did they for him, because Andrew and Jacob were still dead, and on some days, maybe most, their paths to recovery felt as though they'd only gotten longer. With the three-day weekend coming to an end, Ava would soon begin to dread her brother's return to school, one of those places that, despite her letters begging for change, seemed no safer than it was on the afternoon the teenager with the gun pulled up to her playground.

On the bed, Ava slumped across her new teddy bear. Mary, noticing the sudden shift in her daughter's disposition, walked over and sat beside her. "What's wrong?" she whispered, rubbing Ava's shoulder. As Mary leaned down, the necklace she wore in Jacob's memory dangled from her neck, just above the bed. Ava reached her hand out toward it.

"It's my fault," the girl said.

That wasn't true, her mother insisted. "None of y'all did anything wrong." Mary, her face now rigid with apprehension, stroked her daughter's hair. She told her it was okay, but Ava didn't seem to believe her. What would happen next, her mother couldn't know. She'd seen Ava's sadness transform into anger, and much worse, many times before. The girl sat back up on the bed, but her eyes remained low. Mary leaned over to her again. She had another idea. "I'm glad you got to talk to Ty today, right?" Mary asked, as if to remind the girl of the conversation with her friend, the one who understood her. Ava nodded yes, then finally looked up, and for that moment, at least, the darkness passed.

EPILOGUE

On a mild spring evening more than two months after the corona-virus pandemic began, a child inside a Southeast Washington apart-ment pulled a gun out of a drawer, just as Tyshaun had done years earlier in his father's bedroom three miles away. The child handed the gun to a friend, who was eight. Like Tyshaun, that boy thought it was a toy. Unlike Tyshaun, the boy fired it.

The round struck My'onna Hinton, age four, tearing into one side of her neck and popping out the other. With his hands and clothes wet with her blood, the boy ran to the apartment building next door and found the girl's mother, who called 911.

"I didn't mean to do it," he told the woman. "I'm sorry."

By the time she found her daughter, the gun and the adult it belonged to were gone. My'onna would live, but she'd never be the same. The bullet snapped a bone in her neck, leaving her spinal cord damaged. For days, My'onna, who loved nothing more than to dance, could not move her hands.

The novel coronavirus that consumed much of our everyday lives in 2020 pushed gun violence, an American epidemic long before

COVID-19, out of many people's minds. But it never went away, and without reform, it never will. Just as South Carolinians began to fixate on COVID-19's spread in Ava's home state, a three-year-old there found a loaded gun in a bedroom and shot himself in the head. Not long after, a man killed his girlfriend and two of her children, ages twelve and fifteen, because he feared the woman would break up with him. And three weeks before My'onna was shot in DC, two gunmen fired a dozen rounds into a home in Columbia, wounding a thirteen-year-old girl and killing her brother Knowledge Sims. He was seven.

"When is enough enough?" Columbia's police chief asked at a press conference afterward.

That's always been the question. How many children have to die or witness a killing or watch a family member be lowered into the earth before we say, *enough*? Of course, for Greg Gregory, the conservative, gun-owning state senator from South Carolina, the answer came well before all those shootings that coincided with the virus's arrival in his state. Gregory decided he could take no more on February 14, 2018, the day of the slaughter six hundred miles south at Marjory Stoneman Douglas High. Unable to stomach the status quo any longer, he at last spoke up, and he's kept speaking ever since.

There's no one I've interviewed on the subject of guns whose perspective I find more instructive than Gregory's, because he understands better than anyone I know the faction of Americans—both voters and politicians—standing in the way of change. For most of his life, he was one of them. Gregory grew up infatuated with guns, and he's heard, or made, every imaginable argument defending them in the decades since. He told me his reversal was driven, above all, by his humanity, but a desire to *preserve* the Second Amendment also motivates him now. In the swelling ranks of mothers demanding reform, he sensed a determination that would eventually overtake the will of that faction of conservative Americans with whom he'd lived all his life. And what then? If one side had always refused to compromise, how could they expect the other to do any different when the power was theirs alone?

It doesn't have to come to that, though, and like Gregory, no one should want it to. America needs change not years or decades from now—if and when that "tide" he foresees washes over Capitol Hill— but *today*, because with each passing minute, the harm to our youngest citizens grows.

This book does not call for revolution or a repeal of the Second Amendment. Included here are true stories about children who have either died or endured tremendous pain because of gun violence that society has allowed to continue. I did not write this as an appeal to Democrats or a condemnation of Republicans, but instead, as a call to action for anyone in this country who cares about their children. The proposals outlined in these pages are based in reporting and fact, and they will, unequivocally, save lives.

Still, nothing I've argued for will end this scourge. There is no vaccine for gun violence in America. But in the same way that a single mask can protect a person from a virus, a single reform or study or responsible choice can protect a person from a bullet. So, what if we can reduce the number of gun deaths from thirty thousand a year to twenty thousand? What if, in the coming decade, we can salvage the futures of a thousand high-schoolers or a hundred middle-schoolers or a dozen kindergartners? What if we can spare the next My'onna or Knowledge, Ava or Tyshaun?

READERS SOMETIMES ASK me what new policies or initiatives would do the most to protect our children, and after years of reporting on this subject, I have arrived at three answers, only one of which mirrors what many liberal lawmakers have campaigned for over the past decade. That one is obvious: every person who buys a gun should undergo a background check. There are no sensible, good-faith arguments to be made against that regulation, which more than 90 percent of gun owners support. Former ATF special agent David

Chipman described universal background checks as "the most effective way to absolutely upend firearms trafficking," and that should matter to every law-abiding citizen, regardless of politics, because trafficked guns are used every day to kill and maim children and their parents. At present, licensed dealers are required to check customers' backgrounds before every sale, but that does little to prevent criminals from purchasing (directly or indirectly) dozens of weapons without any oversight at gun shows and on the internet.

It's important to understand, too, that universal background checks are intended to mitigate the damage done by the hundreds of millions of guns already in circulation, which, for now, should be our primary concern. This means, for example, that banning extended magazines and assault-style rifles—rational efforts that follow nearly every mass shooting—are not the chief priorities. Though such prohibitions are supported by most Americans, and might seem obvious in a civilized society, today, in this one, they are not the quickest or best ways to reduce the most harm.

That leads to my second answer: we must make a substantial investment in educating gun owners on how critical it is to prevent children from accessing their deadly weapons, and when kids do use those firearms to harm themselves or others because of gun owners' negligence, we must hold the adults responsible.

That's what DC Police chief Peter Newsham intended to do to the person whose pistol that eight-year-old used to accidentally shoot My'onna. "Firearm ownership comes with enormous responsibility, which extends to protecting people who live with the gun owner—especially children," Newsham told me. "Unquestionably, an irresponsible adult is the reason why My'onna's life has been changed forever."

If children did not have access to guns, thousands of them would be rescued each year from death or disfigurement and thousands more from a lifetime of guilt over firing the round that struck their friend or sibling. If children did not have access to guns, thousands of others who pressed the barrels to their temples and pulled the triggers might still be alive. If children did not have access to guns, well more than half the school shootings over the past twenty years would never have happened.

It is an issue on which people's minds can be changed. Jonathan Paxton learned that in the weeks and months after Tyler, his son, shot himself with a loaded revolver in his parents' bedroom. Not once had Jonathan considered that his son might hurt himself, just as several of Jonathan's friends had never considered the possibility with their own kids. Bob Maxwell, the police officer who'd responded to the gruesome scene, began, for the first time, to lock up his service weapon when he returned home from work. But, Jonathan told me, he wasn't the only one.

"My one friend in particular—he had a glass-covered wooden gun case. Well, you could bust the glass and get whatever you want. You know the lock is to keep an honest person out. Somebody that wants in is going to get in. You know a child that wants in there and can see is going to get in there. Hammer, whatever," Jonathan said. After Tyler died, the man bought a new safe and didn't give the key code to anyone, not even his wife.

"I don't know what to say to that. You know, basically he's saying I failed, so he's not going to fail," Jonathan continued, aware that what those men received was an education, the same kind that he so desperately wished he'd gotten eleven years earlier, when his one and only child came into the world.

It bears repeating that this is an idea supported by more than opinion or devastating anecdotes: in the RAND Corporation's review of eighteen different gun policies, the one backed by the most convincing evidence was, by far, child access prevention laws.

Which brings me to my third answer: to know what else will best protect children from gun violence, we need more research, and we need it now. Just between February and late April 2020, the federal government spent $6.4 billion in response to COVID-19—or about

$140,000 per death up to that point. It was a reasonable reaction to a contagion that threatened to take hundreds of thousands of lives, but compare that investment to the support for research into gun violence, which has killed more than 350,000 Americans over the past decade. After years of refusing to fund any research, Congress at last devoted $25 million to it in 2019—or about $640 per death that year.

This isn't complicated. We cannot know what will and won't work if we make no effort to find out.

IT WAS THE night of July 4, 2020, and Tyshaun's mother, Donna, was sitting in her cousin's backyard scrolling through Instagram when a friend's post stopped her. A boy had just been shot and killed in Southeast. He was eleven years old. Donna's heartbeat quickened. Tyshaun was eleven, and earlier that day, he'd gone to a friend's house in Southeast. She called his phone, but he didn't pick up. She called a second time, but still, no answer. She called again, then again and again. Nothing. Five minutes later, her phone rang. It was Tyshaun.

"Where are you?" she demanded.

With his friend, he told her, watching fireworks.

"Mom, why are you yelling?" he asked.

"I just wanted to hear your voice," she told him, but he would soon learn the truth, and with it came the feelings he knew so well—fear for his own life, at first, and then despair, for his father, the life that was no longer there.

I would like to write, after all these years, that Tyshaun doesn't need to be afraid of a stray bullet anymore, just as I would like to write that Ava's bouts of fury and anguish have subsided. That Tyshaun's brother, AJ, hasn't been grappling with the permanence of death since he was two. That Ava's brother, Cameron, isn't now dealing with his own fits of anger. That Jacob's sister, Zoey, doesn't obsess over how he died, and that his brother, Spencer, has some recollection of how he lived. That the students at Eagle Academy will never again draw pictures of shootings and gravestones or that the students at Townville Elementary will never again duck when a balloon pops. That Ava's classmate Siena Kibilko doesn't spend a single moment planning for the next shooting at her school, and that LB isn't still overcome with shame because of what the last one did to him. That Karson Robinson doesn't feel guilty that he couldn't save his dear friend on the playground, and that Collin Edwards doesn't feel sad that he struggles to remember him at all. That their old teacher, Meghan Hollingsworth, could convince her own kids not to worry so much about her. That in a home not far from Townville, Tyler Paxton never took the .357 from the safe. That Tiffany Wright, the former Supreme Court clerk, doesn't sleep with a bottle of pepper spray in her nightstand. That Kaitlyn Towles, whose ninth-grade friend was shot seventeen times, persuaded the people in charge of Washington, DC, to invest in the therapy and support her Anacostia High classmates so badly need. That Emma Gonzalez and Edna Chavez and Zion Kelly, the young activists who never intended to be, won't have to keep giving speeches about the people they loved and lost. That Derek Turner and Jesse Osborne never got ahold of those pistols. That Andrew McPhatter and Jacob Hall are still alive.

I would like to write all of that, but I can't, and I can't because America didn't say *enough* in time for any of them, and until it does, there will be no end to the pain that gun violence inflicts on our children.

This book is based largely on personal observations and hundreds of interviews. I witnessed many of the scenes described firsthand, including the vast majority involving Ava and Tyshaun after the shootings that changed their lives. I reconstructed other scenes based on the accounts of witnesses, police reports, audio recordings, court records and testimony, among other sources. I've cited in the notes the studies, articles, and records that also aided my reporting.

ACKNOWLEDGMENTS

This book exists because families who have endured extraordinary anguish told me, a stranger with a notebook, "Yes," and not just to hours of painful conversation, but to weeks of reporting in their homes, schools, and churches, even when those families were living through their worst moments. To Tyshaun McPhatter, Donna Johnson, and Jessica Jackson; Ava, Cameron, Mary, and David Olsen; Zoey, Spencer, and Renae Hall and Sandra and Stephen McAdams; Collin and Stephanie Edwards; Siena, Emma, Marylea, and Greg Kibilko; Karson Robinson and Kayla Edmonds; LB, Nanny, and Papa; AJ McPhatter and Benica McManus; Zah'Kyi Bynum and Ciera; Olivia and Jonathan Paxton; Meghan and Trevor Hollingsworth; Denise Fredericks, Kerry Burriss, Joanne Avery, and Angie Langdale; Kaitlyn Towles; Javon and Mariama Davies; Gabrielle and MaKenzie Woody; Ajani Dartiguenave and Claudia Charles; Samantha Haviland; Nicole Hockley; Tiffany Wright; and so many others—thank you for your bravery and your trust.

Thanks, too, to the dozens of sources not listed above but whose contributions and expertise were so essential.

I am blessed to have worked with a number of brilliant people on this project, but three, in particular, made it possible. It began in 2015, not with me but with Lynda Robinson, my extraordinary editor at the *Post*, who asked if I was interested in pursuing a series on children and violence, because she thought I might have a knack for reporting on kids who experienced trauma. No one has had a more significant impact on my career than Lynda, and her guidance on this book, from concept to manuscript, was indispensable. I am forever in her debt. When the first piece in the series that she had proposed finally published in 2017, David McCormick emailed me, asking if I'd thought about expanding my work into a book. I hadn't, and probably never would have, without his influence. Beyond an agent, he has been a coach, encourager, and friend. From our first conversation, Denise Oswald, the executive editor at Ecco, embraced my vision for this book, but she also saw beyond it, pushing me to make the words sharper and the ideas more meaningful. She took a chance on me, and I am grateful.

I also deeply appreciate the support from the *Post* and a great many of my colleagues and friends. Thanks to David's team at McCormick Literary and to the wonderful people at Ecco, including Allison Saltzman, Caitlin Mulrooney-Lyski, Meghan Deans, Miriam Parker, Nikki Baldauf, Jenna Dolan, and, especially, Norma Barksdale, whose patience knows no end. Thanks to Steven Rich for his prodigious talents as a data journalist, for his commitment to analyzing campus shootings with rigor, and for the luxurious piece of furniture I hope he one day makes me (google "databae woodshop"). Thanks to Ricky Carioti for taking on the first leg of this journey with me. Thanks to Peter Hermann for covering gun violence in DC with such dedication. Thanks to Paul Duggan for the history lessons. Thanks to Jim Webster for his keen eye. Thanks to Marc Fisher for his exceptional insight and for reading the manuscript and making it better. Thanks to the terrific editors at the *Post*—Mike Semel, Monica Norton, Tracy Grant, Cameron Barr, and Marty Baron—for believing in this work and allowing me the time to do it. Thanks to Josh du Lac for seeing something in me way back when. Thanks to my pals on the Starship, on WhatsApp, and in the thread. Thanks to Mike Foley, Ted Spiker, John Marvel, and Ian Fisher, who have been there from the start (Go Gators). Thanks to my parents, Nan and Ed, for being the best people I will ever know; to my late grandmother, Ruth, for teaching me empathy; to my brother, Edward, for eternal devotion. Thanks to God, for grace I do not deserve. And thanks, finally, to Jenn Alberta, my wife and best friend, for her grit, her wisdom, and her unflinching encouragement. This wouldn't have happened without you.

NOTES

Chapter 1: "I Hate Guns"

6 has made no progress: Rebecca M. Cunningham, Maureen A. Walton, and Patrick M. Carter, "The Major Causes of Death in Children and Adolescents in the United States," *New England Journal of Medicine* 379 (December 2018): https://www.nejm.org/doi/full/10.1056/NEJM sr1804754.

6 about thirty thousand kids and teens: "Underlying Cause of Death, 1999–2008," database, CDC Wonder, Centers for Disease Control and Prevention, https://wonder.cdc.gov/ucd-icd10.html.

6 among the world's high-income countries: Erin Grinshteyn and David Hemenway, "Violent Death Rates: The US Compared with Other High-Income OECD Countries," *American Journal of Medicine* 129, no. 8 (March 2016): https://www.amjmed.com/article/S0002-9343 (15)01030-X/fulltext#sec2.2.

6 concluded that older teens: Ashish P. Thakrar et al., "Child Mortality in the US and 19 OECD Comparator Nations: A 50-Year Time-Trend Analysis," *Health Affairs* 37, no. 1 (January 2018): https://www .healthaffairs.org/doi/pdf/10.1377/hlthaff.2017.0767.

6 nearly four hundred million: Aaron Karp, "Estimating Global Civilian-

Held Firearms Numbers," Small Arms Survey, June 2018, http://www
.smallarmssurvey.org/fileadmin/docs/T-Briefing-Papers/SAS-BP
-Civilian-Firearms-Numbers.pdf.

6 "It's not as if a nineteen-year-old": Craig Lambert, "Death by the
Barrel," *Harvard Magazine*, September/October 2004, https://harvard
magazine.com/2004/09/death-by-the-barrel.html.

7 killed by guns since 1968: Chelsea Bailey, "More Americans Killed by
Guns Since 1968 than in All U.S. Wars—Combined," *NBC News*, October 4, 2017, https://www.nbcnews.com/news/amp/ncna807156.

7 kids who witness an attack: Kimberly J. Mitchell et al., "Weapon In-
volvement in the Victimization of Children," *Pediatrics* 136, no. 1 (July
2015): https://pediatrics.aappublications.org/content/136/1/10.

7 kids who simply lived: Patrick Sharkey, "The Acute Effect of Local Homicides on Children's Cognitive Performance," *Proceedings of the National Academy of Sciences of the United States of America* 107, no. 26
(May 2010): https://www.pnas.org/content/107/26/11733.

7 where a murder had occurred: Maggie Fox, "Murder Rates Affect IQ
Test Scores: Study," Reuters, June 14, 2010, https://www.reuters.com
/article/us-violence-children/murder-rates-affect-iq-tests-scores-study
-idUSTRE65D5VW20100614.

Chapter 3: "I Can't Believe He Went Through with It"

37 referred to as "Project Rainbow": Helen Carter, "Manchester Teenagers
Planned Columbine-style Attack, Jury Told," *Guardian*, September 2, 2009,
https://www.theguardian.com/uk/2009/sep/02/manchester-teenagers
-columbine-style-attack.

37 misguided belief in a myth: "Inside the Online Subculture of Columbiners," CBC Radio, February 20, 2015, https://www.cbc.ca/radio
/day6/episode-221-inside-the-world-of-columbiners-kidults-radical
-homemakers-and-more-1.2961895/inside-the-online-subculture-of
-columbiners-1.2961908.

37 one person told researchers: Jenni Raitanen and Atte Oksanen, "Global
Online Subculture Surrounding School Shootings," *American Behavioral Scientist* 62, no. 2 (January 2018): https://journals.sagepub.com
/doi/abs/10.1177/0002764218755835.

38 at least forty-three school shooters: Peter Langman, "The Influence of Columbine," SchoolShooters.info, February 20, 2019, https://schoolshooters
.info/sites/default/files/columbine_influence_tabloid_1.2.pdf.

41 site that has been: Jonathan Allen, "U.S. Mayors Say Thousands of

Guns Sold Illegally Online," Reuters, December 12, 2013, reuters.com /article/us-usa-shooting-mayors/u-s-mayors-say-thousands-of-guns -sold-illegally-online-idUSBRE9BB1CR20131213.

44 perhaps the youngest in history: Roger Rosenblatt, "The Killing of Kayla," *Time*, March 5, 2000, http://content.time.com/time/magazine /article/0,9171,40342,00.html.

44 who murdered her former girlfriend: Nohelani Graf, "Family of Accused School Shooter Breaks Silence," ABC 15, February 16, 2016, https://www.abc15.com/news/region-west-valley/glendale/glendale -school-shooting-family-of-accused-shooter-at-independence-high -school-breaks-silence.

44 killing her and a student: Sonya Hamasaki and Darran Simon, "Student One of 3 Dead in San Bernardino School Shooting," CNN, April 11, 2017, https://www.cnn.com/2017/04/10/us/san-bernardino-school -shooting/index.html.

45 investigators presented a slide: "Marjory Stoneman Douglas High School Public Safety Commission Part 2," Florida Channel, updated November 13, 2018, https://thefloridachannel.org/videos/11-13-18-marjory -stoneman-douglas-high-school-public-safety-commission-part -2/.

45 Langman has catalogued: Peter Langman, "School Shooters: The Warning Signs," SchoolShooters.info, February 12, 2016, https://school shooters.info/sites/default/files/school_shooters_warning_signs_1.2 _0.pdf.

45 before she persuaded a boy: Ray Stern, "Glendale Boy Who Provided Gun in High School Shooting May Be Charged," *Phoenix New Times*, February 26, 2016, https://www.phoenixnewtimes.com/news /glendale-boy-who-provided-gun-in-high-school-shooting-may-be -charged-8092217.

45 history of brutal violence: Joe Nelson, "San Bernardino School Shooter Had History of Violence," *San Bernardino Sun*, April 12, 2017, https:// www.sbsun.com/2017/04/12/san-bernardino-school-shooter-had -history-of-violence/.

46 half-brother later testified: Nikie Mayo, "School shooter Jesse Osborne was abused by the father he killed, half-brother testifies," *Greenville News*, November 13, 2019, https://www.greenvilleonline.com /story/news/local/south-carolina/2019/11/13/townville-school-shooter -jesse-osborne-sentencing-hearing-second-day-jacob-hall-anderson -county-sc/2522120001/.

Chapter 4: "You Have to Separate the Guns from the Kids"

55 The caller into C-SPAN: "User Clip: David Hemenway on Gun Control," C-SPAN, October 19, 2017, https://www.c-span.org/video/?c468 6913/user-clip-david-hemenway-gun-control.

56 people feeling suicidal: Paul S. F. Yip et al., "Means Restriction for Suicide Prevention," *Lancet* 379, no. 9,834 (June 2012): https://www .thelancet.com/journals/lancet/article/PIIS0140-6736(12)60521-2 /fulltext.

56 that made a revelatory discovery: Anita Knopov et al., "Household Gun Ownership and Youth Suicide Rates at the State Level, 2005– 2015," *American Journal of Preventive Medicine* 56, no. 3 (March 2019): https://www.ncbi.nlm.nih.gov/pubmed/30661885.

57 tend to turn to methods: Mark Thompson, "Why Are So Many Female Veterans Killing Themselves?" Pogo.org, October 16, 2017, https:// www.pogo.org/analysis/2017/10/why-are-so-many-female-veterans -killing-themselves/.

57 six times more likely: "Firearm Suicide in the United States," Everytown for Gun Safety, updated August 30, 2019, https://everytownresearch .org/firearm-suicide/#foot_note_18.

57 "more comfortable with firearms": Emily Wax-Thibodeaux, "VA Addresses Suicide by Gun Problem Among Female Veterans," *Washington Post*, October 8, 2015, https://www.washingtonpost.com/news/federal -eye/wp/2015/10/08/women-veterans-have-such-a-high-success-rate -in-committing-suicide-because-they-use-guns/.

57 within *five minutes* of deciding: Thomas R. Simon et al., "Characteristics of Impulsive Suicide Attempts and Attempters," *Suicide and Life-Threatening Behavior* 32, no. 1 (January 2011): https://onlinelibrary .wiley.com/doi/abs/10.1521/suli.32.1.5.49.24212.

57 half the nation's suicide deaths: "Guns and Suicide," Giffords, https:// giffords.org/issue/guns-and-suicide/.

58 nine in ten who survive: "Attempters' Longterm Survival," Harvard T. H. Chan School of Public Health, https://www.hsph.harvard.edu /means-matter/means-matter/survival/.

58 almost ten thousand children: CDC, "Underlying Cause of Death, 1999–2018."

61 as much as a third: Susan Scutti, "Locking Up Guns Could Reduce Teen and Childhood Firearm Deaths by a Third," CNN, May 13, 2019, https:// www.cnn.com/2019/05/13/health/locked-up-guns-child-deaths-study /index.html.

61 survey of gun-owning families: Frances Baxley and Matthew Miller,

"Parental Misperceptions About Children and Firearms," *Archives of Pediatrics and Adolescent Medicine* 160, no. 5 (May 2006): https://jamanetwork.com/journals/jamapediatrics/fullarticle/204929.

61 4.6 million children: Deborah Azrael et al., "Firearm Storage in Gun-Owning Households with Children: Results of a 2015 National Survey," *Journal of Urban Health* 95, no. 1 (May 10, 2018): https://www.thetrace.org/wp-content/uploads/2018/05/Firearm-Storage-in-Households-with-Children_JUH.pdf.

61 by the RAND Corporation: "The Effects of Child-Access Prevention Laws," RAND Corporation, updated April 22, 2020, https://www.rand.org/research/gun-policy/analysis/child-access-prevention.html.

61 Just thirty states have adopted: "Child Access Prevention," Giffords Law Center, https://lawcenter.giffords.org/gun-laws/policy-areas/child-consumer-safety/child-access-prevention/#footnote_1_460.

63 he suspected his stance: Andrew Wolfson, "'They Are Damaged': Plea Deal Unlikely for Marshall County Shooting Suspect," *Louisville Courier Journal*, January 17, 2019, https://www.courier-journal.com/story/news/crime/2019/01/17/marshall-county-school-shooting-trial-likely-over-plea-deal/2525586002/.

65 the need to wear seat belts: "Policy Impact: Seat Belts," Motor Vehicle Safety, Centers for Disease Control and Prevention, https://www.cdc.gov/motorvehiclesafety/seatbeltbrief/index.html.

65 opposed regulations: Leo C. Wolinsky, "Big Lobbies Clash in Fight on Seat Belts: Hearings Open Today as California Joins Auto Safety Debate," *Los Angeles Times*, February 19, 1985, https://www.latimes.com/archives/la-xpm-1985-02-19-mn-546-story.html.

Chapter 5: "I Hope My Daddy's Okay"

70 401 homicides in the District of Columbia: "Tracking D.C.-area Homicides," *Washington Post*, n.d., https://www.washingtonpost.com/graphics/local/homicides/.

72 to foster more than 140 children: Courtland Milloy, "A D.C. Adoption Success Story," *Washington Post*, February 18, 2009, https://www.washingtonpost.com/wp-dyn/content/article/2009/02/17/AR2009021702992.html?nav=E8.

78 In a separate review: Serena Lei, Tim Meko, and Ben Southgate, "Mapping Gunshots Near DC Schools," Urban Institute, https://apps.urban.org/features/everydayviolence/.

79 Years of research show: Patrick Fowler, "Community Violence: A Meta-analysis on the Effect of Exposure and Mental Health Outcomes of

Children and Adolescents," *Development and Psychopathology* 21, no. 1 (January 2009): https://www.cambridge.org/core/journals/development -and-psychopathology/article/community-violence-a-metaanalysis-on -the-effect-of-exposure-and-mental-health-outcomes-of-children-and -adolescents/A460C5BCCC50A19B4D53D772C76261DE.

Chapter 6: "It's Nothing to Get a Gun"

91 until it peaked at 482: Paul Duggan, "In D.C., Bullets Leave Another Child Fatherless," *Washington Post*, September 15, 2013, https://www .washingtonpost.com/sf/local/2013/09/15/in-d-c-bullets-leave-another -child-fatherless/?utm_term=.2123deb7f158.

92 appointed a financial control board: Paul Duggan, "'Why Would I Leave? It's My Home': In Kenilworth, a D.C. Neighborhood on the Brink of Gentrification, the Past Is About to Meet the Future," *Washington Post*, November 25, 2016, https://www.washingtonpost.com /sf/local/2016/11/25/why-would-i-leave-its-my-home/?utm_term =.96ffeb4b4577.

94 an eight-year period in Chicago: Ben Green, Thibaut Horel, and Andrew V. Papachristos, "Modeling Contagion Through Social Networks to Explain and Predict Gunshot Violence in Chicago, 2006 to 2014," *JAMA Internal Medicine* 177, no. 3 (January 3, 2017): https:// scholar.harvard.edu/files/bgreen/files/jama-iternmed-17.pdf.

97 more than 5,100 illegal guns: "Firearms Trace Data—2018," Bureau of Alcohol, Tobacco, Firearms and Explosives, updated August 26, 2019, https://www.atf.gov/resource-center/firearms-trace-data-2018.

97 earned a D rating: "Virginia Gun Laws," Giffords Law Center, https:// lawcenter.giffords.org/gun-laws/state-law/virginia/.

98 surveyed thousands of prison inmates: Mariel Alper and Lauren Glaze, "Source and Use of Firearms Involved in Crimes: Survey of Prison Inmates, 2016," U.S. Department of Justice, Bureau of Justice Statistics, last modified January 2019, https://www.bjs.gov/content/pub/pdf /suficspi16.pdf.

98 a quarter of a million guns: "About 1.4 Million Guns Stolen During Household Burglaries and Other Property Crimes from 2005 through 2010," U.S. Department of Justice, Bureau of Justice Statistics, last modified November 8, 2012, https://www.bjs.gov/content/pub/press /fshbopc0510pr.cfm.

98 double the government's estimate: Brian Freskos, "Guns Are Stolen in America Up to Once Every Minute. Owners Who Leave Their Weapons

in Cars Make It Easy for Thieves," *Trace*, September 21, 2016, https://www.thetrace.org/2016/09/stolen-guns-cars-trucks-us-atlanta/.

98 few states require stores: Brian Freskos, "Easy Targets: Tracking Stolen Firearms Through the Black Market, from Gun Store Thefts to Crime Scenes," *Trace*, February 2019, https://www.thetrace.org/features/gun-store-theft-trafficking-atf/.

98 nearly half of gun owners: Julia A. Wolfson et al., "The US Public's Preference for Safer Guns," *American Journal of Public Health* 106, no. 3 (March 2016): https://www.ncbi.nlm.nih.gov/pmc/articles/PMC4815965/.

100 Its annual budget: "Fact Sheet—Facts and Figures for Fiscal Year 2018," Bureau of Alcohol, Tobacco, Firearms and Explosives, last modified May 2019, https://www.atf.gov/resource-center/fact-sheet/fact-sheet-facts-and-figures-fiscal-year-2018.

101 stopped by a dice game: Peter Hermann and Rachel Weiner, "He Put 224 Guns on the Streets. His Family Would Pay a Price," *Washington Post*, January 24, 2019, https://www.washingtonpost.com/local/public-safety/he-put-224-guns-on-the-streets-his-family-would-pay-a-price/2019/01/23/68cd2520-1a57-11e9-8813-cb9dec761e73_story.html.

102 Taiyania Aaliyah Thompson: Peter Hermann, "A D.C. Girl Was Killed Just After Turning 16. Her Teenage Father Was Slain When She Was an Infant," *Washington Post*, January 29, 2018, https://www.washingtonpost.com/local/public-safety/a-dc-teen-was-killed-a-month-after-turning-16-her-father-was-slain-at-17/2018/01/29/aa4e820e-051e-11e8-94e8-e8b8600ade23_story.html.

102 Steve Slaughter: Paul Duggan, "Slow-motion Massacre," *Washington Post*, November 12, 2018, https://www.washingtonpost.com/news/local/wp/2018/11/12/feature/a-craving-for-snacks-brought-three-d-c-boys-out-on-a-frigid-night-then-gunfire-changed-everything/.

102 Karon Brown: Keith L. Alexander, Peter Hermann, and Clarence Williams, "'We're Tired of Kids Being Shot': As Family and Community Grieve, Police Search for Gunman Who Killed 11-Year-Old D.C. Boy," *Washington Post*, July 20, 2019, https://www.washingtonpost.com/local/public-safety/were-tired-of-kids-being-shot-as-family-and-community-grieve-police-search-for-gunman-who-killed-11-year-old-dc-boypolice-think-a-driver-tried-to-save-the-boy-from-a-fight-but-then-a-gunman-fired/2019/07/19/bb818d56-aa2b-11e9-86dd-d7f0e60391e9_story.html.

102 Makiyah Wilson: Michael Brice-Saddler, Justin Jouvenal, and Perry Stein, "'Please Don't Let My Baby Die': Mother Holds 10-Year-Old as She Dies Following Shooting at D.C. Apartment Complex, Witnesses Say," *Washington Post*, July 17, 2018, https://www.washingtonpost.com /pb/local/public-safety/10-year-old-girl-dies-in-northeast-dc-shooting -four-adults-wounded/2018/07/17/8bf1a600-89b3-11e8-85ae-511bc1 146b0b_story.html?commentID=&outputType=comment.

102 weeks before he died: Peter Hermann, "In the Weeks Before He Was Killed, He Wrote a Poem. 'In D.C., It's Nothing but People Trying to Take Your Life Away'," *Washington Post*, July 23, 2019, https://www .washingtonpost.com/local/public-safety/in-the-weeks-before-he-was -killed-he-wrote-a-poem-in-dc-its-nothing-but-people-trying-to-take -your-life-away/2019/07/23/231c731a-ad8b-11e9-bc5c-e73b603e7f38 _story.html.

Chapter 7: "Can You Stop Violence?"

107 fifteen-year-old honor student: Antonio Olivo and Jenna Portnoy, "15-Year-Old Killed Sunday Was 'Beloved Student' at D.C. Charter School," *Washington Post*, May 27, 2019, https://www.washingtonpost .com/local/public-safety/teen-boy-killed-in-dc-shooting-identified-as -honor-roll-student-at-somerset-prep/2019/05/27/882b3a48-808b-11e9 -933d-7501070ee669_story.html.

107 more than 90 percent: "Guns," Gallup, https://news.gallup.com/poll/1645 /guns.aspx.

108 spent more than $30 million: Maggie Haberman, Annie Karni, and Danny Hakim, "N.R.A. Gets Results on Gun Laws in One Phone Call with Trump," *New York Times*, August 22, 2019, https://www.nytimes .com/2019/08/20/us/politics/trump-gun-control-nra.html.

109 The president called it: Jonathan Weisman, "Senate Blocks Drive for Gun Control," *New York Times*, April 17, 2013, https://www.nytimes .com/2013/04/18/us/politics/senate-obama-gun-control.html.

109 Prime Minister Jacinda Ardern said: Praveen Menon, "New Zealand Votes to Amend Gun Laws After Christchurch Attack," Reuters, April 10, 2019, https://in.reuters.com/article/newzealand-shooting-parliament/new -zealand-votes-for-gun-law-changes-after-christchurch-attack-idINKC N1RM0X6.

110 explained Robert Spitzer: Robert J. Spitzer, "The Gun-Safety Issue Is Actually Helping Democrats," *New York Times*, November 12, 2018, https://www.nytimes.com/2018/11/12/opinion/gun-control-congress -mass-shooting.html.

111 existential fissures: Beth Reinhard et al., "NRA Money Flowed to Board Members Amid Allegedly Lavish Spending by Top Officials and Vendors," *Washington Post*, June 9, 2019, https://www.washingtonpost.com /investigations/nra-money-flowed-to-board-members-amid-allegedly -lavish-spending-by-top-officials-and-vendors/2019/06/09/3eafe160-81 86-11e9-9a67-a687ca99fb3d_story.html.

112 survey by Johns Hopkins University: Colleen L. Barry et al., "Public Support for Gun Violence Prevention Policies Among Gun Owners and Non-Gun Owners in 2017," *American Journal of Public Health* 108, no. 7 (July 1, 2018): https://ajph.aphapublications.org/doi/10.2105/AJPH .2018.304432.

112 A separate poll revealed: "APM Survey: Americans' Views on Key Gun Policies," American Public Media, last modified August 20, 2019, https://www.apmresearchlab.org/gun-survey-red-flag.

112 39,000 young people: Alexandra Rubenstein et al., "Alarming Trends in Mortality from Firearms Among United States Schoolchildren," *American Journal of Medicine* 132, no. 8 (August 2019): https://www.amjmed .com/article/S0002-9343(19)30176-7/pdf.

113 stricter firearms laws: Monika K. Goyal et al., "State Gun Laws and Pediatric Firearm-Related Mortality," *Pediatrics* 144, no. 2 (August 2019): https://pediatrics.aappublications.org/content/144/2/e20183283.

113 set out to understand: "Gun Policy Research Review," Gun Policy in America, RAND Corporation, https://www.rand.org/research/gun -policy/analysis.html.

114 published a study: Arthur L. Kellermann et al., "Gun Ownership as a Risk Factor for Homicide in the Home," *New England Journal of Medicine* 329 (October 1993): https://www.nejm.org/doi/full/10.1056/NE JM199310073291506.

115 revealed the enormous consequences: David E. Stark and Nigam H. Shah, "Funding and Publication of Research on Gun Violence and Other Leading Causes of Death," *Journal of the American Medical Association* 317, no. 1 (January 3, 2017): https://jamanetwork.com/journals /jama/article-abstract/2595514.

116 Dickey once explained: Rachel Martin, "Two Sides Come Together on Gun Research Funding," *NPR*, December 6, 2015, https://www.npr .org/2015/12/06/458661944/two-sides-come-together-on-gun-research -funding.

117 one of those interviews: Martin, "Two Sides Come Together on Gun Research Funding."

119 during a botched robbery: Peter Hermann, "D.C. Teen Shot During

Attempted Robbery Fought Back, Police Said. Both He and His Assail-ant Were Killed," *Washington Post*, September 21, 2017, https://www .washingtonpost.com/local/public-safety/man-stabbed-in-brentwood -neighborhood-has-died-dc-police-say/2017/09/21/27aefa06-9ebf-11e7 -9083-fbfddf6804c2_story.html.

124 placed it on the table: Jamie Lovegrove, "U.S. Rep. Ralph Norman Pulls Out Loaded Gun in Constituent Meeting to Make Point About Safety," *Post and Courier*, April 6, 2018, https://www.postandcourier .com/politics/u-s-rep-ralph-norman-pulls-out-loaded-gun-in/article _ea97bda0-39d3-11e8-b120-3b253f2be91e.html.

125 he told a reporter: Tim Smith, "Senator Shuts Door on More Gun Hear-ings This Year," *State*, April 3, 2016, https://www.thestate.com/news /politics-government/state-politics/article69782867.html.

125 an op-ed defending both positions: Mike Spies and Larry Martin, "I'm a Republican Lawmaker in the Deep South. These Are the Gun Laws I Can Support," *Trace*, May 6, 2016, https://www.thetrace.org/2016/05 /senator-larry-martin-south-carolina-permitless-carry/.

125 a widely shared op-ed: Greg Gregory, "OPINION: It's Past Time to Address Mass Murder in America," *Greenville News*, March 16, 2018, https://www.greenvilleonline.com/story/opinion/2018/03/16/opinion -its-past-time-address-mass-murder-america/424833002/.

127 less than a third: Tom W. Smith and Jaesok Son, "General Social Survey: Trends in Gun Ownership in the United States, 1972–2014," *NORC at the University of Chicago*, March 2015, https://www.norc.org /PDFs/GSS%20Reports/GSS_Trends%20in%20Gun%20Ownership _US_1972-2014.pdf.

128 Eighty percent of the state: Caitlin Byrd, "Poll Shows South Carolina Overwhelmingly Supports Closing 'Charleston Loophole,'" *Post and Courier*, March 21, 2019, https://www.postandcourier.com/politics/poll -shows-south-carolina-overwhelmingly-supports-closing-charleston -loophole/article_810d626a-4b46-11e9-b336-d77962703e10.html.

Chapter 10: "There's No Guarantee I'm Going to Live"

194 shot him seventeen times: Peter Hermann and Keith L. Alexander, "'Are They Coming?' Teen Asked Bystander Before He Was Shot 17 Times in Stairwell," *Washington Post*, December 19, 2018, https://www .washingtonpost.com/local/public-safety/are-they-coming-teen -asked-bystander-before-he-was-shot-17-times-in-stairwell/2018/12/19 /fdc8d2c2-03a6-11e9-9122-82e98f91ee6f_story.html.

194 80 percent of the student body: Perry Stein, "Two Friends Shot Dead in

the Neighborhood. What Could He Do? Keep Writing Music," *Washington Post*, April 20, 2019, https://www.washingtonpost.com/local /education/two-friends-shot-dead-in-the-neighborhood-what-could -he-do-keep-writing-music/2019/04/20/768c82a2-56f0-11e9-9136-f8e 636f1f6df_story.html.

196 develop PTSD: Fowler et al., "Community Violence."

196 worse on tests: Patrick Sharkey, "The Acute Effect of Local Homicides on Children's Cognitive Performance," *Proceedings of the National Academy of Sciences* 107, no. 26 (June 2010): https://www.pnas.org/content /107/26/11733.

196 health of their hearts: Anna W. Wright et al., "Systematic Review: Exposure to Community Violence and Physical Health Outcomes in Youth," *Journal of Pediatric Psychology* 42, no. 4 (May 2017): https://www.ncbi .nlm.nih.gov/pubmed/27794530.

197 hugely disproportionate number: Joy Resmovits, "Black Preschool Kids Get Suspended Much More Frequently than White Preschool Kids, U.S. Survey Says," *Los Angeles Times*, June 6, 2016, https://www.latimes .com/local/education/la-na-suspension-rates-preschool-crdc-20 160606-snap-story.html.

199 single trusted adult: Mark A. Bellis et al., "Does Continuous Trusted Adult Support in Childhood Impart Life-Course Resilience Against Adverse Childhood Experiences—A Retrospective Study on Adult Health-Harming Behaviours and Mental Well-Being," *BMC Psychiatry* 17, no. 1 (December 2017): https://www.ncbi.nlm.nih.gov/pubmed /28335746.

**Chapter 11: "It's More than Just Protecting
Children from Bullet Holes"**

205 BB gun at Fremont High: Tammy Real-McKeighan, "Students Talk About Being Inside School During Lockdown," *Fremont Tribune*, November 29, 2018, https://fremonttribune.com/news/local/students-talk -about-being-inside-school-during-lockdown/article_a0941112-910f -524a-af28-5247a0fe9806.html.

206 sixth-grader at Bailey Middle: Emma Kennedy, "ECSO: Bailey Middle School Eighth-Grader Arrested for Comment that Caused Lockdowns," *Pensacola New Journal*, February 28, 2018, https://www.pnj .com/story/news/crime/2018/02/28/bailey-middle-hellen-caro -elementary-lockdown-ecso-8th-grader-charged-after-saying-gun -bailey/380745002/.

206 campus at Susan E. Wagner High: Maura Grunlund, "Lockdown Over:

Students Dismissed After Unfounded Gun Report Prompts Panic at Susan Wagner," *Staten Island Advance*, February 28, 2018, https://www.silive.com/news/2018/02/wagner_high_school_on_lockdown.html#incart_2box_silive-homepage-featured.

209 feared a shooting: Nikki Graf, "A Majority of U.S. Teens Fear a Shooting Could Happen at Their School, and Most Parents Share Their Concern," Pew Research Center, April 18, 2018, https://www.pewresearch.org/fact-tank/2018/04/18/a-majority-of-u-s-teens-fear-a-shooting-could-happen-at-their-school-and-most-parents-share-their-concern/.

212 "code red": Michael Williams, "Seminole Officials Announce New School Lockdown Procedures in Wake of Drill Scare at Lake Brantley High," *Orlando Sentinel*, February 8, 2019, https://www.orlandosentinel.com/news/breaking-news/os-ne-new-seminole-lockdown-policies-20190208-story.html.

Chapter 12: "Are You Going to Keep Kids Safe?"

223 offered no specifics: Moriah Balingit, "White House Weighs in on Fatal Kentucky School Shooting," *Washington Post*, January 24, 2018, https://www.washingtonpost.com/news/education/wp/2018/01/24/white-house-weighs-in-on-fatal-kentucky-school-shooting/.

225 condemned the student walkout: "TWISC: In Session March 14, 2018," SouthCarolinaETV, YouTube, last modified March 14, 2018, https://www.youtube.com/watch?v=qk1mYiFjhHE.

Chapter 13: "That's Twenty-nine Thousand Dollars a Kid"

227 writing an op-ed: JoAnne Avery, "OPINION: 'As a School Leader, I Am Frustrated . . . ,'" *Independent Mail*, March 12, 2018, https://www.independentmail.com/story/opinion/2018/03/12/opinion-school-leader-am-frustrated/416080002/.

228 $3 billion market: "School Security Systems Industry—US Market Overview," IHS Markit, February 26, 2018, https://technology.ihs.com/600401/school-security-systems-industry-us-market-overview.

228 shooter insurance: Jonathan Berr, "Schools Are Now Buying Insurance Against Mass Shootings," CBS News, June 8, 2018, https://www.cbsnews.com/news/schools-are-now-buying-insurance-against-mass-shootings/.

233 organize a coup: Anthony Faiola, Shawn Boburg, and Ana Vanessa Herrero, "Venezuela raid: How an ex-Green Beret and a defecting general

planned to capture Maduro," *Washington Post*, May 10, 2020, https://www.washingtonpost.com/world/the_americas/venezuela-raid-jordan-goudreau-cliver-alcala-maduro/2020/05/10/767c3386-9194-11ea-9322-a29e75effc93_story.html.

236 At Huffman: Carol Robinson, "Wrongful Death Lawsuit Filed in Shooting Death of Courtlin Arrington at Huffman High School," AL.com, May 15, 2018, https://www.al.com/news/birmingham/2018/05/wrongful_death_lawsuit_filed_i_1.html.

236 At Freeman: "Freeman High School Shooting: Suspect Said He Was Bullied, Police Documents Say," CBS News, September 14, 2017, https://www.cbsnews.com/news/freeman-high-school-shooting-suspect-said-he-was-bullied-police-documents-say/.

238 YouTube video: "ALICE Training Video—Middle School Students," ResponseOptions, YouTube, last modified August 10, 2012, https://www.youtube.com/watch?v=k6ksnSzsy6M.

240 federal instructions: "Guide for Developing High-Quality School Emergency Operations Plans," U.S. Department of Education, June 2013, https://rems.ed.gov/docs/REMS_K-12_Guide_508.pdf.

241 produce a guide: "Best Practice Considerations for Schools in Active Shooter and Other Armed Assailant Drills," National Association of School Psychologists, updated April 2017, https://www.nasponline.org/resources-and-publications/resources-and-podcasts/school-climate-safety-and-crisis/systems-level-prevention/best-practice-considerations-for-schools-in-active-shooter-and-other-armed-assailant-drills.

242 buckets of river stones: Peggy Lee, "Superintendent Says Students Are Armed with Rocks in Case of a School Shooting," WNEP, March 22, 2018, https://www.wnep.com/article/news/local/schuylkill-county/superintendent-says-students-are-armed-with-rocks-in-case-of-a-school-shooting/523-2f5ccaca-d44e-4dd6-a12e-a66501241767.

242 Sam Strahan: Chandrika Narayan, "Student Died After Confronting Shooter at Spokane School," CNN, September 14, 2017, https://www.cnn.com/2017/09/14/us/student-killed-confronting-shooter-trnd/index.html.

243 she once wrote: Nicole Hockley and Madison Feller, "Nicole Hockley Lost Her Son at Sandy Hook. Then She Had to Send Her Surviving Son Back to School," *Elle*, March 6, 2018, https://www.elle.com/culture/career-politics/a19053193/sandy-hook-shooting-parkland-gun-safety-president-trump/.

244 lockdown drills: Elizabeth J. Zhe and Amanda B. Nickerson, "Effects

of an Intruder Crisis Drill on Children's Knowledge, Anxiety, and Perceptions of School Safety," *School Psychology Review* 36, no. 3 (2007): https://eric.ed.gov/?id=EJ788357.

Chapter 14: "Remember, You Can't See Daddy Anymore"

254 the study reported: Jocelyn R. Smith, "Unequal Burdens of Loss: Examining the Frequency and Timing of Homicide Deaths Experienced by Young Black Men Across the Life Course," *American Journal of Public Health* 105, no. S3 (July 1, 2015): https://ajph.aphapublications.org/doi/full/10.2105/AJPH.2014.302535.

254 "lifelong racial inequality": Debra Umberson et al., "Death of Family Members as an Overlooked Source of Racial Disadvantage in the United States," *Proceedings of the National Academy of Sciences* 114, no. 5 (January 23, 2017): https://www.pnas.org/content/early/2017/01/17/1605599114#abstract-2.

Chapter 15: "I Cannot Promise You that It Will Be Easy"

270 analysis of resilience: Kristen Yule, Jessica Houston and John Grych, "Resilience in Children Exposed to Violence: A Meta-analysis of Protective Factors Across Ecological Contexts," *Clinical Child and Family Psychology Review* 22, no. 3 (September 2019): https://link.springer.com/article/10.1007/s10567-019-00293-1.

272 Holocaust survivors: Roberta R. Greene, "Holocaust Survivors: A Study in Resilience," *Journal of Gerontological Social Work* 37, no. 1 (2002): https://www.tandfonline.com/doi/abs/10.1300/J083v37n01_02.

Epilogue

287 the boy fired it: Peter Hermann, "Little Girl Slowly Recovering After Being Accidentally Shot by Another Child," *Washington Post*, June 13, 2020, https://www.washingtonpost.com/local/public-safety/little-girl-slowly-recovering-after-being-accidentally-shot-by-another-child/2020/06/13/232d2156-a9c5-11ea-9063-e69bd6520940_story.html.

288 found a loaded gun: "Police: Boy, 3, Who Shot Himself in the Head Improving," Associated Press, March 5, 2020, https://apnews.com/2805410d4692dbe80823930fc0c00d66.

288 man killed his girlfriend: Kiana Miller, Laurel Mallory, and Joe Gorchow, "Report: Surviving Children Detail Terrifying Account of Murder-Suicide at home Near St. Matthews," WISTV.com, https://www.wistv

.com/2020/05/18/surviving-children-detail-terrifying-account-murder
-suicide-home-near-st-matthews/.

289 90 percent of gun owners: "U.S. Support For Gun Control Tops 2–1, Highest Ever, Quinnipiac University National Poll Finds; Let Dreamers Stay, 80 Percent Of Voters Say," Quinnipiac University Poll, https:// poll.qu.edu/national/release-detail?ReleaseID=2521.

290 rational efforts: "Large Capacity Magazines," Giffords Law Center, https:// lawcenter.giffords.org/gun-laws/policy-areas/hardware-ammunition /large-capacity-magazines/.

290 supported by most Americans: "Guns," Gallup, https://news.gallup.com /poll/1645/guns.aspx.

290 thousands of them would be rescued: "The Effects of Child-Access Prevention Laws," RAND Corporation, updated April 22, 2020, https:// www.rand.org/research/gun-policy/analysis/child-access-prevention .html.

291 spent $6.4 billion in response: Aaron Boyd, "Federal Spending on COVID-19 Doubles in Last 10 Days," Nextgov, April, 23, 2020, https:// www.nextgov.com/cio-briefing/2020/04/federal-spending-covid-19 -doubles-last-10-days/164838/.

292 more than 350,000 Americans: "Underlying Cause of Death, 1999– 2018," database, CDC Wonder, Centers for Disease Control and Prevention, accessed June 30, 2020, https://wonder.cdc.gov/ucd-icd10.html.

292 $640 per death that year: "Past Summary Ledgers," Gun Violence Archive, https://www.gunviolencearchive.org/past-tolls.

INDEX